ELECTROPHYSIOLOGY OF MIND

OXFORD PSYCHOLOGY SERIES

Editors

Nicholas J. Mackintosh   James L. McGaugh
Timothy Shallice   Endel Tulving
Anne Treisman   Lawrence Weiskrantz

Electrophysiology of Mind

Event-Related Brain Potentials and Cognition

Edited by

MICHAEL D. RUGG

Professor of Psychology
University of St Andrews

and

MICHAEL G. H. COLES

Professor of Psychology, Department of Psychology and
Beckman Institute, University of Illinois
at Urbana-Champaign

OXFORD PSYCHOLOGY SERIES
NO. 25

OXFORD   NEW YORK   TOKYO
OXFORD UNIVERSITY PRESS

Oxford University Press, Great Clarendon Street, Oxford OX2 6DP
Oxford New York
Athens Auckland Bangkok Bogota Bombay
Buenos Aires Calcutta Cape Town Dar es Salaam
Delhi Florence Hong Kong Istanbul Karachi
Kuala Lumpur Madras Madrid Melbourne
Mexico City Nairobi Paris Singapore
Taipei Tokyo Toronto Warsaw

and associated companies in
Berlin Ibadan

Oxford is a trade mark of Oxford University Press

Published in the United States by
Oxford University Press Inc., New York

© Oxford University Press, 1995
First published 1995
First published in paperback 1996
Reprinted 1997

A catalogue record for this book is available from the British Library

Library of Congress Cataloging in Publication Data
(Data available)

ISBN 0 19 852416 1

Printed and bound in Great Britain by
Biddles Ltd, Guildford and King's Lynn

Foreword

Michael I. Posner

Professor of Psychology, University of Oregon

Mental chronometry has been defined as the time-course of information pro-cessing in the nervous system (Posner 1978). This splendid volume reviews a productive period of research aimed at connecting brain and mind through the use of scalp-recorded brain potentials to record the temporal course of informa-tion processing in the human brain.

The successive deflections of the EEG time-locked to appropriate signals have been successfully linked to many psychological processes involved in attention, memory, and motor control, as the reader of this book will find out. The intro-ductory chapter provides an overview of these components and Chapter 2 examines the logic for linking them to psychological processes. The editors of the volume have done an extremely valuable service in delineating these rules, which will be invaluable guides for the next wave of chronometric studies using event-related potentials (ERPs).

Only a few short years ago, or anyway it seems to someone of my age, ERP studies were seen as irrelevant to the study of brain or mind, as merely a kind of artefact like amplifying the signal from a bowl of jelly or listening to a computer signal with a stethoscope. This generation of researchers, as should be clear to readers of this volume, have addressed that issue and shown convincingly that the time-dependent electrical signal can be used to study and illuminate central psychological issues.

Chapters 3–6, by world leaders in specific areas of research, give excellent reviews of what has been discovered about attention, information processing dynamics, memory, and language by the use of ERPs. Everyone will have their own favourite examples of progress in this area, but I especially enjoyed accounts of the mechanisms of spatial attention, of continuous transfer of information from sensory to motor systems, and of how lexical and sentence information combine to determine meaning. The writers convey a feeling of progress, both in reliability of measurement and in the theoretical contributions to cognitive psychology.

Despite the considerable gains in knowledge demonstrated in this volume, I personally believe that the greatest contributions of ERPs lie ahead. New neuroimaging methods like positron emission tomography (PET) and functional magnetic resonance imaging (fMRI) have revealed the spatial location of many putative generators of cognitive processes (Posner and Raichle 1994). It is now possible to study in some detail the communication between these generators by examining the time-dependent scalp activity that can be related to them (Gevins *et al.* 1994; Tucker *et al.* 1994). One may wonder why it is useful to connect

ERPs to PET or fMRI. Haven't these new methods rendered the old ones obsolete? The fact is that any measure that relies on changes in the vascular system is not going to reflect the temporal accuracy needed for chronometric studies. There is now a large effort to provide secure links between a functional anatomy developed from methods like PET and fMRI with time-dependent measures. Some of the flavour of this effort is present in Chapter 3 of the current volume. The effort to relate areas of blood flow change to scalp electrical activity will benefit from the same careful analysis of linkage that has been discussed in Chapter 2 of this book. I believe data to date are encouraging. Moreover, new recording devices (Tucker 1993) and algorithms for bootstrapping from scalp distribution to generators (Scherg 1989) give some promise that ERPs can be used to hypothesize localized areas that give rise to their components. The prospect of seeing areas of brain activity wax and wane during the learning and performance of high-level skills makes the years ahead appear full of promise.

Another new aspect of the relationship between ERPs and other brain imaging methods is the ability to check the results by examining the convergence of various methods. Just as links between ERPs and cognitive methods have been useful in bolstering faith in chronometric analysis of brain potentials, so it will be import-ant to check putative generators obtained from ERPs with new neuroimaging methods. The impressive sets of tools that are now available to study these problems will have to be matched by better theoretical analysis. It is for that goal that the current volume will be of special importance.

This volume is a statement of what has been found out. It provides strong evidence that cognitive psychology can benefit from the use of brain electrical activity. Does it also help in understanding the operating of the human brain? Neuroscience studies of alert monkeys during learning and after injury have given evidence of plasticity even in basic sensory processes (Recanzone *et al.* 1992). The use of ERPs in conjunction with neuroimaging will allow the study of the plasticity of the human brain during the execution of human skills like those discussed in this book. These studies could lead to further development of theories of how the human brain works as various levels of skill are acquired. A genuine cognitive neuroscience should have much to say about the properties of the human brain that constrain the ability to acquire and execute high-level skills that people perform. If ERPs are to contribute to such a development new experiments will have to be based on the findings and concepts reviewed in this volume. From this perspective the book that Rugg, Coles, and their collaborators have produced can serve both as a summary of where we have been and also as a pointer to the way ahead.

REFERENCES

Gevins, A., Cutillo, B., DuRousseau, D., Le, J., Leong, H., Martin, N., Smith, M. E., Bressler, S., Brickett, P., McLaughlin, J., Barbero, N., and Laxer, K. (1994). Imaging the spatiotemporal dynamics of cognition with high resolution evoked poten-tial methods. *Human Brain Mapping*, 1, 101–16.

Posner, M. I. (1978). *Chronometric explorations of mind*. Erlbaum, Hillsdale NJ.

Posner, M. I. and Raichle, M. E. (1994). *Images of mind*. Scientific American Library, New York.

Recanzone, G. H., Merzenich, M. M., and Schreiner, C. E. (1992). Changes in the distributed temporal response properties of S1 cortical neurons reflect improvements in performance on a temporally based tactile discrimination task. *Journal of Neurophysiology*, 67, 1071–91.

Scherg, M. (1989). Fundamentals of dipole source analysis. In *Auditory evoked magnetic fields and potentials: advances in audiology* (ed. F. Grandoli and G. L. Romani), pp. 1–30. Karger, Basel.

Tucker, D. M. (1993). The geodesic sensor net. *Electroencephalography and Clinical Neurophysiology*, 87, 154–63.

Tucker, D. M., Liotti, M., Potts, G. F., Russell, G. S., and Posner, M. I. (1994). Spatiotemporal analysis of brain electrical fields. *Human Brain Mapping*, 1, 134–52.

Preface

The subject of this book is the event-related brain potential (ERP) and its use in studies of cognitive processing in human subjects. Our principal motivation for putting the book together is to draw attention to the considerable corpus of research that uses the ERP approach to address issues relevant to present-day cognitive psychology. ERP studies far outnumber those conducted along similar lines with other psychophysiological techniques and, over the years, ERP studies have increasingly been conducted in theoretical contexts derived directly from cognitive psychology. Furthermore, the relative maturity of the ERP field has led to the development of a substantial degree of consensus about the methodological standards appropriate for cognitive ERP work. Unfortunately, it has also led to the development of a technical vocabulary and 'subculture' that, while facilitating communication among cognoscenti, has, we suspect, acted to reduce the impact of ERP studies among the wider psychological community. One aim of this book is to remedy this situation by making ERP research more accessible to that community.

With these considerations in mind, the first two chapters of the book provide a basic introduction to ERP research. These chapters include a review of ERP methodology and the concept of an ERP component, as well as an account of the rationale for the use of ERPs in cognitive psychology, the advantages this brings over the employment exclusively of behavioural indices of processing, and the major difficulties that afflict the interpretation of ERP data. We also briefly consider the ERP in relation to other techniques for studying brain–cognition relationships. Subsequent chapters review ERP work in four areas—attention, mental chronometry, memory, and language—that are both central to the concerns of human experimental and cognitive psychology and which have been the subject of significant ERP research. Our hope is that the book will not only provide a useful survey and review of work in these areas for those already knowledgeable about ERP research, but will also prove valuable to others, less familiar with the field, who are curious about the contribution that ERP studies have made or might make to cognitive studies.

The interval between the book's conception and production has been unusually long. We originally discussed the possibility of doing a book together during a visit by Rugg to Champaign in 1984. While it was our initial intention to write a complete book together, it soon became apparent that this would entail far more time than either of us could afford to devote to such a project. Thus, we are fortunate to have been able to call on distinguished colleagues with expertise in areas that needed to be covered and whose general approach to ERP research is compatible with ours. Ron Mangun and Steve Hillyard, and Lee Osterhout and Phil Holcomb agreed to join the project in 1990.

We began writing our own contributions to the book during Rugg's second visit to Champaign in 1991, a visit that was sponsored in part by the Beckman

Institute at the University of Illinois. Other significant writing occurred while Coles was on sabbatical leave in 1993 in Germany (at the University of Tübingen), a leave made possible in part by an award from the Alexander von Humboldt Foundation and in part by the University of Illinois. Niels Birbaumer, Wolfgang Miltner, and their colleagues at Tübingen provided a most congenial environment for this endeavour. At different times in 1993 we both spent a month at the Max Planck Institute for Psycholinguistics and the Nijmegen Institute for Cognition and Information, both in Nijmegen, The Netherlands. Considerable progress on our chapters was made during these visits. We thank especially Colin Brown, Ton Coenen, and Peter Hagoort for their hospitality during our stays in Nijmegen.

At various stages of writing our jointly authored chapters, we solicited comments from colleagues; these included Jeff Miller at the University of California, San Diego, and Richard Schweikert, Robert Proctor, and their students at Purdue University, Juliet Holdstock and Ruth Mark at the University of St Andrews, and Art Kramer and Greg Miller at the University of Illinois.

We also thank Betty Heggemeier in Champaign for assistance in all phases of the project, along with Steve Holland who prepared the figures in Chapters 1 and 2. We must also acknowledge the Wellcome Trust (Rugg) and the National Institute for Mental Health (Coles) for their continuing financial support of our research.

Finally, we thank Mike Posner for agreeing to write the Foreword. He has played a major role in the development of the field of cognitive neuroscience and is uniquely qualified to consider the place of ERP research in this context.

St Andrews, Scotland   M. D. R.
Champaign, Illinois   M. G. H. C.
May 1994

Contents

Contributors

Michael G. H. Coles
Department of Psychology, University of Illinois, 603 E. Daniel Street, Champaign, IL 61820, USA.

Steven A. Hillyard
Department of Neurosciences, University of California, San Diego, La Jolla, CA 92903, USA.

Phillip J. Holcomb
Tufts University, 490 Boston Avenue, Medford, MA 02155, USA.

George R. Mangun
Department of Psychology and Center for Neuroscience, University of California, Davis, Davis, CA 95616, USA.

Lee Osterhout
Department of Psychology, University of Washington, Seattle, WA 98195, USA.

Leun J. Otten
Department of Psychology, University of Illinois, 663 E. Daniel Street, Champaign, IL 61820, USA.

Michael D. Rugg
School of Psychology, University of St Andrews, Fife, KY16 9JU, UK.

Marten K. Scheffers
Department of Psychology, University of Illinois, 663 E. Daniel Street, Champaign, IL 61820, USA.

Henderikus G. O. M. Smid
Department of Clinical Neurophysiology, Otto von Guericke University, Leipziger Strasse, D-39120 Magdeburg, Germany.

1 Event-related brain potentials: an introduction

Michael G. H. Coles and Michael D. Rugg

1.1 INTRODUCTION

This book is concerned with the intersection of two research areas: event-related brain potentials (ERPs) and cognitive psychology. In particular, we will be considering what has been learned and what might be learned about human cognitive function by measuring the electrical activity of the brain through electrodes placed on the scalp. In this first chapter we focus on the methodology of ERP research and on the problem of isolating ERP components, while in Chapter 2 we review issues that arise in making inferences from ERPs about cognition.

We begin by considering how an ERP signal is obtained, as well as how such a signal is analysed. We consider at some length the issue of the definition of a component and we provide a brief review of some of the more well-known components. This latter review is intended to give a historical context for cognitive ERP research and the chapter as a whole should provide the reader with some understanding of the vocabulary of the ERP researcher and the 'lore' of the cognitive electrophysiologist.

1.2 ERP RECORDING AND ANALYSIS

In this section we review some of the basic facts and concepts germane to ERP recording and analysis. (Portions of this section are derived from Coles *et al.* (1990); see also Allison *et al.* (1986), Nunez (1981), and Picton (1985), for further information.)

1.2.1 Derivation

When a pair of electrodes are attached to the surface of the human scalp and connected to a differential amplifier, the output of the amplifier reveals a pattern of variation in voltage over time. This voltage variation is known as the 'electro-encephalogram' (or EEG). The amplitude of the normal EEG can vary between approximately -100 and $+100$ μV, and its frequency ranges to 40 Hz or more.

Suppose that we present a stimulus to a human subject while recording the EEG. We can define an epoch of the EEG that is time-locked to the stimulus. For example, the epoch may begin 100 ms before the onset of the stimulus and end 1000 ms later. Within this epoch, there may be voltage changes that are specifically related to the brain's response to the stimulus. It is these voltage changes that constitute the event-related potential, or ERP.

In early research involving these measures of brain potential, the term 'evoked potential', or EP, was used because it was believed that the potentials reflected brain activity that was strictly 'evoked' by the presentation of the stimulus, activity related to basic sensory processes. As we shall see, it is now proposed that at least some of these potentials are related to 'a variety of processes that are *invoked* by the psychological demands of the situation' (Donchin *et al.* 1978, p. 350). The realization that the potentials reflected more than just evoked activity led to the use of the more neutral term 'event-related'.

1.2.2 The generation of the ERP

It is generally accepted that the ERP reflects activity originating within the brain (although see Section 1.2.5 on artefacts). However, the relationship between what is going on in the brain and what we observe at the scalp is not completely understood. Nevertheless, the following points appear to be clear (see Nunez (1981), Scherg and Picton (1991), and Wood (1987) for more detailed discussions of the physiological determinants of ERP waveforms). First, ERPs recorded from the scalp represent net electrical fields associated with the activity of sizeable populations of neurons. Second, and relatedly, the individual neurons that comprise such a population must be synchronously active, and have a certain geometric configuration, if they are to produce fields that can be measured at the scalp. In particular, the neurons must be configured in such a way that their individual electrical fields summate to yield a dipolar field (a field with positive and negative charges between which current flows). Such configurations are known as 'open fields' and usually involve the alignment of neurons in a parallel orientation. Finally, biophysical and neurophysiological considerations strongly suggest that scalp-recorded ERP waveforms are principally a reflection of post-synaptic (dendritic) potentials, rather than of axonal action potentials (Allison *et al.* 1986).

Consideration of the neural processes that we probably detect in the ERP has important consequences for their interpretation. First, there is undoubtedly much neural activity that is never apparent at the scalp. In many neuronal populations, even those with an 'open field' configuration, activity might be insufficiently synchronous to generate an electrical field that can be recorded at a distance. In some structures, such as the cerebral cortex, the geometric arrangement of neurons is conducive to the summation and propagation of their electrical activity because the neurons share the same orientation, perpendicular to the cortical surface. However, in other structures, such as the thalamus, the arrangement of neurons almost certainly guarantees their invisibility to distant recording electrodes. They are arranged in such a way as to produce no detectable field outside them.

The resultant selectivity of the ERP is both an advantage and a disadvantage. If we observed the totality of brain activity at the scalp, the resultant measures arguably would be so complex as to be difficult or impossible to analyse. However, we need always to be aware that there are almost certainly numerous functionally important neural processes that cannot be detected using the ERP technique.

1.2.3 Recording issues

As we noted earlier, to obtain an ERP one needs to record the difference in voltage between two electrode sites; but where should the electrodes be placed? At present, the most common practice is to employ what is referred to as a 'common reference' recording procedure. This involves connecting each member of an array of scalp electrodes to a single 'reference', comprising either one other electrode or perhaps a pair of electrodes that have been linked together (as with the popular 'linked mastoid' reference, which consists of a linked pair of electrodes, one on each mastoid bone located behind each ear). The reference site is chosen so as to be relatively uninfluenced by the electrical activity of experimental interest. Recordings are based on the difference in voltage between each 'exploring' electrode and the same (common) reference electrode(s). More complex recording arrangements are also possible and are occasionally employed. These can involve computing voltage differences between subsets of adjacent electrodes (as in 'current-source density' analysis: Nunez 1990; Perrin *et al.* 1989), or subtracting the across-electrode mean voltage (as determined with respect to a common reference) from each electrode to yield recordings with respect to an 'average reference' (Lehmann 1987). Such procedures are used to accentuate or 'sharpen' regional differences in scalp fields, with the hope that this will allow greater insight into the likely locus of the generators of the fields.

Electrode locations are generally described with reference to the 10–20 system (Jasper 1958; and see Fig. 1.1). In this system, the location of an electrode is specified in terms of its proximity to particular regions of the brain (frontal, 'central', temporal, parietal, and occipital) and of its location in the lateral plane (odd number for left, the subscript z for midline, and even numbers for right). Thus, Pz defines a midline electrode location over the parietal lobe, while F3 defines a left frontal site. Although these electrode descriptors refer to particular brain areas, it is important to note that activity recorded at any particular scalp site is not necessarily attributable to activity in brain regions in close proximity to that site. This is because the brain acts as a volume conductor, meaning that electrical activity generated in one area can be detected at distant locations.

In recent years there has been an increased interest in the use of ERPs to make inferences about what is going on inside the brain (see Section 1.3.1.1). Because the techniques required to make these inferences require that the electrical fields on the scalp be sampled at a high spatial frequency, the 10–20 system has been enhanced by the use of both non-standard locations and a higher density of electrodes (e.g. Tucker 1993).

1.2.4 Conditioning the signal

The EEG includes frequencies that are often outside those that are of interest to the ERP researcher. For this reason, the amplifiers used to record the ERP usually

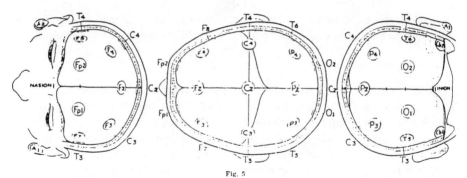

Fig. 5

Frontal superior and posterior views showing all the standard electrode positions as described in the text.

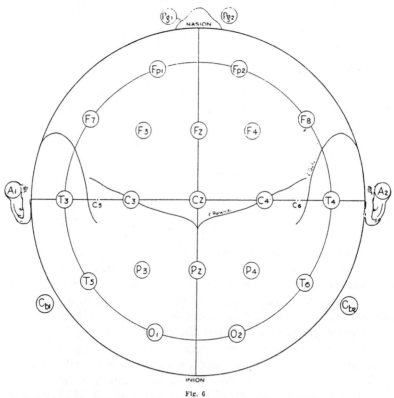

Fig. 6

A single plane projection of the head, showing all standard positions and the location of the Rolandic and Sylvian fissures. The outer circle was drawn at the level of the nasion and inion. The inner circle represents the temporal line of electrodes. This diagram provides a useful stamp for the indication of electrode placements in routine recording.

Fig. 1.1 The 10–20 system for electrode placement. The principal locations are defined in terms of the relative distances (in 10 or 20 percentile values) along two major axes: the anterior–posterior axis (from nasion to inion), and the coronal axis (from left to right post-auricular points). Other locations are defined in relation to these principal locations. The original legend for this figure reads as follows: 'A single plane projection of the head,

include optional filter settings that allow the investigator to attenuate activity above and below selected frequencies. Of particular importance in this regard is high-frequency activity that is attributable to muscle (for example, of the jaws) rather than brain activity, and activity at the line (mains) frequency (60 or 50 Hz). Low-frequency activity can also be attenuated ('high-pass' filtering); however, care must be taken to ensure that low-frequency activity in the ERP waveform is not significantly distorted by such filtering.

1.2.5 Artefacts

The filtering procedures described in the previous section can sometimes be used to attenuate artefactual activity that arises from sources other than the brain. However, there are two major sources of artefact, movements of the eyes and eyelids, that cannot be dealt with in this way. This is because these movements occur at the same frequencies as important features of the ERP waveforms. Eye-movement and eye-blink artefacts arise because the eyeball functions like an electrical dipole, with positive and negative charge on either side. Movements of the eye therefore produce fluctuating electrical fields that are propagated back across the scalp. These fields are picked up by scalp electrodes and contaminate the recording of brain activity. To deal with these artefacts, investigators use one of several approaches. First, they may instruct subjects to maintain their gaze at a fixation point and to avoid blinking except at designated times when task events are not present. The problem with this approach is that it may impose a secondary task on the subject (the task of not moving their eyes), and this may interfere with the subject's performance on the primary task of interest. Second, investigators may discard all EEG epochs for which eye movements or blinks are detected. The problem here is that there may be an insufficient number of artefact-free trials for tasks that require eye movements for their successful performance or for some populations (for example the young and the aged) that have trouble keeping their eyes still. In the face of these difficulties, investigators have resorted to a third approach that involves estimation and removal of the contribution of the eye movements and blinks to the ERP signal (for example Gratton *et al.* 1983). The advantage of correcting the ERP signal in this way is that one can retain all the ERP data, even when substantial eye movements are present. Brunia *et al.* (1989) report the results of a comparison among six different correction procedures, and the reader who is interested in more information is referred to this article.

1.2.6 Extracting the signal

As we have noted, the ERP is set of voltage changes contained within an epoch of EEG that is time-locked to some event. In most cases, these changes are small

showing all standard positions and the location of the Rolandic and Sylvian fissures. The outer circle was drawn at the level of the nasion and inion. The inner circle represents the temporal line of electrodes. This diagram provides a useful stamp for the indication of electrode placements in routine recording.' (From Jasper (1958): Fig. 6, p. 374. Copyright © 1958 Elsevier Science Ireland Ltd., reprinted by permission.)

(on the order of microvolts) in relation to the EEG waveform (which is on the order of tens of microvolts) in which they are embedded. For this reason, it is necessary to employ signal processing techniques to extract the 'signal' (the time-locked ERP) from the 'noise' (the background EEG). By far the most commonly used signal extraction technique is averaging. This involves recording a number of EEG epochs, each of which is time-locked to repetitions of the same event (or event class). The digital EEG values for each time-point in the epoch are then averaged to yield a single vector of values representing the average activity at each time-point. This is the average event-related potential (see Fig. 1.2). Given the assumption that EEG activity not time-locked to the event will vary randomly across epochs, this 'background' EEG will tend to average to zero, and the residual waveform after averaging should therefore largely represent activity that bears a fixed temporal relationship to the event across epochs.

One of the disadvantages of the averaging procedure is that it cannot provide

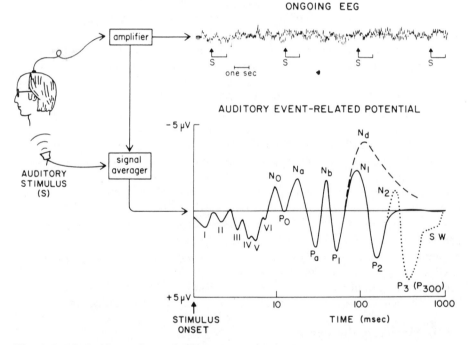

Fig. 1.2 'Idealized waveform of the computer-averaged auditory event-related potential (ERP) to brief sound. The ERP is generally too small to be detected in the ongoing EEG (top) and requires computer averaging over many stimulus presentations to achieve adequate signal/noise ratios. The logarithmic time display allows visualization of the early brainstem responses (Waves I–VI), the midlatency components (No, Po, Na, Pa, Nb), the "vertex potential" waves (P1, N1, P2), and task-related endogenous components (Nd, N2, P300, and slow wave).' (From Hillyard and Kutas (1983): Fig. 1, p. 35. Reproduced with permission from the *Annual Review of Psychology*, Volume 34, © 1983 by Annual Reviews.)

a direct estimate of the ERP elicited by individual events. For this reason, the resulting average ERP cannot be compared directly with other measures, such as reaction time, that can be derived from individual experimental trials. Furthermore, the average waveform may not, in fact, resemble the actual waveform that is recorded on an individual trial. For example, if the amplitude of a particular waveform feature on individual trials has a bimodal distribution, then the average amplitude will not correspond to the actual amplitude of any individual trial. Similar problems will occur if the latency of a particular waveform feature has a bimodal distribution. If this kind of situation obtains, then it is difficult to interpret an amplitude difference between two average waveforms. Such a difference could be due to a difference in latency variability or to a difference in the proportion of trials in the two modes of a bimodal amplitude distribution, rather than to a real change in amplitude on individual trials.

Because of these problems with signal averaging, there have been many attempts to devise other signal extraction procedures that can provide an estimate of the ERP for each event of interest. The most primitive of these involves the use of analogue or digital filters which attenuate frequencies in the EEG that are either higher or lower than those contained in the ERP signal of interest. More complex filters involve cross-correlation procedures that effectively search the epoch on each trial for regions of maximal correspondence with a predefined template. Thus, if one expects an epoch to contain an ERP of a particular kind (that is, a waveform with a characteristic shape), one can determine the portion of the epoch that corresponds best to this template (Glaser and Ruchkin 1976; Woody 1967). The template can be established on a priori grounds, or it can be derived empirically using a technique such as stepwise discriminant function analysis (Squires and Donchin 1976). The template might also take account of the expected distribution of the ERP across the scalp, in which case the filter responds to activity that has a particular topography (Gratton *et al.* 1989). While these techniques for generating measures of the ERP on individual trials show some promise, this promise has as yet only been realized for the largest ERP deflections.

1.3 ERP COMPONENTS AND THEIR MEASUREMENT

Probably no other issue in the methodology of ERP research has aroused more controversy than the question of 'what is an ERP component?'. On the face of it, an answer to the question would seem to be relatively straightforward. After extracting the signal using one of the procedures described in the previous section, one needs merely to focus on some feature of the resulting waveform (for example, a peak or trough), and this feature then becomes the component of interest. In this case, measurement of the feature can be accomplished in a relatively simple fashion merely by determining its amplitude (in μV) and latency (in ms). Amplitude can be measured in relation to some other feature of the waveform (in which case it is referred to as a 'peak-to-peak' measure) or in relation to a baseline (usually defined as the mean voltage level for some period preceding the stimulus or event). Latency can then be measured in terms of the temporal relationship between the feature of the waveform and the stimulus or event of interest. Unfortunately, in at least some circumstances, there are problems with this simple approach to component definition and measurement, and in the next section we shall review these problems and attempts to solve them (see also Donchin *et al.* 1978; Picton and Stuss 1980; Rugg in press).

1.3.1 Defining and extracting ERP components

The greatest impediment to the simple approach mentioned above is 'component overlap'. Component overlap refers to the fact that the waveform we observe by measuring the voltage at the scalp results from the summation of electrical activity that may be generated by several different sources in the brain. As we noted earlier, the brain is a conducting medium. Thus, activity generated in one spatial location may be propagated through the brain tissue and be detectable at other locations. The single voltage we measure at a particular electrode at a particular time may well be attributable to the activity of a variety of different generators in different spatial locations.

One consequence of volume conduction is that there need be no direct correspondence between the timing of the distinctive features of an ERP waveform (that is, its peaks and troughs) and the temporal characteristics of the neural systems whose activity is reflected by the waveform. For example, an ERP peak with a latency of 200 ms, might reflect the activity not of a single neural generator maximally active at that time, but the combined activity of two (or more) generators, maximally active before and after 200 ms, but with fields that summate to a maximum at that time. The ambiguity surrounding the interpretation of peaks and troughs in ERP waveforms has led to the proposal that these features should be described by the theoretically neutral term 'deflection', the term 'component' being reserved for features of the waveform that can be attributed to the activity of specific neuronal populations (Näätänen and Picton 1987).

For researches such as Näätänen and Picton (1987), who adopt what might be called the 'physiological' approach to component definition, a defining characteristic of an ERP component is its anatomical source within the brain. According to this view, then, to measure a particular ERP component, we must have a method of making the contributing sources unambiguous. For other ERP researchers (e.g. Donchin 1979, 1981), who adopt what might be called the 'functional' approach to ERP definition, an ERP component is defined more in terms of the information processing operation with which it is correlated. Thus, components are defined in terms of the cognitive function thought to be performed by the brain systems whose activity is recorded at the scalp. The 'cognitive function' is specified by the nature of independent variables whose manipulation effects the component, and by the relationships observed between the component and other measures (e.g. overt behavioral measures like response speed and accuracy). According to this view, it is entirely possible for a component to be identified with a particular feature of the waveform that reflects the activity of multiple generators within the brain, so long as these generators constitute a functionally homogeneous system.

Although it is easy to describe physiological and psychological approaches to component definition as if they are mutually exclusive, it should be noted that for many investigators both approaches play a role. For example, in what has become a classic approach to component definition, Donchin *et al.* (1978) argued that a component should be defined by a combination of its polarity, its characteristic latency, its distribution across the scalp, and its sensitivity to characteristic experimental manipulations. Note that polarity and distribution imply a consistency in physiological source, while latency and sensitivity imply a consistency in psychological function.

1.3.1.1 *Physiological approaches to component identification*

Recent years have seen increased interest in attempts to identify the intracranial sources of the electrical activity recorded at the scalp. A variety of different kinds of approaches have been used to inform source questions. These include: intracranial recording in humans (e.g. Halgren *et al.* 1980; McCarthy and Wood 1987), whereby electrical activitity recorded from electrodes placed inside the brain is related to scalp activity; the use of PET and other functional neuroimaging techniques, to relate the scalp ERP to localized neural activity detected in analogous tasks (see Compton *et al.* 1991 and Chapter 2); the development of animal models (e.g. Pineda and Swick 1992) that permit one to apply the techniques of neuroscience (e.g. lesions, neurochemistry, and single- and multiple-unit recordings) to the study of neural systems in animals that may correspond to the systems responsible for ERP generation in humans; and studies of neurological cases, that allow one to identify relationships between brain lesions and distortions in scalp electrical activity (see Knight (1991) and Rugg (1992, in press) for reviews of this approach). Data from these different approaches can be used to constrain both the locus and number of sources for a given ERP effect, although the information they provide is somewhat indirect.

There has, however, been steady progress in the development of more direct techniques that allow ERP sources to be inferred directly from scalp fields themselves. Among the most advanced of these techniques is the Brain Electrical Source Analysis procedure (BESA: Scherg 1990). This procedure starts from the assumptions that the ERP waveform represents the summation of the activity of a number of different sources of fixed location within the brain, and that these sources can be appropriately modelled as 'equivalent dipoles'. A BESA 'solution' consists of the specification of these sources in terms of their number, location, orientation, and the time-courses and relative strengths of their activity. Such solutions can be assessed by computing the scalp fields that they would generate, and determining the 'goodness of fit' between these predicted fields and those observed empirically.

An important feature of the BESA procedure is that the location and other parameters of putative sources can be constrained by the experimenter in the light of, for instance, anatomical knowledge, or of information obtained from a complementary technique such as PET scanning. A second important feature of the BESA procedure is that the contribution made by each source to the ERP can be regarded as an independent ERP component. Hence the technique provides, at least in principle, a means of reducing and describing ERP data in terms of the parameters of a relatively small number of underlying components, each associated with its own putative generator in the brain.

Because of the increasing availability of programs implementing 'source localization' procedures such as BESA, physiological approaches to the decomposition and quantification of ERP waveforms are likely to grow in popularity. Although these procedures undoubtedly provide a useful tool for the reduction and quantification of ERP data, it is as well to remember that such techniques are no panacea for some of the problems afflicting ERP research. First, when used in the hypothesis-generating mode, they do not solve the 'inverse problem' — that is, they do not provide a unique solution to account for the distribution of the scalp activity on the basis of the activity of a number of intracranial sources. Indeed, it is quite possible using, say, the BESA procedure to come up with more than one plausible, well-fitting configuration of sources for the same ERP data set. Second, the techniques are predicated on the assumption that it is physiologically meaningful to characterize ERP generators mathematically as 'equivalent dipoles'; ideal generators that, from a distance, behave as if they give rise to a classic dipolar electromagnetic field. While the approximation of active neural tissue to a single equivalent dipole is appropriate when the area of tissue is relatively small, this may not be so for larger areas. Note especially that, for mathematical reasons, the locus of the equivalent dipole for a large volume of active neural tissue (with a large number of neurons with parallel processes) will appear to be deeper within the brain than the neural tissue which it represents.

1.3.1.2 Psychological approaches to component identification

From a psychological perspective, the principal problem when decomposing ERP waveforms is posed by the need to select a specific feature of the waveform that is related to a specific psychological process. If one adopts any but the most simple view of the information processing system, then one would expect that different processing operations are likely to be occurring in parallel, and therefore that any particular 'surface' feature of the waveform, like a peak or trough, could reflect more than one process.

When conceptualized in this way, it can be seen that the one obvious approach to the problem of component overlap is to subtract waveforms obtained in different experimental conditions to 'isolate' the component whose presence differentiates between the conditions. Whatever is different between the two waveforms is the component of interest, and this component is then identified with whatever cognitive process is believed to differ between the conditions. Many different components have been identifed in this way including the Nd or Processing

Negativity (see Hillyard and Hansen (1986); Näätänen (1992); and see Chapter 3), the Mismatch Negativity (see Näätänen 1992; and Chapter 3), and the Dm (see Paller *et al.* 1987; and see Chapter 5). Furthermore, this approach has also been adopted in PET studies to isolate patterns of brain metabolism that are associated with specific cognitive operations and processes (see Chapter 2).

To readers who are cognitive psychologists, this 'subtractive' approach will be reminiscent of the Donderian approach to the measurement of stage durations (e.g. Donders 1868/1969; and see Chapter 4). Of course, the assumptions that underlie this approach, particularly that of 'pure insertion', are also applicable to the subtraction procedure when applied to ERPs. In the ERP context, 'pure insertion' refers to the assumption that one can create two conditions such that the conditions differ only in the process of interest and are equivalent with respect to all other processes. It would clearly be inadvisable to use the subtraction procedure to extract components if the 'pure insertion' assumption cannot be demonstrably supported.

An additional problem for the use of the subtraction procedure in ERP research is that any difference in the latency of the same component in the two conditions will produce a deflection in the subtraction waveforms. This would suggest that there is a component when, in fact, the waveforms differ only with respect to the latency of the same component.

Other attempts to develop methods for component extraction have tried to exploit patterns of covariation in ERP data sets. The most popular such method is Principal Components Analysis (or PCA; see Donchin and Heffley (1978) for a thorough description of the procedure as applied to ERP data). The purpose of PCA is to identify common sources of variance in a set of data. For the ERP researcher, these data comprise values representing variation in the voltage over time during the recording epoch, variation in voltage across different electrode locations, and variation in voltage across different experimental manipulations. As we have noted, variation in ERP voltage across the scalp is attributed to the locus of the source(s) of the ERP in the brain, while variation in voltage as a function of experimental manipulation is attributed to variation in the psychological processes that are engaged in a situation. The purpose of PCA in this context is to identify aspects of the waveform that show covariation over both experimental conditions and scalp locations. Thus, PCA can be regarded as a hybrid approach that embodies features of both physiological and psychological approaches to component definition.

When PCA is applied to a set of ERP data, it yields a set of 'components', each of which is characterized by a vector of weights, one weight for each time-point in the waveform. These weights can be thought of as a linear filter that 'enhances' the waveform at some time-points and some scalp locations, while attenuating the waveform at other time-points and locations. When the values for a particular waveform are multiplied by the weights, and the resulting values are summed (to yield 'factor scores'), we have a measure of the degree to which the component is present in that waveform. These factor scores are then used as 'amplitude' measures of the component.

It is important to note that PCA is a procedure that merely identifies patterns of covariance in a set of waveforms. These patterns of covariance or components still need to be interpreted by the researcher. This is usually accomplished with reference to the polarity, latency, and distribution of the component, as well as to its sensitivity to experimental manipulations (Donchin *et al.* 1978).

From around the mid 1970s to mid 1980s PCA was perhaps the single most popular analytical method in cognitive ERP research. Since that time the technique has become less popular, at least in part because of two problems that limit its application. First, as with the subtraction procedure described earlier, PCA may yield spurious components if the latency of a component varies with experimental conditions. Second, a simulation study by Wood and McCarthy (1984) suggested that, when applied to ERP-like data, the PCA procedure tends to 'misallocate' variance between extracted components. Some of the variance that should have been attributed to one component (given the way the simulated data set was constructed) became associated with a second, supposedly orthogonal component. In the light of these findings, it would be unwise at present to use PCA as the sole means of component identification or quantification. Further work is required to determine the pervasiveness of the the misallocation problem using a wider range of data sets, both simulated and real.

1.3.1.3. Summary

In this section we have considered two central issues in ERP methodology, the identification and the extraction of components. Whether a component is defined in terms of the brain system that generates it, or the psychological process it manifests, the problem of component overlap must be confronted. Particular brain systems and particular cognitive processes are unlikely to be activated in isolation, and we therefore need procedures that will allow us to make unambiguous (to 'disambiguate') the components whose activity contributes to the observed waveform. We have reviewed techniques that approach the problem from either the physiological or the psychological domain or both, and it is evident that the ultimate solution has not been reached. A promising approach would be to devise a technique that, like PCA, can incorporate both physiological and psychological definitions. However, unlike PCA, the technique would have to be able to handle the problems of latency variability and misallocation of variance. Although this perfect solution is not yet a reality, it is nevertheless the case that considerable progress has been made, and, in the next section, we review the more common of the ERP components that have been identified so far using the 'less-than-perfect' techniques currently available.

1.3.2 A compendium of ERP components

In this section we provide a brief review of some of the more commonly recorded components. The review provides some historical perspective. In most cases we reproduce the waveforms that were provided in the papers that contained the initial reports of the components and we provide a brief narrative description of the paradigms. Following other reviews of this kind (for example, see Donchin *et al.* 1978), we find it convenient to categorize ERP components in terms of those that precede and those that follow events, whose occurrence can be defined in relation to external criteria, like the time of presentation of a particular stimulus or the time at which an overt behavioural response is executed. The need for an external criterion is occasioned by the fact that we must decide where in the ongoing EEG we should look for our ERPs. As we noted earlier, the ERPs are small in relation to the background EEG signal and we must therefore use averaging or some other technique to extract the ERP signal from the EEG noise. These signal extraction techniques require that the search for the ERP is confined to a particular epoch that is defined with reference to an external criterion. In the case of the event-preceding components, this means that one looks backward in time from the external criterion for the ERP that precedes the event in question. Of course, this should not imply that we believe in backward causation — rather, we just have no way of knowing when the antecedent causal event occurred. (For a discussion of this issue in the context of movement-related potentials, see Libet (1985) and associated commentary.)

1.3.2.1 Event-preceding components

Readiness potential (bereitschaftspotential) This component was first identified by Kornhuber and Deeke (1965) in their studies of voluntary movements. As can be seen in Fig. 1.3, there is a slow, ramp-like negative shift that precedes the actual production of a voluntary hand movement by as much as 1000 ms. The negativity is maximal at precentral electrode sites, and it peaks (about 10–15 μV) at about the time of overt movement. In Fig. 1.3 we see that, as the time of the impending

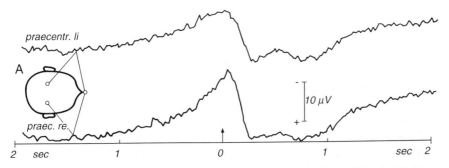

Fig. 1.3 'Brain potential changes during voluntary movement of the left hand. Movement onset . . . indicated by the arrow. Negative potential during preparation, positive potential after movement with larger amplitude over the contralateral (right) brain hemisphere. Unipolar derivation with the precentral regions referenced against the nose. Average of 512 movements. Negative is up. Left of 0 = time before movement onset in the electromyogram. Vp. G. F.' (From Kornhuber and Deeke (1965): Fig. 1, panel A, p. 4. Copyright © 1965 Springer-Verlag, reprinted by permission. Figure legend translated by Amy Adamson.)

movement approaches, the negativity becomes larger over the right scalp site, contralateral to the left-hand movement. Vaughan and his colleagues (for example Vaughan *et al.* 1968), who independently observed the same component, showed that this lateralized effect was evident for arm, hand, and finger movements. In fact, the precise scalp distribution of this component, has been linked to the somatotopic arrangement of motor cortex. This component, especially its lateralized aspect (referred to as the Lateralized Readiness Potentials LRP), has been related to motor preparation (see Coles 1989; and Chapter 4).

The Contingent Negative Variation (CNV)   The CNV was first observed by Walter and his colleagues (Walter *et al.* 1964). Their paradigm involved the presentation of pairs of stimuli, separated by a time interval, and the establishment of a contingency between the stimuli. In the original experiments, the first stimulus was a click, the second, a flickering light, and the subject was required to make a button-press response to the light. The interval between click and flicker was one sec. As can be seen in Fig. 1.4 (panel D), during the interval between click and flicker, a slow negative wave occurs. The wave can be as large as 20 μV, and it is maximal over fronto-central regions. It has a ramp-like shape and tends to reach its maximum negativity at around the time of the second stimulus. This is the CNV. As can be seen by comparing panel D with the other panels in Fig. 1.4, the CNV is not evident when the click or light were presented alone or when they were paired without the response requirement. The CNV was originally described as an 'expectancy' wave, although more recently it has been linked to motoric and non-motoric preparatory processes (see O-wave and E-wave below).

The O-wave and the E-wave   Several years after the discovery of the CNV, Loveless and Sanford (1974) conducted an experiment that suggested that the CNV was actually composed of at least two components. These two components 'emerged' when the interval between the two stimuli was extended beyond the 1 s originally used by Walter and his colleagues (Walter *et al.* 1964). As can be seen in Fig. 1.5, at intervals of 6 and 15 s there is evidently an initial negative-going response following the first stimulus and a later negative shift that precedes the second stimulus. Loveless and Sanford labelled the early response the 'O-wave', indicating their belief that the response was a sign of orienting, while they labelled the later wave the 'E-wave'. Loveless and Sandford noted the similarity between the E-wave and the readiness potential described by Kornhuber and Deeke. Indeed, some investigators have claimed that the E-wave is the readiness potential and that the requirement that the subject respond to the second stimulus is critical for the E-wave to occur. Others have argued for the existence of non-motoric E-waves that are associated with preparation for the processing of sensory information or performance feedback. For a discussion of these issues, see, for example, Brunia (1993), Harter and Anllo-Vento (1991), Rohrbaugh and Gaillard (1983), or Simons (1988).

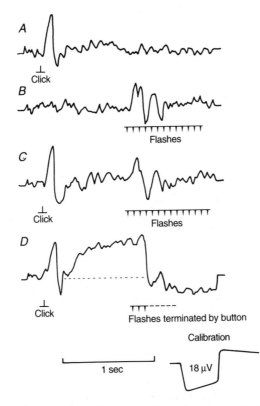

Fig. 1.4 'Averages of responses to 12 presentations. A, response in fronto-vertical region to clicks; B, flicker; C, clicks followed by flicker; D, clicks followed by flicker terminated by the subject pressing a button as instructed. The contingent negative variation (CNV) appears following the conditional response and submerges the negative component of the imperative response.' (From Walter *et al.* (1964): Fig. 1, p. 381. Reprinted with permission of *Nature*. Copyright © 1964 Macmillan Magazine Ltd.)

1.3.2.2 *Event-following components*

For the sake of classification, it has proved useful to distinguish between two classes of components that follow events. On the one hand there are a set of components whose characteristics (amplitude, latency, and distribution) seem to depend on the physical properties of sensory stimuli, such as their modality and intensity. These are *exogenous* components. It has been claimed that their characteristics are immune to variations in the subject's state and to the nature of the interaction between the subject and the stimulus — that is, that they are not influenced by 'cognitive' manipulations. On the other hand there is another set of components whose characteristics (and indeed whose very existence) depends on the nature of the subject's interaction with the stimulus. These components vary as a function of such factors as attention, task relevance, and the nature of

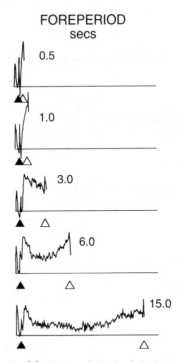

Fig. 1.5 'CNVs . . . at each of five intervals (0.5, 1.0, 3.0, 6.0, and 15.0 sec.) between warning signal (▲) and imperative signal (△) in a regular series. Each plot has been terminated after the major peak of the evoked response to the imperative signal. The baseline is the average level of the EEG during a period of 1 sec. preceding the warning signal. A calibration pulse of −20 μV is shown at the beginning of each plot.' (From Loveless and Sanford (1974): Fig. 4, panel (a), p. 58. Copyright © 1974. Elsevier Science Publishers, reprinted by permission.)

the processing required by the stimulus, and some can be elicited even in the absence of an external event, as, for example, when an expected stimulus does not occur (e.g. Sutton *et al.* 1967). These are the *endogenous* components.

Like most dichotomies, the endogenous–exogenous distinction has proved to be an oversimplification of the real state of affairs. Almost all the early 'sensory' components have been shown to be modifiable by cognitive manipulations (e.g. attention) and many of the later 'cognitive' components have been shown to be influenced by the physical attributes of the eliciting conditions (e.g. modality of the stimulus). For this reason it appears to be more accurate to conceive of an exogenous–endogenous *dimension* that is roughly coextensive with time. Thus, those ERP components that occur within the first 100 ms of stimulus presentation tend to be more exogenous, while those occurring later tend to be more endogenous. In the following review, components are discussed in approximate order of their latencies and, thus, in order of increasing sensitivity to cognitive factors.

Sensory components   Sensory stimuli in all modalities are associated with a series of deflections in the ERP that are related to the transmission of sensory information from the peripheral sensory system to the cortex and/or the arrival of that information in the cortex. For some modalities the latencies of the earliest of these deflections are extremely short (a few milliseconds) and, in this case, the deflections undoubtedly reflect the transmission of sensory information in the sensory pathways. For example, for auditory stimuli one can detect the so-called 'brainstem' responses that have a latency of less than 10 ms and, as their name implies, these deflections correspond to the activation of various nuclei in the brainstem that are associated with the transmission of auditory information. Later deflections (with latencies up to 100 ms) correspond to the arrival of this information in various regions of the cortex. A similar situation obtains with somatosensory stimuli. However, for visual stimuli only the later deflections seem to be evident, presumably because the neurons in the sensory relay nuclei (e.g. the lateral geniculate nucleus) are configured such that they constitute closed fields, and thus their activity is not observable at the scalp. Although, for all modalities, many of these sensory components are modifiable by, for example, attentional manipulations, the components are also 'obligatory' in the sense that they will be observed in every individual and on every occasion unless the sensory systems in question are compromised in some way.

Nd/processing negativity   While the sensory components reviewed in the previous section are obligatory, the 'Nd' (or negative difference wave; see Hillyard and Hansen (1986) and Chapter 3) and the 'processing negativity' (Näätänen *et al.* 1978) provide a classic example of the optional, endogenous or more cognitive nature of some ERP components. The Nd and processing negativity are descriptors of the same component, although the claims about the functional significance of the component are somewhat different. 'Nd' emphasizes the polarity and operation used to identify the component, the Nd being isolated by taking the difference between two ERP waveforms that are elicited in response to the same physical stimulus. The critical comparison is between ERPs for the same stimulus when it is attended versus when it is unattended. 'Processing negativity' emphasizes the fact that the component is related to some form of extra processing accorded to attended events on the basis of a preceding selection process.

The typical paradigm involves the presentation of streams of stimuli at fast presentation rates, with the stimuli varying as a function of one or more critical attributes. For example, in the classic experiment by Hillyard and his colleagues (Hillyard *et al.* 1973), subjects heard a sequence of tone pips of 800 Hz in the left ear and a sequence of 1500 Hz tone pips in the right ear, in both cases with interstimulus intervals of between 250 and 1250 ms. About one-tenth of the tone pips in each ear were of a slightly higher frequency (840 Hz and 1560 Hz), and the subjects' task was to attend to one ear and count the number of these target higher-frequency tones. In some conditions, they attended to the right ear and in others to the left ear. In experiment 1, the two tone pip sequences were independent, while in experiment 2, a single sequence was used, with an interstimulus interval

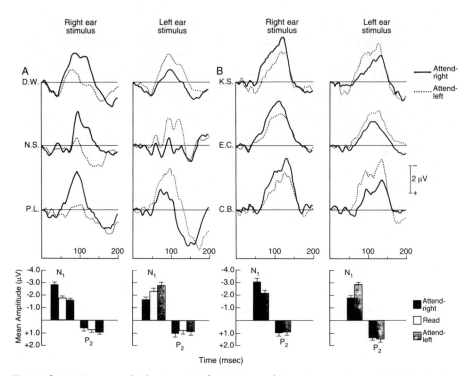

Fig. 1.6 '(a) Vertex evoked potentials from three subjects in experiment 1. Each tracing is the averaged response to all 1024 stimuli that were presented to each ear under attend-right (solid lines) and attend-left (dotted lines) conditions. Stimulus onset is at beginning of tracing. Baselines were drawn through the mean voltage over 0 to 10 ms. Bar graphs give the mean and standard error (10 subjects) of the baseline to peak amplitudes of N_1 and P_2 evoked via each ear under all three experimental conditions. (b) Evoked potentials from three subjects in experiment 2, with bar graphs giving mean amplitudes over all ten subjects.' (From Hillyard *et al.* (1973): Fig. 1, p. 178. *Science*, Volume 182. Copyright © by the AAAS, reprinted by permission.)

of between 100 and 800 ms and each tone being delivered to either right or left ear. The critical comparison (shown in Fig. 1.6) is between the ERPs for attended and unattended stimuli presented in a particular ear. As can be seen in the figure, the attended ERPs were more negative than the unattended ERPs, and this difference was maximal at around 100 ms after stimulus presentation. Hillyard and his colleagues concluded that the effect of attention was to modulate the amplitude of the N1 component, reflecting the fact that, when unattended, sensory input was excluded from further processing. This view can be contrasted with that of Näätänen and his colleagues (e.g. Näätänen *et al.*, 1978), who have argued that the effect of attention is to add a negative shift to the unattended ERP, a shift that is not specifically time-locked to the N1 component. They have claimed that this negative shift was associated with the processing of the target stimulus dimension. Although variations in the paradigms used by Hillyard and by Näätänen, with respect to the interstimulus interval, e.g., may be responsible in part for the differences in interpretation of 'the attention effect', disagreements still persist. These are considered in Chapter 3 and in Näätänen's recent synthesis (Näätänen 1992).

Mismatch negativity and the N2   At about 200 ms following the presentation of some classes of visual and auditory events, a negative component is evident in the ERP waveform. This negative component is referred to as the N200 or N2, although, as several investigators have argued, there may in fact be several different components that are present in the waveform at this time (see Pritchard *et al.* 1991 for a review). The critical condition for the elicitation of this component is that the event must deviate in some way from the prevailing context.

As with the P300 (see below), the typical paradigm involves the presentation of a series of events, with each event belonging to one or other of two or more classes. One class of events is improbable, and the presentation of these rare events elicits the N200. In a classic set of studies by Näätänen and his colleagues (Näätänen *et al.* 1978), probable and improbable events were distinguished first by their intensity (Experiment 1: 1000 Hz tone pips of either 70 or 80 dB) and then by their frequency (Experiment 2: 70 dB tone pips of either 1000 or 1140 Hz). As in the selective attention experiment described in the previous section, the tone pips could occur in either ear and, in different conditions, the subject was instructed to attend to one of the two ears and count the number of rare stimuli presented in the attended ear. To observe the mismatch negativity it is customary to subtract the ERP for the probable events (standards) from the ERP for the improbable events (signals). Of course, this can be done separately for events presented in the attended and in the unattended ear. Figure 1.7 shows the difference waveforms obtained by Näätänen and his colleagues (1978). As can be seen in this figure, the difference waveforms reveal a negativity that peaks at about 200 ms for both left- and right-ear stimuli. Importantly, this negativity is present for both Experiments 1 and 2 (that is for both intensity and pitch deviance) and for both attended and unattended conditions. In the attended condition, the negativity is followed by a positivity (the P300) which we shall discuss in the next section.

The fact that this mismatch negativity (also referred to as the N2a) is present even when the stimuli are unattended, led Näätänen and his colleagues to suggest that it reflects the automatic detection of physical deviance. Indeed, the mismatch negativity appears to be critically dependent on physical deviance of the current stimulus from the prevailing context, and several studies have illustrated that its amplitude is sensitive to the degree of deviance. However, the idea that the component reflects purely automatic processes has been challenged recently by Woldorff *et al.* (1991), who showed that its amplitude may be influenced by attention. Again, this is a controversial area and the interested reader should consult Chapter 3 for further information. Note that the mismatch negativity should not be confused with the second N200 component (the N2b), whose presence depends on the events being task relevant. In many circumstances, this component appears to covary with a later positive component, the P300, or P3b.

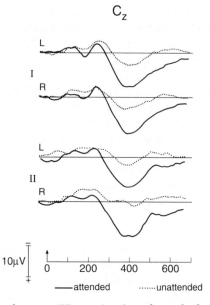

Fig. 1.7 'The difference between EPs to signals and standards (averaged across Ss) . . . for the left (L) and right (R) ear when attended and when unattended. These differences were obtained by subtracting the corresponding time points of the EP to standards from the EP to signals. I refs to Experiment 1, II to Experiment 2.' (From Näätänen *et al.* (1978): Fig. 4, left panel (C_z electrode). Copyright © 1978 Elsevier Science Publishers, reprinted with permission.)

P300, P3, P3a, and P3b   Probably no other component has received as much attention as the P300 and related positive deflections. This is partly because of its size (5–20 μV) and because of the ease with which it can be elicited. In the classic original experiment by Sutton and his colleagues (Sutton *et al.* 1965), subjects were presented with a series of pairs of stimuli, a cueing stimulus and a test stimulus. The test stimuli could be clicks or light flashes. For some pairs, the cueing stimulus was always followed by the same test stimulus and the subject could thus be certain about the sensory quality of the stimulus before it occurred. For other pairs, the cueing stimulus could be followed by either visual or auditory test stimuli. After the presentation of each cueing stimulus, the subject had to guess the modality of the forthcoming test stimulus. The critical comparison concerned the ERPs following test stimuli in certain and uncertain conditions. As can be seen in Fig. 1.8, these ERPS differ in a number of ways. However, the most salient differentiating characteristic is the positivity that peaks at around 300 ms. This is the P300 or P3b.

In subsequent research, the standard paradigm evolved to one in which a series of events are presented to the subject, and the events comprise two classes. One class is generally rarer than the other—hence the name 'oddball task'—and the subject is required to respond in some way to the rarer of the two events. The

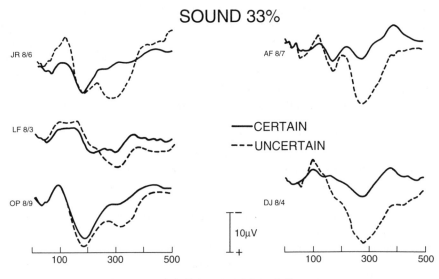

SOUND 33%

—CERTAIN
---UNCERTAIN

TIME (MILLISECONDS)

Fig. 1.8 'Average waveforms for certain and uncertain (P=.33) sounds for five subjects.' (From Sutton *et al.* (1965): Fig. 1, p. 1187. *Science*, Volume 150. Copyright © 1965 by the AAAS, reprinted by permission.)

ERP component consists of positive deflection, that is maximal over the parietal/central area, that has a latency of at least 300 ms and as much as 900 ms. This latency variability is controlled by the ease with which an event can be categorized as belonging to one of the two classes, the more difficult the categorization, the longer the latency. For this reason, it has been argued that the latency of the P300 can be used as a measure of 'stimulus evaluation time' (e.g. see Donchin and Coles 1988*a*,*b*; and Chapter 4 for a review). In tasks with a simple 'oddball' structure, the amplitude of the component depends on probability; the rarer the event, the larger the P300. It also depends on the amount of information extracted from the event. These and other considerations have given rise to the proposal that the P300 reflects a process of context or memory updating by which the current model of the environment is modified as a function of incoming information (e.g. see Donchin and Coles 1988*a*,*b*; and Chapter 4 for a review). Several investigators (e.g. Johnson 1986) have pointed out that the P300 does not appear to be a unitary component and, instead, may represent the activity of a widely distributed system whose constituent parts may be more or less coupled depending on the situation. More precise knowledge of the functional significance of this component or complex of components will have to wait until more information is available about the neural systems involved.

One part of this complex that has been distinguished is the so-called P3a. If a third 'novel' event is introduced into the oddball task, a positive component, different from the classical P300, can be observed. Novelty is defined in the context of the other two events: e.g., a 'dog-bark' in the context of high and low tones. Such novel stimuli elicit a large positivity with a latency that is earlier than that of the target-evoked P300, and a scalp distribution that is more oriented towards the front of the scalp (e.g. see Knight *et al.*, 1989). This component is sometimes referred to as the 'frontal P3' or the 'P3a' to distinguish it from the classic, parietally distributed P300 described in the previous paragraph. The classic P300 is then referred to as the 'P3b' or 'parietal P3'. It is apparent that the P3a and P3b are dependent on the integrity of different brain regions, since Knight and his colleagues have shown that P3a (but not P3b) is influenced by lesions of the frontal cortex. The P3a has been linked to processes involved in the involuntary capture of attention by salient events (Knight 1991).

N400   While the N200 family of components are elicited in response to events that are physically deviant from the prevailing context, the N400 component is sensitive to deviance in relation to much more abstract attributes of the eliciting stimulus, such as meaning. The component was first observed by Kutas and Hillyard (1980) in their classic studies of sentence processing. Subjects were required to read sentences comprised of about seven words, with each word being presented individually at 1 s intervals. In some sentences, the final word was semantically inappropriate but syntactically correct, while in other sentences the final word was larger in letter size than the preceding words. Of course, there were also normal sentences that ended with normal sized, semantically appropriate words. As can be seen in Fig. 1.9, semantically deviant final words elicited a negative deflection with a latency of about 400 ms (the N400), while physically deviant words (in larger type) were associated with the classic P300 (with a latency 0f 560 ms).

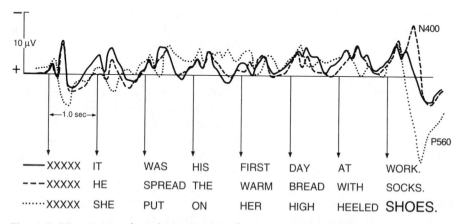

Fig. 1.9 'The timing of word presentations for three sample sentences and typical ERP waveforms recorded over the entire seven-word sentence, averaged over three subjects (in experiment 2 (dashed and solid lines) and three subjects in experiment 3 (dotted line).' (From Kutas and Hillyard (1980): Fig. 1, panel (A), p. 203. *Science*, Volume 207. Copyright © 1980 by the AAAS, reprinted by permission.)

Neither component was evident when the sentence terminated with a word that was both semantically and physically congruous with the preceding words.

Subsequent work has shown that the amplitude of the component is an inverse function of the semantic relatedness between a word and its sentence context, and that it can be elicited in semantic priming paradigms. Furthermore, large N400s are observed in response to isolated words (words with no context), when such words are processed to the level of their identity. Thus, the N400 appears to be a 'default' component, evoked by words whose meaning is unrelated to, or not predicted by, the prior context of the words. The effect of priming, whether contextual or semantic, is to attenuate the component. The dependence of the N400 on semantic relatedness has made it an important tool for the study of on-line semantic processing in written and spoken language (see Chapter 6). However, the N400 is also sensitive to a wide range of non-semantic relationships between words such as phonological or orthographic relatedness (e.g. Rugg and Barrett 1987). N400-like components have also been observed in response to non-verbal stimuli, such as pictures (Barrett and Rugg 1990). Current theories of the functional significance of N400 are discussed in Chapters 5 and 6.

REFERENCES

Allison, T., Wood, C. C., and McCarthy, G. M. (1986). The central nervous system. In *Psychophysiology: systems, processes, and applications* (ed. M. G. H. Coles, E. Donchin, and S. W. Porges), pp. 5–25. Guilford, New York.

Barrett, S. E. and Rugg, M. D. (1990). Event-related potentials and the phonological matching of pictures. *Brain and Language*, **38**, 424–37.

Brunia, C. H. M. (1993). Waiting in readiness: gating in attention and motor preparation. *Psychophysiology*, **30**, 327–39.

Brunia, C. H. M. *et al.* (1989). Correcting ocular artifacts in the EEG: a comparison of several methods. *Journal of Psychophysiology*, **3**, 1–50.

Coles, M. G. H. (1989). Modern mind-brain reading: psychophysiology, physiology and cognition. *Psychophysiology*, **26**, 251–69.

Coles, M. G. H., Gratton, G., and Fabiani, M. (1990). Event-related brain potentials. In *Principles of psychophysiology: physical, social, and inferential elements* (ed. J. T. Cacioppo and L. G. Tassinary), pp. 413–55. Cambridge University Press, Cambridge, UK.

Compton, P., Grossenbacher, P., Posner, M. I., and Tucker, D. M. (1991). A cognitive anatomical approach to attention in lexical access. *Journal of Cognitive Neuroscience*, **3**, 304–12.

Donchin, E. (1979). Event-related brain potentials: a tool in the study of human information processing. In *Evoked potentials and behavior* (ed. H. Begleiter), pp. 13–75. Plenum, New York.

Donchin, E. (1981). Surprise! . . . surprise? *Psychophysiology*, **18**, 493–513.

Donchin, E. and Coles, M. G. H. (1988*a*). Is the P300 component a manifestation of context updating? *Behavioral and Brain Sciences*, **11**, 355–72.

Donchin, E. and Coles, M. G. H. (1988*b*). On the conceptual foundations of cognitive psychophysiology. *Behavioral and Brain Sciences*, **11**, 406–17.

Donchin, E. and Heffley, E. (1978). Multivariate analysis of event-related potential data:

a tutorial review. In *Multidisciplinary perspectives in event-related potential research* (ed. D. Otto), pp. 555–72. US Goverment Printing Office, Washington, DC.

Donchin, E., Ritter, W., and McCallum, C. (1978). Cognitive psychophysiology: the endogenous components of the ERP. In *Brain event-related potentials in man* (ed. E. Callaway, P. Tueting, and S. H. Koslow), pp. 349–411. Academic New York.

Donders, F. C. (1868/1969). On the speed of mental processes. In *Attention and performance II* (ed. and trans. W. G. Koster), pp. 412–31. North-Holland, Amsterdam.

Glaser, E. M. and Ruchkin, D. S. (1976). *Principles of neurobiological signal analysis.* Academic, New York.

Gratton, G., Coles, M. G. H., and Donchin, E. (1983). A new method for off-line remova of ocular artifact. *Electroencephalography and Clinical Neurophysiology*, **55**, 468–84.

Gratton, G., Coles, M. G. H., and Donchin, E. (1989). A procedure for using multi-electrode information in the analysis of components of the event-related potential: vector filter. *Psychophysiology*, **26**, 222–32.

Halgren, E., Squires, N. K., Wilson, C. L., Rohrbaugh, J. W., Babb, T. L., and Crandall, P. H. (1980). Endogenous potentials generated in the human hippocampal formation and amygdala by infrequent events. *Science*, **210**, 803–805.

Harter, M. R. and Anllo-Vento, L. (1991). Visual-spatial attention: preparation and selection in children and adults. In *Event-related potentials of the brain* (EEG Suppl. 42), (ed. C. H. M. Brunia, G. Mulder, and M. N. Verbaten), pp. 183–94. Elsevier, Amsterdam.

Hillyard, S. A. and Hansen, J. C. (1986). Attention: electrophysiological approaches. In *Psychophysiology: systems, processes, and applications* (ed. M. G. H. Coles, E. Donchin and S. W. Porges), pp. 227–43. Guilford, New York.

Hillyard, S. A., and Kutas, M. (1983). Electrophysiology of cognitive processing. *Annual Review of Psychology*, **34**, 33–61.

Hillyard, S. A., Hink, R. F., Schwent, V. L., and Picton, T. W. (1973) Electrical signs of selective attention in the human brain. *Science*, **182**, 177–80.

Jasper, H. (1958). The ten twenty electrode system of the International Federation. *Electroencephalography and Clinical Neurophysiology*, **10**, 371–5.

Johnson, R., Jr. (1986). A triarchic model of P300 amplitude. *Psychophysiology*, **23**, 367–84.

Knight, R. T. (1991). Evoked potential studies of attention capacity in human frontal lobe lesions. In *Frontal lobe function and dysfunction* (ed. H. S. Levin, H. M. Eisenberg, and A. L. Benton), pp. 139–53. Oxford University Press, New York.

Knight, R. T., Scabini, D., Woods, D. L., and Clayworth, C. C. (1989). Contributions of temporal-parietal junction to the human auditory P3. *Brain Research*, **502**, 109–16.

Kornhuber, H. H. and Deecke, L. (1965). Hirnpotentialanderungen bei Willkurbewe-gungen und passiven Bewegungen des Menschen: Bereitschaftspotential und reafferente Potentiale. *Pfulgers Archiv*, **284**, 1–17.

Kutas, M. and Hillyard, S. A. (1980). Reading senseless sentences: brain potentials reflect semantic incongruity. *Science*, **207**, 203–5.

Lehmann, D. (1987). Principles of spatial analysis. In *Handbook of electrophysiology and clinical neurophysiology: Vol. 1. Methods of analysis of brain electrical and magnetic signals* (ed. A. S. Gevins and A. Remond), pp. 309–54. Elsevier, Amsterdam.

Libet, B. (1985). Unconscious cerebral initiative and the role of conscious will in voluntary action. *Behavioral and Brain Sciences*, **8**, 529–66.

Loveless, N. E. and Sanford, A. J. (1974) Effects of age on the contingent negative variation and preparatory set in a reaction-time task. *Journal of Gerontology*, **29**, 52–63.

McCarthy, G. and Wood, C. C. (1987). Intracranial recordings of endogenous ERPs in humans. *Electroencephalography and Clinical Neurophysiology*, Supplement, 39, 331–7.

Näätänen, R. (1992). *Attention and brain function*. Erlbaum, Hillsdale, NJ.

Näätänen, R. and Picton, T. W. (1987). The N1 wave of the human electric and magnetic response to sound: a review and an analysis of the component structure. *Psychophysiology*, 24, 375–425.

Näätänen, R., Gaillard, A. W. K., and Mantysalo, S. (1978) The N1 effect of selective attention reinterpreted. *Acta Psychologica*, 42, 313–29.

Nunez, P. L. (1981). *Electric fields of the brain: the neurophysics of EEG*. Oxford University Press, London.

Nunez, P. L. (1990). Physical principles and neurophysiological mechanisms underlying event-related potentials. In *Event-related brain potentials* (ed. J. W. Rohrbaugh, R. Parasuramen, and R. Johnson), pp. 19–36. Oxford University Press, New York.

Paller, K. A., Kutas, M., and Mayes, A. (1987). Neural correlates of encoding in an incidental learning paradigm. *Electroencephalography and Clinical Neurophysiology*, 67, 360–71.

Perrin, F., Pernier, J., Bertrand, O., and Echallier, J. F. (1989). Spherical spline for scalp potential and current density mapping. *Electroencephalography and Clinical Neurophysiology*, 72, 184–7.

Picton, T. W. (1985). The recording and measurement of evoked potentials. In *A textbook of clinical neurophysiology* (ed. A. M. Halliday, S. R. Butler, and R. Paul), pp. 23–40. Wiley, New York.

Picton, T. W. and Stuss, D. T. (1980). The component structure of the human event-related potentials. In *Motivation, motor and sensory process of the brain. Progress in brain research* (ed. H. H. Kornhuber and L. Deecke), pp. 17–49. Elsevier, Amsterdam.

Pineda, J. A. and Swick, D. (1992). Visual P3-like potentials in squirrel monkey: effects of a noradrenergic agonist. *Brain Research Bulletin*, 28, 485–91.

Pritchard, W. S., Shappell, S. A., and Brandt, M. E. (1991). Psychophysiology N200/ N400: a review and classification scheme. In *Advances in psychophysiology*, Vol. 4, (ed. J. R. Jennings, P. K. Ackles, and M. G. H. Coles), pp. 43–106. Jessica Kingsley, London.

Rohrbaugh, J. and Gaillard, A. W. K. (1983). Sensory and motor aspects of the contingent negative variation. In *Tutorials in event-related potentials research: endogenous components* (ed. A. W. K. Gaillard and W. Ritter), pp. 269–310. North-Holland, Amsterdam.

Rugg, M. D. (1992). Event-related potentials in clinical neuropsychology. In *The handbook of neuropsychological assessment* (ed. J. R. Crawford, W. A. McKinlay, and D. M. Parker), pp. 393–412. Erlbaum, Hillsdale, NJ.

Rugg, M. D. Cognitive event-related potentials: intracerebral and lesion studies. In *Handbook of neuropsychology*, Vol. 9, (ed. R. Johnson, J. C. Baron, J. Grafman, and J. Hendler). Elsevier, Amsterdam. (In press.)

Rugg, M. D. and Barrett, S. E. (1987). Event-related potentials and the interaction between orthographic and phonological information in a rhyme-judgment task. *Brain and Language*, 32, 336–61.

Scherg, M. (1990). Fundamentals of dipole source potential analysis. In *Auditory evoked magnetic fields and electric potentials. Advances in audiology*, Vol. 6, (ed. F. Grandori, M. Hoke, and G. L. Romani), pp. 40–69. Karger, Basel.

Scherg, M. and Picton, T. W. (1991). Separation and identification of event-related potential components by brain electric source analysis. In *Event-related brain research*, EEG Suppl. 42, (ed. C. H. Brunia, G. Mulder, and M. N. Verbaten), pp. 24–37. Elsevier, Amsterdam.

Simons, R. F. (1988). Event-related slow brain potentials: a perspective from ANS psychophysiology. In *Advances in psychophysiology*, Vol. 3, (ed. P. I. Ackles, J. R. Jennings, and M. G. H. Coles), pp. 223–67. JAI Press, Greenwich, CT.

Squires, K. C. and Donchin, E. (1976). Beyond averaging: the use of discriminant functions to recognize event-related potentials elicited by single auditory stimuli. *Electroencephalography and Clinical Neurophysiology*, 41, 449–59.

Sutton, S., Braren, M., Zubin, J., and John, E. R. (1965). Evoked potential correlates of stimulus uncertainty. *Science*, 150, 1187–8.

Sutton, S., Tueting, P., Zubin, J., and John, E. R. (1967). Information delivery and the sensory evoked potential. **Science**, 155, 1436–9.

Tucker, D. (1993). Spatial sampling of head electrical fields: the geodesic electrode net. *Electroencephalography and Clinical Neurophysiology*, 87, 154–63.

Vaughan, H. G., jun., Costa, L. D., and Ritter, W. (1968). Topography of the human motor potential. *Electroencephalography and Clinical Neurophysiology*, 25, 1–10.

Walter, W. G., Cooper, R., Aldridge, V. J., McCallum, W. C., and Winter, A. L. (1964). Contingent negative variation: an electrical sign of sensorimotor association and expectancy in the human brain. *Nature*, 230, 380–4.

Woldorff, M. G., Hackley, S. A., and Hillyard, S. A. (1991). The effects of channel-selective attention on the mismatch negativity wave elicited by deviant tones. *Psychophysiology*, 28, 30–42.

Wood, C. C. (1987). Generators of event-related potentials. In *A textbook of clinical neurophysiology* (ed. A. M. Halliday, S. R. Butler, and R. Paul), pp. 535–67. Wiley, New York.

Wood, C. C. and McCarthy, G. (1984). Principal component of event-related potentials: simulation studies demonstrate misallocation of variance across components. *Electroenecphalography and Clinical Neurophysiology*, 59, 249–60.

Woody, C. D. (1967). Characterization of an adaptive filter for the analysis of variable latency neuroelectrical signaineering, *Medical and Biological Engineering*, 5, 539–53.

2 The ERP and cognitive psychology: conceptual issues

Michael D. Rugg and Michael G. H. Coles

2.1 THE ERP IN COGNITIVE PSYCHOLOGY

For many cognitive psychologists, particularly those who work within the information processing framework, the goal of cognitive psychology is to identify the cognitive processes that mediate between the environment and overt behaviour, the representations on which these processes operate, the ways in which they interact, and their temporal properties. The conventional methodologies of cognitive psychology do not permit cognitive processes and representations to be observed directly. Instead, they must be inferred by a judicious selection of experimental manipulations, and by an analysis of the effects of these manipulations on overt behaviour.

Given that cognitive processes are implemented by the brain, it seems to make sense to explore the possibility that measures of brain activity can provide insights into their nature. The ERP appears to be a good candidate in this regard, not least because it can be recorded at the time these processes are supposedly occurring. And as we have seen in Chapter 1, there is sufficient variability in the features of the ERP, both in time and space, to suggest that it might accommodate at least some of the richness of the neural activity associated with cognitive processing. The use of the word 'might' in the preceding sentence is intentional. It is entirely possible that those aspects of brain activity that we can detect through our scalp electrodes are inconsequential with respect to the processes that are of interest to the cognitive psychologist. Thus only empirical investigation will determine whether, in fact, measures of the ERP can provide insights at the functional level.

2.2 OTHER PHYSIOLOGICAL MEASURES OF COGNITIVE PROCESSING

The ERP is one of a number of physiological measures of activity in the central nervous system that can be used in cognitive studies. Related measures include parameters of the spontaneous EEG, and the magnetic homologues of the ERP and EEG (magnetoencephalographic indices). These electrical and magnetic measures have in common the desirable property that they can provide records of brain activity at essentially any scale of temporal resolution. This is especially

advantageous for the study of fast-acting processes underlying the rapid identification and categorization of stimuli; processes commonly studied in behavioural
experiments by reaction-time techniques. However, measures of electrical and
magnetic fields both suffer from the fact that the localization of their intracranial
sources is a difficult undertaking (see Chapter 1). As a result, at present we know
little about the brain systems responsible for endogenous, task-sensitive electrical
and magnetic activity, although there are good grounds for optimism (Rugg in
press; Swick *et al.* 1994).

In the last decade or so techniques have been developed that make it possible
to image the brain's metabolic activity directly, the most important of which is
positron emission tomography (PET; Raichle 1990). Using radioactive tracers
with short half-lives (e.g. $H_2^{15}O$) to obtain PET images of cerebral blood flow,
small task-specific changes in flow can be localized with an accuracy of less than
a centimetre. The application of PET to the study of cognitive processing relies
on the principle that one can localize differences in regional cerebral blood flow
between experimental conditions designed to differ solely with respect to the
cognitive operation(s) of interest. On the assumption that changes in blood flow
signify changes in neural activity at the same location, the technique allows brain
regions differing in activity as a function of experimental condition to be identified. In a typical 'cognitive activation' study, multiple scans are obtained from
each subject in a range of experimental conditions. The scans are normalized to
a standard stereotaxic space, and differences in flow between a pair of conditions
are revealed by subtracting the scans obtained in each condition, and performing
across-subject statistical comparisons to identify regions in which blood flow
differs significantly. The PET technique has been used to draw inferences about
the neuroanatomic correlates of cognitive processes implicated in activities such
as word and face recognition (Howard *et al.* 1992; Sergent *et al.* 1992), selective
visual attention (Corbetta *et al.* 1990), and memory (Paulesu *et al.* 1993; Squire
et al. 1992).

Unlike the electrical and magnetic measures discussed above, PET and related
techniques allow task-related changes in brain activity (or more accurately, those
components of such activity associated with detectable changes in blood flow) to
be localized with a high degree of precision. In its present state of development,
however, the temporal resolution of the PET technique is several tens of seconds,
some three orders of magnitude greater than what can be achieved using electrical
or magnetic recordings of brain activity. Recent developments in functional
magnetic resonance imaging (fMRI) offer the prospect of imaging changes in
regional blood flow/volume over very much shorter intervals than those currently
possible with PET (e.g. McCarthy *et al.* 1993). In addition, fMRI can overcome
the restrictions imposed by the need to limit radiation dosage, and to employ
experimental designs in which the conditions are blocked rather than mixed. None
the less, so long as the dependent variable in functional neuroimaging is a correlate
of blood flow or volume, the response time of the cerebral vasculature (more
than 1 s; see Friston *et al.* (1993) for a review) sets a physiological limit on the
temporal resolution that can be achieved. This resolution is too coarse, probably

by about two orders of magnitude, to track cognitively related neural activity in real-time.

PET and related functional neuroimaging techniques clearly have a central role to play in identifying brain regions that may contribute to the implementation of different cognitive operations. However, because of their lack of temporal resolution, these techniques are currently of limited value in the study of the dynamics of cognitive processes and their neural substrates. They also suffer from a number of more practical disadvantages, not least among which are their great expense and high level of technological complexity.

In spite of these disadvantages, the very high spatial resolution that can be achieved in functional neuroimaging studies means that such studies may have an important bearing on the interpretation of ERP data. To the extent that, say, PET and ERP measures can be obtained under comparable experimental conditions, it might be possible to exploit the PET findings to develop hypotheses about the likely neural origins of task-sensitive features of the ERP. Unfortunately, integrating ERP and functional neuroimaging data does not promise to be easy, since the neurobiological constraints that determine whether an experimental manipulation will lead to a measurable effect are fundamentally different for the two techniques.

As outlined in more detail in Chapter 1 (Section 1.2.2), ERP waveforms are reflections of synchronous activity in neuronal populations oriented so as to produce an electrical field on the scalp. Asynchronous activity, or activity in populations unfavourably oriented with respect to the scalp, will therefore not be detected. However, neuronal activity with the appropriate properties need only persist for a few tens of milliseconds during the course of the processing of a stimulus to be observable in an ERP. By contrast, to be detected by a functional neuroimaging technique, neural activity, and thus its associated metabolic correlates, need not be synchronous or time-locked to an event at all. The activity must, however, be present over a sufficiently large fraction of the scanning period to show up above background 'noise'. It remains to be seen whether, in practice, the different preconditions for detecting task- and/or stimulus-evoked changes in ERP and metabolic measures are a significant obstacle to the integration of data from the two techniques. In the present state of knowledge, it would be unwise to assume that it is invariably the case that the same brain regions are responsible for task-related changes in the two kinds of measure, no matter how similar the procedures employed to obtain the two data sets.

2.3 MAKING INFERENCES FROM ERPS

In the following two subsections, we examine the functional inferences that can be made from ERP data and the assumptions upon which these inferences are based. In the first subsection, we focus on current practice, and catalogue, in order of the number and complexity of their supporting assumptions, the inferences that are commonly made on the basis of cognitive ERP data. In the subsequent subsection, we step back a little, and examine in more detail the basic assumptions underlying attempts to draw functional conclusions from ERP data.

Although the discussions below focus on ERPs, many of the issues raised are no less germane to attempts to understand human cognitive function using other physiological measures, such as those derived from functional neuroimaging techniques. This is especially true of the issues surrounding the difficulties, discussed in Section 2.3.2.2, of establishing the *functional significance* of a biological correlate of a hypothesized cognitive process. That is, of determining the causal role, in information processing terms, of brain activity reflected by a physiological measure.

2.3.1 Making inferences from ERPs I

For the purposes of illustration, consider the situation in which we record an ERP from subjects in two different conditions, A and B, and obtain the two average waveforms shown in Fig. 2.1 (see Coles *et al.* (1991) for further discussion of this issue).

1. *Level 1*. At the most basic level, we can infer from Fig. 2.1 that the two conditions have different effects on the ERP. Such an inference depends solely on the application of a conventional statistical test to measures of some feature of the waveform. If we assume that the ERP represents some facet of neural activity, and that cognitive processes are manifested in this neural activity, then we can also infer that the cognitive processing associated with the two conditions in some way differs. Inferences as to how the processing is different depend on a conceptual analysis of the differences between the two conditions.

2. *Level 2*. Inspection of Fig. 2.1 reveals that the waveforms for the two conditions begin to differ about 150 ms after the onset of the eliciting event. Appropriate statistical tests can be applied to determine the latency at which the

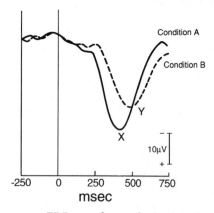

Fig. 2.1 Hypothetical average ERP waveforms obtained under two experimental conditions, A and B. There are a number of differences between these waveforms, for example in the latency and amplitude of the peaks marked X and Y, and these differences provide the basis for inferences about the processing differences between the two conditions. See text for further details.

waveforms do in fact differ. If we again assume that the ERP represents some facet of neural activity, and that some cognitive process is manifested in this activity, then we can make the inference that, by at least 150 ms, the processing in the two conditions is different. It is important to note that the ERP difference only places an *upper* bound on the time by which processing is different. It is entirely possible that processing begins to differ at an earlier point in time, but that such a difference is not evident in the ERP. In spite of this limitation, the finding that a pair of ERPs differ at a particular point in time can in principle be used to provide important constraints on the time-course of processing. As with Level 1, the complexity of Level 2 inferences can be enhanced by a conceptual analysis of the differences between the two conditions.

3. *Level 3.* It is possible to take advantage of the spatial dimension of ERPs to enlarge upon Level 1 and Level 2 type inferences by searching for evidence of parallel processes. For example, suppose it was found that one experimental variable affected ERPs at the Pz electrode in a characteristic fashion, while another variable simultaneously gave rise to a different kind of ERP effect at the Fz site. Such a finding would arguably provide good evidence that the variables in question engaged neurally (and thus perhaps functionally) different processes that over-lapped in time. By the same token, differences in distribution over the scalp of the waveforms elicited in the two conditions could constitute evidence that the two conditions engaged non-equivalent neural/functional processes.

4. *Level 4.* As can be seen in Fig. 2.1, the waveforms differ with respect to the latency of a positive peak, labelled X and Y. The reliability of this difference can be established using standard statistical procedures. If we know what process is manifested by this positive peak, then we can infer that the two conditions differ with respect to this process. Whereas for the preceding inferences specification of the process depends on a conceptual analysis of the differences between the two conditions, Level 4 inferences depend on prior information about the functional significance of the waveform feature. For example, on the basis of a variety of studies, it has been claimed that positive peaks of the kind shown in Fig. 2.1 (referred to as P300s or P3bs; see Chapter 1) do not occur until after the event has been fully evaluated (e.g. Donchin and Coles 1988*a,b*). If this claim is accepted, then one can infer that stimulus evaluation processes take longer in condition B than in condition A. Of course, this inference also depends on the assumption that all the other factors that could influence the latency of the positive peaks are equivalent across the two conditions.

5. *Level 5.* In Fig. 2.1 it is also the case that the size or amplitude of the positive peaks is different in the two conditions. Again this can be supported by statistical tests applied to some amplitude measure. If we know that variations in the size of the component reflect variations in the degree to which some process is invoked, then we can infer that the two conditions differ in this regard. As with Level 4 inferences, this kind of knowledge is gained by independent studies that have explored both the 'determinants' and 'consequences' of amplitude variation. These studies have as their aim a specification of the kinds of experimental variables

whose manipulation influences the amplitude of a component, as well as a description of the relationship between amplitude variability and some other aspect of the subject's behaviour (for example, reaction time). These kinds of data are then used to generate a theory that specifies the cognitive process that is related to the component. In the case of the P300 or P3b, it has been proposed that amplitude variations reflect variations in the degree to which a representation of the experimental context is updated. If this proposal is accepted, then the differences between conditions shown in Fig. 2.1 can support the inference that updating processes are greater in condition A than B (see Donchin (1981) and Donchin and Coles (1988*a,b*) for an amplification of these arguments).

2.3.2 Making Inferences from ERPs II

As we discussed in the preceding sections, inferences can be drawn from ERP data at a number of different levels. These inferences are dependent on specific sets of assumptions about the relationship between ERPs, cognitive processes, and brain activity. In this subsection, we discuss some of the more general issues that constrain the functional interpretation of ERP (and other physiological) data.

One simple but important constraint, already alluded to, comes from the asymmetry between what can be concluded from the presence versus the absence of an effect of an experimental variable. A reliable difference between ERPs as a function of an experimental manipulation demonstrates that the manipulation engendered differential brain activity. But the absence of such a difference does not permit the opposite conclusion, namely, that the manipulation in question did not give rise to differential brain activity. Differences in activity may well have occurred, but with too small an amplitude to be detectable at the scalp, or in tissue unfavourably configured for the generation of field potentials. Thus to draw strong conclusions on the basis of null effects, it is not sufficient merely to determine that two experimental conditions yield statistically indistinguishable ERP waveforms. Rather, it is necessary to have a strong pre-experimental hypothesis that predicts the likely size of the ERP difference to be expected if the hypothesis of a null effect is invalid, and an experimental design of sufficient power to detect this difference should it exist.

In the previous subsection, the different kinds of inference that can be drawn from ERP data were ordered with respect to the number and complexity of their supporting assumptions. The simplest case, it was argued, occurs when ERP data are used merely as a means of establishing whether two or more experimental conditions are associated with differential processing. It is instructive to consider in more detail the assumptions that underlie this apparently straightforward application of ERP data.

2.3.2.1 *Inter-domain mapping*

The rationale for employing ERPs to determine whether two conditions have different effects upon the nervous system is unproblematic. Assuming that the study has been properly designed and conducted, it is indisputable that reliably different ERP waveforms signify that their respective eliciting events were associated with differential activity in the nervous system. Difficulties arise though when such differences are to be interpreted functionally, in other words, in terms of their causal relationship to any differences in cognitive processing engendered by the experimental manipulation in question. Any attempt to differentiate functionally distinct states with physiological data requires a theoretical framework in which physical and functional states of the nervous system can be interrelated. Without such a framework, however vague or loosely defined, there can be no basis for the use of any form of physiological data as a means of differentiating cognitive processes.

We assume that, like ourselves, most of our readers adhere to some sort of materialist position, in which it is accepted as axiomatic that cognitive processes or states are caused exclusively by physical activity in the nervous system. Such a position dictates that two or more functional states cannot be associated with the same physical state. But this does not preclude the possibility that the same functional state can be caused by more than one physical state. (This possibility has been seriously proposed, and held up as a reason why biological measures cannot be used to differentiate cognitive states and processes (Mehler *et al.* 1984).) Thus even the simplest inference that we feel can be drawn from ERP data (Section 2.3.1) is predicated on a specific, strong assumption about the relationship between neural and cognitive processes. The assumption in question is that the same functional state does not arise from qualitatively different forms of neural activity. Although it can be argued that this assumption is both defensible and parsimonious, it is open to empirical refutation.

A further problem in using physiological data to differentiate functional states centres on the question of the criteria that should be adopted to decide when such data signify functionally distinct processes, rather than the same process(es) active to differing degrees. It is generally (and usually implicitly) assumed that ERP effects that differ from one another in their relative amplitudes, but not in their patterns of distribution across the scalp, signify variations in the 'degree' or 'intensity' of the engagement of a common cognitive process (or set of processes). That is, it is assumed that different levels of activation of a common set of ERP generators are indicative of different levels of activation of the same functional states/processes. This may be a reasonable assumption, but again it must be remembered that it is at present no more than an assumption.

It follows from this assumption that to establish that an experimental manipulation has a qualitative rather than a quantitative influence on cognitive processing, ERP differences must be attributable to something other than changes in the activity of the same neural generator(s). In practice, this amounts to the demonstration that two experimental treatments are associated with ERPs that have different distributions over the scalp. Only when such differences in distribution are found can it be asserted that the experimental treatments gave rise to different patterns of neural activity, raising the possibility that they were associated with different functional processes.

It is important to note, however, that differing ERP scalp distributions provide a necessary but not a sufficient condition for the conclusion that functionally distinct processes have been identified. One reason for this is that it is unclear at present just how different two distributions have to be (or, equivalently, how different in location the underlying generators have to be) before the conclusion that they reflect different functional states is justified. Should one treat *any* reliable difference in ERP scalp distributions, no matter how subtle, as functionally significant? And if so, what criteria should be used to determine the sensitivity of the search for such differences? For example, all other things being equal, the probability of detecting differences in scalp distribution will increase with the number of recording channels employed. Hence the findings from two studies, identical other than for the number of scalp sites from which ERPs were recorded, could lead to quite different conclusions about the functional equivalence of the experimental conditions investigated.

In fact, there are grounds for thinking that differences in ERP scalp distributions need not always signify the engagement of qualitatively different cognitive processes. For example, consider a hypothetical experiment in which ERPs were recorded to concrete and abstract words presented in a lexical decision task, and that the scalp distribution of these ERPs differed. One conclusion might be that this difference indicated that the cognitive processes engaged in this task by the two classes of word were qualitatively different. Suppose, however, that the neural representations of concrete and abstract words do not entirely overlap anatomically (Coltheart 1985). If so, the difference in scalp distribution between ERPs evoked by the two classes of word might reflect the consequences of engaging processes that, although functionally equivalent, are active at non-overlapping brain loci. This example serves to illustrate the general point that if ERPs are sensitive to the *content* of a cognitive operation as well as to its *identity*, ambiguities will arise in the interpretation of scalp distribution differences whenever the critical eliciting items are not or cannot be counterbalanced over experimental conditions, and, whenever there are grounds for believing that the neural representations of the different item classes are anatomically distinct.

The foregoing discussion is arguably most relevant to attempts to interpret fairly small and subtle differences in ERP scalp distributions, since it seems unlikely that the loci of the neural substrates of the representations of, say, words with different semantic properties are likely to be entirely non-overlapping at the level of spatial resolution that can be achieved with scalp ERPs. But what of large and dramatic differences in the scalp distribution of two or more ERP effects? These too do not necessarily signify the engagement of different functional processes in the experimental conditions in question, as can be illustrated by the following example drawn from work on attention-related modulations of visual ERPs.

Attention-related changes in the early components of the visual ERP show different scalp distributions depending on the visual field in which the evoking stimulus is presented, in that the changes are maximal over the hemiscalp contralateral to the stimulated field (see Chapter 3). This finding has not, however, led many people to conclude that functionally distinct processes underlie visual attention to stimuli in the left and right visual fields! Rather, the data are generally interpreted as evidence for the functional equivalence of attentional processes independently represented in each hemisphere. Note that since the direction of attention to the left visual field has different behavioural consequences from attention directed to the right field, this example does not violate the assumption, mentioned above, that the same functional state cannot arise from qualitatively different forms of neural activity. It does, however, serve to emphasize that there is more to the differentiation of functionally distinct processes than the mere demonstration that two experimental conditions are associated with different patterns of neural activity. It also illustrates the important role that can be played in the interpretation of ERP data by biological knowledge, in this case knowledge of the neuroanatomy of the visual pathways.

2.3.2.2 *Establishing functional significance*

More complex inferences from ERP data encounter further difficulties. These centre on the problem of establishing the functional significance of ERP effects, that is, of describing the neural activity reflected by an ERP effect in terms of the role of that activity in the instantiation of a specific cognitive operation or process. Even on the (highly simplifying) assumption that every distinct cognitive process is associated with a unique set of neural processes, specifying the relationship between the two domains is a formidable problem.

First, we once again have to acknowledge that ERPs provide information about only a fraction of the neural activity associated with the processing of a stimulus. Thus, the 'ERP signature' of any putative cognitive process is likely to be far from the equivalent of its 'neural signature'. So, as already pointed out, a failure to find ERP evidence for differential cognitive processing is of itself often likely to be of rather little theoretical significance.

Second, attempts to interrelate neural activity and cognitive processes have to confront the problem that functional or information processing accounts of performance on a particular task can take many different forms. Such accounts differ in their levels of analysis and abstraction (e.g. Marr's (1982) discussion of the different levels of explanation that can be applied to visual object recognition) and, more fundamentally, in their assumptions about such basic questions as whether adequate functional accounts of behaviour are possible without commitment to some kind of 'symbolic' processing architecture (see, for example, Smolensky (1988) and associated commentaries). Serious attempts to assign functional significance to task-related variations in neural activity must therefore confront the following issues. First, given the nature of the neural activity in question (in the case of ERPs, presumed to be synchronous changes in polarization of relatively large neuronal populations), what level of description is most appropriate for an attempt to assign functional significance to the activity? For example, within Marr's (1982) scheme, should the description be articulated at the 'computational' or 'algorithmic' level? Second, within what framework should the description be articulated? While functional accounts based upon differing processing architectures and assumptions are sometimes thought of as complement-ary rather than competitive, it seems unlikely that all functionally plausible accounts are equally amenable to investigation and elucidation by physiological measures such as the ERP.

These issues have yet to receive much in the way of serious attention (although see Donchin and Coles 1988*a*). Indeed it can be argued, with some justification, that at the current stage of development of the field the lack of progress on this front is of little hindrance. This situation is, however, likely to change dramatically if significant progress can be made on the issue discussed next.

2.3.2.3 *From correlation to causation*

At the present time, the major difficulty in determining the functional significance of ERP data arguably comes from the 'correlational' nature of the types of studies that are typically conducted. A sufficiently large number of ingenious experiments might permit the conclusion that changes in, say, the amplitude of some ERP component are closely associated with variations in the degree that a putative cognitive process is active. Nevertheless, it is hard to see how such a relationship, however tight, could ever permit the conclusion that the neural processes responsible for the generation of the component in question also contributed to the instantia-tion of that process. This is because it is hard to imagine how an experiment that involved the manipulation of a cognitive variable could be designed so as to rule out the possibility that an ERP effect was merely a *consequence* of the variation in the manipulated process, and reflected more directly variation in some other process, contingent on the one being manipulated.

For many purposes, knowing that variance in an ERP effect is closely correlated with variation in the degree of engagement of a specific cognitive process may well be adequate. Such knowledge is not dependent on information about the neural bases of either the ERP effect or the cognitive process with which it is associated, and it is sufficient to allow ERPs to be used, say, as a covert index of processing in the absence of behavioural measures. However, for other purposes, correlational relationships are clearly insufficient. To obtain maximum benefit from chronometric applications of ERPs, for example, it is necessary to know the identity of the cognitive process(es) directly reflected by an ERP effect. At present it is rarely possible in such studies to assume that one is doing more than measuring the time-course of a index that, while correlated with the process of interest, is displaced in time from it by an unknown amount (hence the caveat regarding the interpretation of the time of onset of ERP differences in Section 2.3.1).

How can correlational statements about ERPs and cognitive processes be re-placed with causal/functional statements? It is illustrative in this context to note that exactly the same difficulty afflicts other, arguably more direct, measures of task- and stimulus-related neural activity. Take for example the technique of single-neuron recording. Such recordings from visual cortical regions of monkeys have identified populations of neurons that are differentially sensitive to a variety of stimulus attributes (Zeki 1993). However, as in the case of correlations between ERPs and behaviour, correlations between single-neuron activity and stimulus attributes can do no more than suggest the likely functions carried out by a given neuronal population. To address functional questions directly, it is necessary to look to evidence from other sources, such as the effects of lesions and, more recently, microstimulation. For example, area MT of the monkey visual cortex contains a high density of cells directionally sensitive to movement. This observation suggests that these cells might have a causal role in movement perception, but the correlational nature of the data mean that, by themselves, they can be no more than suggestive. It turns out though that not only do lesions of MT significantly (albeit temporarily) impair the ability to detect and discriminate motion (Wurtz *et al.*, 1990), but stimulation of MT neurons biases animals' responses in a motion detection task in a highly systematic fashion (Salzman *et al.*, 1990). On the basis of such evidence, it seems reasonable to conclude that single-unit recordings of motion-sensitive cells in MT are indeed indexing neuronal activity that has a causal role in movement perception. Similar kinds of evidence are necessary to elucidate the functional role of any attribute-sensitive neuronal population.

The above example illustrates two points. First, it emphasizes that the problem of elucidating the functional significance of a physiological correlate of information processing is by no means unique to ERP data. Second, it shows that to go beyond correlational statements about ERPs and cognitive processes it is necessary to test directly for the existence of causal relationships between the physiological activity being measured and the cognitive process with which it is correlated. Such experiments require that the neural system(s) thought to be responsible for a particular ERP effect be manipulated, and the functional consequences of such manipulations be observed. While it seems very unlikely that microstimulation will ever be a technique applicable to humans, studies of patients who have suffered lesions is obviously practical and, no doubt, other methods of interfering with the normal functioning of the brain, such as pharmacological manipulations, will also prove to be of value.

The upshot of the preceding discussion is that we are unlikely to have a complete understanding of the functional significance of ERPs until we can identify the neural structures and processes responsible for their generation. It will then be possible to determine the functional consequences of changes in the neural activity directly reflected by a given ERP waveform. It will also allow ERP research to be integrated fully with the large and ever-expanding database about the neural bases of cognition. Such an integration would permit knowledge about the functional role of different neural structures to inform hypotheses about the functional significance of different ERP effects.

The biological knowledge of ERP generators needed to accomplish this integration can be gained from various sources. We have already mentioned (Chapter 1, Section 1.3.1.1) that techniques are now being developed that allow the generators of ERP components to be characterized as multiple discrete sources of neural activity, which can be 'localized' within the brain, perhaps with the aid of findings from functional neuroimaging studies. A converging source of information comes from the systematic study of the effects of focal brain lesions. Such studies are especially important because they can both provide information about the role of different brain regions in the modulation and generation of ERPs, and allow specific hypotheses about the relationship between ERP effects and cognitive processes to be tested (Rugg 1992, in press). By way of example, suppose that the N400 ERP component (see Chapters 1 and 6) was believed to reflect the cognitive processes necessary for normal language comprehension. It would then follow that brain damage sufficient to cause dysfunction of these processes should be associated with an abnormal N400. Failure to find this relationship would negate the hypothesis linking N400 to comprehension, irrespective of how closely correlated N400 amplitude and measures of comprehension might be under normal circumstances. Parenthetically, it is worth noting that this application of the lesion method is asymmetric. Confirmation of the relationship would not necessarily mean that the hypothesis was correct. It would still be necessary to show that N400 is insensitive to lesions that do not interfere with comprehension, and that the component does not index some process *contingent* on comprehension, rather than contributing to it (see Rugg (1992) for further discussion of these issues).

2.4 CONCLUSIONS

We have argued that establishing the functional significance of cognitive ERPs requires the identification both of their cognitive correlates and their neural origins. Progress on each of these fronts is accelerating rapidly; cognitive ERP research has never been more closely integrated with 'mainstream' cognitive psychology than at the present time, and studies utilizing such methods as source analysis procedures and analysis of lesion effects are becoming increasingly common (Rugg in press; Swick *et al.* 1994).

Even at its present stage of development, and notwithstanding the problems of interpretation discussed in this chapter, we believe that the ERP technique has already made a significant contribution in several areas of cognitive enquiry. We hope that the remainder of the book will lead readers to the same conclusion.

REFERENCES

Coles, M. G. H., De Jong, R., Gehring, W. J., and Gratton, G. (1991). Continuous versus discrete information processing: evidence from movement-related potentials. In *Event-related brain research (EEG Suppl. 42)*, (ed. C. H. M. Brunia, G. Mulder, and M. N. Verbaten) pp. 260–9 Elsevier, Amsterdam.

Coltheart, M. (1985). Right hemisphere reading revisited. *Behavioural and Brain Sciences*, 8, 363–79.

Corbetta, M, Miezin, F. M, Dobmeyer, S., Shulman, G. L., and Petersen, S. E. (1990).

Attentional modulation of neural processing of shape, color, and velocity in humans. *Science*, **248**, 1556–9.

Donchin, E. (1981). Surprise! . . . Surprise? *Psychophysiology*, **18**, 493–513.

Donchin, E. and Coles, M. G. H. (1988*a*). Is the P300 component a manifestation of context updating. *The Behavioral and Brain Sciences*, **11**, 355–72.

Donchin, E. and Coles, M. G. H. (1988*b*). On the conceptual foundations of cognitive psychophysiology: a reply to comments. *Behavioral and Brain Sciences*, **11**, 406–25.

Friston, K. J., Jezzard, P., and Turner, R. (1993). The analysis of functional MRI time-series. *Human brain mapping*, **1**, 153–71.

Howard, D., Patterson, K., Wise, R., Brown, W. D., Friston, K., Weiller, C., and Frackowiak, R. (1992). The cortical localisation of the lexicons: PET evidence. *Brain*, **155**, 1769–82.

McCarthy, G., Blamire, A. M., Rottman, D. L., Gruetter, R., and Shulman, R. G. (1993). Echo-planar magnetic resonance imaging studies of frontal cortex activation during word generation in humans. *Proceedings of the National Academy of Sciences of the USA*, **90**, 4952–6.

Marr, D. (1982). *Vision*. Freeman, San Francisco.

Mehler, J., Morton, J., and Jusczyk, P. W. (1984). On reducing language to biology. *Cognitive Neuropsychology*, **1**, 83–116.

Paulesu, E., Frith, C. D., and Frackowiak, R. S. J. (1993). The neural correlates of the verbal component of working memory. *Nature*, **362**, 324–44.

Raichle, M. (1990). Exploring the mind with dynamic imaging. *Seminars in the Neurosciences*, **2**, 307–15.

Rugg, M. D. (1992). Event-related potentials in clinical neuropsychology. In *The Handbook of Neuropsychological Assessment*, (ed. J. R. Crawford, W. A. McKinlay, and D. M. Parker) pp. 393–412. Erlbaum, Hillsdale, NJ.

Rugg, M. D. Cognitive event-related potentials: intracerebral and lesion studies. In *Handbook of Neuropsychology*, Vol. 10, (ed. J. C. Baron and J. Grafman. Elsevier, Amsterdam. (In press.)

Salzman, C. D., Britten, K. H., and Newsome, W. T. (1990). Cortical microstimulation influences perceptual judgements of motion direction. *Nature*, **346**, 174–7.

Sergent, J., Ohta, S., and MacDonald, B. (1992). Functional neuroanatomy of face and object processing. *Brain*, **115**, 15–36.

Squire, L. R., Ojemann, J. G., Miezin, F. M., Petersen, S. E., Videen, T. O., and Raichle, M. E. (1992). Activation of the hippocampus in normal humans: a functional anatomical study of memory. *Proceedings of the National Academy of Sciences of the USA*, **89**, 1837–41.

Smolensky, P. (1988). On the proper treatment of connectionism. *Behavioural and Brain Sciences*, **11**, 1–74.

Swick, D., Kutas, M., and Neville, H. J. (1994) Localizing the generators of event-related brain potentials. In *Localization and neuroimaging in neuropsychology* (ed. A. Kertesz), pp. 73–122. Academic, San Diego.

Wurtz, R. H., Yamasaki, D. S., Duffy, C. J., and Roy, J.–P. (1990). Functional specialization for visual motion processing in primate cerebral cortex. *Cold Spring Harbor Symposia on Quantitative Biology*, **LV**, 717–27.

Zeki, S. (1993). *A vision of the brain*. Blackwell Scientific, Oxford.

3 Mechanisms and models of selective attention

George R. Mangun and Steven A. Hillyard

3.1 INTRODUCTION

The concept of attention is at once both intuitive and elusive, and after more than 100 years of investigation the study of its psychological and neural mechanisms continues to generate intense controversy (e.g. Allport 1993; Näätänen 1992). A significant development in this area of study has been an increasing success in revealing the neural systems that mediate attentional processes (e.g. Posner and Petersen 1990). The aim of this chapter is to review some of the main themes of research on attentional mechanisms, with particular emphasis on the contributions of electrophysiological studies to current cognitive models of attention. Principally, we will approach attention from the information processing perspective and will concentrate on the sensory-selective aspects of attention. In addition, we will comment on the control systems that are involved in establishing attentional selectivity. References will be made to converging evidence from studies in animals, and to functional imaging studies in humans, but most of the physiological data to be considered will be derived from event-related potential (ERP) studies in humans. A central theme will be the use of physiological information to constrain cognitive theories.

3.1.1 Selective attention

It has long been recognized that events in the external and internal world must compete for control of perception, memory, and behaviour. The mechanisms underlying these aspects of human conscious experience remain to be completely identified, although significant progress has been made in elucidating the role of attentional processes in perception and cognition (e.g. Eriksen and Yeh 1985; Hawkins *et al.* 1990; Hoffman and Nelson 1981; Posner 1980; Prinzmetal *et al.* 1986; Reinitz 1990; Treisman 1988). In recent years there have also been numerous advances in our understanding of the brain systems that give rise to cognitive processes including attention (e.g. Colby 1991; Näätänen 1992; Posner and Petersen 1990).

A key question regarding selective attention concerns the stage of sensory processing at which incoming signals can first be selected or rejected by attentional mechanisms. This issue led theoreticians to the concepts of early (e.g. Broadbent 1958, 1970; Treisman 1969) and late (e.g. Deutsch and Deutsch 1936; Norman

1968) selection as possible mechanisms of attentional control over incoming information. From the psychological standpoint, early selection is taken to mean that the processing of a stimulus need not be completed before the event can be either selected for further processing or rejected as irrelevant. This view implies a bottleneck in information processing in the brain that protects higher, limited-capacity processing systems from being overloaded by irrelevant inputs. In contrast, late selection theorists have argued that both attended and irrelevant stimuli are fully analysed before any selection between them takes place (for a review see Allport (1989)).

This 'levels of selection' question has also been addressed from the perspective of signal detection. In this form, the question is whether attention acts via changes in the sensitivity of the perceptual system or only affects the decision or response criterion applied to attended and unattended events. For example, Posner and his colleagues showed that prior cueing of a stimulus location improved the speed with which a target was detected at the cued location relative to uncued locations (Fig. 3.1). They suggested that a facilitation of sensory/perceptual processing might underlie the speeded reaction times (Posner 1980). However, several investigators have suggested that reaction times (RTs) could differ for stimuli at cued versus uncued locations if different decision criteria were established for responding to each (Müller and Findlay 1987; Shaw 1984; Sperling 1984) (Fig. 3.2).

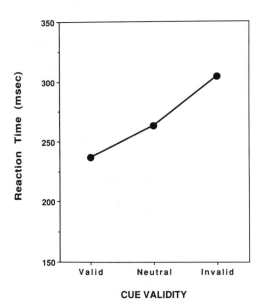

CUE VALIDITY

Fig. 3.1 Reaction times to lateralized target stimuli as a function of precuing. When the prior cue correctly indicated the location of the subsequent target stimulus (valid condition) the reaction times were faster than when the cue incorrectly indicated the target location (invalid trial) or provided no information as to the most likely target location (neutral trial). (Reprinted with permission from Posner *et al.* (1978).)

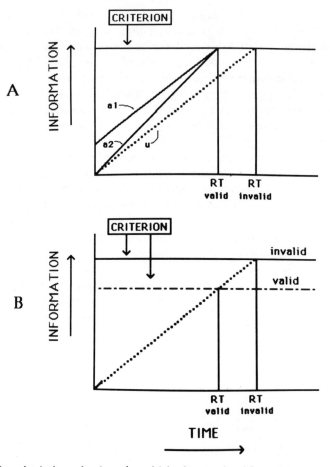

Fig. 3.2 Hypothetical mechanisms by which changes in either sensory-perceptual processing (A, top) or decision/response criterion (B, bottom) could result in faster RTs for validly cued versus invalidly cued targets. If the subjects maintained a fixed decision/response criterion level (top), faster RTs would result if there were changes in the amount (a1) or uptake rate (a2) of information with attention during validly cued trials, because the criterion for emitting a response would be reached sooner. Alternatively, if the amount or rate of sensory-perceptual information remained the same, but the criterion level for emitting a response to the targets changed with valid versus invalid locations, differences in RT would also be obtained (bottom).

Signal detection methods applied to this question have added support to the idea that precueing (and therefore attention) does indeed result in changes in perceptual sensitivity (d'), thereby supporting the notion that attention can act at a relatively early, perceptual level of information processing (Downing 1988; Hawkins *et al.* 1990). It has been pointed out, however, that it is difficult from signal detection methods alone to rule out a late selection process (Müller and Humphreys 1991). Accordingly, these approaches may not inform us unequivocally as to the precise locus of attentional effects within the information processing system. Nor can they specify the neural mechanisms giving rise to increased sensitivity. It is possible, however, to apply psychophysiological methods to address this question and to help identify the intermediate neural events that contribute to the ultimate behavioural output. Indeed, it has been more than two decades since the initial studies demonstrating that sensory inputs were modifiable by attentional processes in humans (Eason *et al.* 1969; Hillyard *et al.* 1973).

3.1.2 Electrophysiological approaches

In humans, event-related potentials (ERPs) are becoming an increasingly useful technique for the study of selective attention and perception. As described elsewhere in this book (see Chapter 1), ERPs are voltage changes recorded from the human scalp that are time-locked to a sensory, motor, or cognitive process, and therefore provide an electrophysiological window onto brain function during cognition. ERPs are well suited for studying attention because they can provide a more complete picture of processing at various levels of the nervous system than can be obtained from behavioural methods alone. In a number of cases, the neural generators of specific ERP components have been identified and characterized. For example, the short-latency auditory ERPs index activity as early as the auditory nerve and reflect activity at various relay stages in the ascending auditory pathway (Fig. 3.3).

A second and very important advantage of ERP recordings in the study of attention is that they provide a measure of the processing of a stimulus in the absence of any requirement that the subject attend to or respond to that stimulus. Thus, it becomes possible to study and compare the processing of both attended and unattended inputs during conditions of strongly focused attention. Finally, the high temporal resolution (of the order of milliseconds) of the ERPs provides important information about the absolute and relative timing of neural/cognitive events that is difficult to infer from behaviour, and that is not available in other physiological methods such as positron emission tomography (PET) or functional magnetic resonance imaging (fMRI). These issues are discussed in greater detail in Chapter 2.

In the remainder of this chapter, we will consider the evidence obtained from electrophysiological studies of selective attention and critically review their implications for understanding the underlying psychological and neural mechanisms of attention in both visual and auditory processing.

3.2 VISUAL–SPATIAL ATTENTION

Electrophysiological methods were first applied successfully to study visual–spatial attention in humans by Robert Eason and his colleagues in the late 1960s. They examined the ERPs elicited by lateralized flash stimuli when those stimuli were actively attended to by the subject, and when they were explicitly ignored (Eason

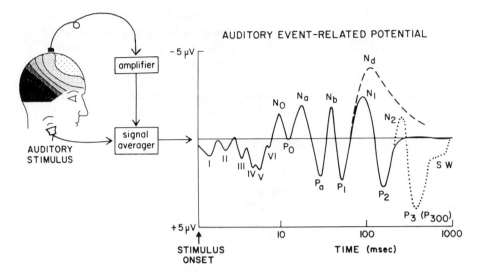

Fig. 3.3 Idealized auditory event-related potential plotted on a log-time scale. Following a sound, a series of highly reproducible voltage deflections can be observed from scalp recordings. Beginning as early as a few milliseconds after the stimulus the action of the auditory nerve can be seen in wave I. Within the first 10 ms seven characteristic waves can be identified that track activity along the ascending auditory brainstem pathway to level of the thalamic relay. Cortical activity is first observed in the time period of 15–50 ms in the midlatency potentials, and these are followed over the next several hundred milliseconds by several components that are related to aspects of both sensory and cognitive processing. (From Hillyard 1993.)

et al. 1969). The finding was that ERPs in the latency range between 100 and 200 ms after the briefly flashed stimulus were altered by the direction of attention in the visual fields. This interesting effect has since been replicated in numerous studies which have also demonstrated attentional modulations of even shorter-latency ERP components (Eason 1981; Mangun and Hillyard 1990*a*; Van Voorhis and Hillyard 1977). The general finding has been that stimuli falling within the 'spotlight' of spatial attention elicit enhanced early P1 (80–120 ms) and N1 (160–200 ms) ERP components over posterior scalp regions (Fig 3.4). Similar selective attention effects have also been described in the auditory (see Section 3.4) and somatosensory modalities; somatosensory studies will not be discussed here, and the interested reader is referred to Näätänen (1992) for an excellent review.

Because of the experimental designs that were employed, these changes in ERP components could not be attributed to global differences in brain state (that is, of arousal and alerting) between conditions of attend versus ignore. Rather, these ERP effects reflect stimulus-selective processing, in that the overall level of arousal is controlled in such experiments by requiring that the subjects perform tasks that are matched in overall difficulty and relevance in each experimental condition. For example, the ERPs elicited by identical physical stimuli are compared when those

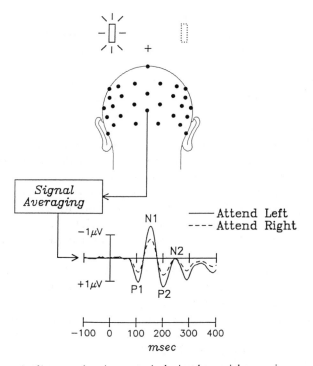

Fig. 3.4 Schematic diagram showing a typical visual–spatial attention experiment with ERP recording. Left- and right-field stimuli are shown flashed one at a time to a subject while fixation is maintained on a central location on the display (+). For the duration of one run (lasting 1–2 min) the subject is instructed to attend exclusively (without looking at) one visual field location while ignoring the other. The task is to detect infrequent target stimuli that differ from non-targets (for example in size). In different runs, the to-be-attended location is either the left or right. Thus, ERPs can be obtained to the left- and right-field stimuli separately when they are attended and ignored (unattended). The effects of attention are the difference in the ERPs to the same physical stimuli (for example left flashes) when attended (attend left) versus ignored (attend right). Thus, in each attention condition the subject maintains similar levels of arousal since in each attention condition a similar task is being required. Only the direction of attention is altered. Typical ERP spatial attention effects are shown at the bottom. The flashed stimulus elicits a series of voltage fluctuations over the occipital scalp and these fluctuations can be identified and are labelled here as the P1, N1, P2 and N2 'components'. Spatial attention effects are seen as amplitude enhancements of the early sensory-evoked P1 and N1 components. Sometimes the subsequent P2 and N2 components are also amplitude modulated.

stimuli are attended to versus when those stimuli are ignored as the subject directs attention to another input channel that contains equivalent stimuli and involves a similar or identical task (Hillyard *et al.* 1973). Thus, attention effects in the ERPs are not merely reflections of non-specific factors such as arousal or differential preparation.

A second methodological procedure necessary to control for the occurrence of non-specific effects is to use stimulus sequences that do not permit the subject to predict whether a forthcoming stimulus belongs to the attended or unattended class. Such knowledge could allow subjects to differentially prepare for the forthcoming stimulus on a trial-by-trial basis which might lead to changes in the global state of the nervous system through increased arousal in anticipation of the attended stimulus. Differences in non-specific arousal could affect the ERPs, but this would not be evidence for selective processing with attention. The possibility that the subjects might predict which stimulus is going to be presented next, and therefore differentially prepare themselves for that stimulus, can be prevented by presenting the attended and unattended stimuli in random order within a set of trials. If the subjects cannot predict which stimulus will occur next, any changes in the ERPs would have to be attributable to stimulus-selective processes and not to trial-by-trial changes in preparatory state or arousal. These issues were debated in early discussions in the literature (e.g. Karlin 1970; Näätänen 1967) and were largely resolved using the controls described above (Hillyard and Picton 1979).

Thus, the ERP findings described above can be attributed to selective rather than non-selective aspects of attention, and they can be interpreted as reflecting a type of 'gain control' mechanism over sensory/perceptual processing (e.g. Eason 1981; Hillyard and Mangun 1987). Presumably, at the neuronal level this reflects changes in the excitability of the sensory neurons coding the physical features of the stimulus and generating the ERPs. Moreover, this gain control must occur through the influence of descending (afferent) neural projections onto the sensory neurons. Such a proposal is based, in part, upon the observation that spatial attention modulates the amplitudes of the P1 and N1 components without significantly affecting their latencies, scalp distributions, or waveshapes. This pattern is consistent with the idea that during the different conditions of attention the same sensory neurons are being activated by the stimulus, but that the attentional gain control mechanism affects the amplitude of this evoked activity.

3.2.1 Spatial cueing of attention: perceptual sensitivity or decision bias?

As noted above, there has been a long-standing controversy over whether cued expectancy in visual–spatial processing leads to improved response performance due to changes in perceptual sensitivity, or instead to alterations in decision and/or response bias (e.g. Hawkins *et al.* 1990; Müller and Findlay 1987; Posner *et al.* 1980; Shaw 1984). If as proposed by Hawkins *et al.* and Posner and colleagues, precueing of the likely location of a target item leads to alterations in perceptual processing, we should be able to observe differences in the electrophysiological indices of such processing in the ERP response to precued and uncued stimuli. We have followed this approach in several experiments (e.g. Mangun *et al.* 1987; Mangun and Hillyard 1991).

The design used in our studies followed that of Posner and colleagues (1978, 1980): each trial began with an arrow presented at fixation for 200 ms. The arrow pointed to either the left or right visual field. Following each arrow by 800 ms was the lateralized target. The arrow correctly indicated the side on which the target would occur with high probability (75 per cent), but on some (25 per cent) of the trials the target occurred in the opposite visual field location (invalid trial). This spatial priming paradigm produces an 'endogenous orienting', since attention is directed by voluntary processes; this is to be contrasted with 'exogenous orienting' wherein attention is captured automatically to the location of a sensory signal (e.g. Jonides 1981; Klein *et al.* 1992).

The predictive value of the cue has been shown to lead to speeded RTs in response to targets that occur at precued locations (see Fig. 3.1). If this effect is due to changes in the perceptual processing of validly and invalidly cued targets, then the early sensory-evoked ERP components should show expectancy-related changes in either amplitude or latency. If, on the other hand, the cueing effects on RT are the result of changes in decision and/or response bias, then one would expect stability of those early ERP components that reflect the sensory–perceptual stages of processing, and instead, changes in the longer-latency ERP components related to decision or action. Thus, we compared, for example, the ERPs to left-field targets when validly versus invalidly cued, as shown in Fig. 3.5. The principal finding was that the early P1 and N1 components of the ERPs were larger in peak amplitude when the evoking stimulus had been precued. These effects were not the result of eye movements toward the cued location because the eyes remained fixed at a central fixation point, and eye movements were monitored; trials containing deviations of fixation were discarded.

These amplitude modulations of early visual ERP components produced by trial-by-trial cueing are similar, if not identical, to those observed in tasks where attention is sustained upon a single visual field location throughout a block of trials while comparable stimuli are flashed to that location and other unattended locations in the visual field (e.g. Eason 1981; Eason *et al.* 1969; Hillyard and Münte 1984; Mangun and Hillyard 1987, 1988, 1990*b*; Neville and Lawson 1987; Rugg *et al.* 1987; Van Voorhis and Hillyard 1977). Such effects have been interpreted as evidence that early sensory processing is affected by spatially directed attention (e.g. Eason 1981; Hillyard and Mangun 1987). Thus, the evidence obtained in the trial-by-trial cueing experiment is consistent with the proposal of Posner and others that expectancy-induced facilitation of RT and perceptual sensitivity (d') could be the result of improvements in early sensory and perceptual processing. These data do not, however, tell us whether the effects observed in behavioural studies of spatial priming are dependent upon early selection mechanisms. For example, it is possible that the reaction time effects of Posner and others might result from changes in decision and response criteria alone (cf. Müller and Findlay 1987). None the less, the finding of amplitude modulations of ERP components with as short a latency as 80–100 ms post-stimulus during expectancy-based cueing strongly suggests a link between sensory–perceptual sensitivity and RT effects. Thus, these data converge with recent findings of changes in perceptual sensitivity (d') for precued targets (e.g. Hawkins *et al.* 1990) and provide information about the neural mechanisms and levels of information processing involved in attentional processing.

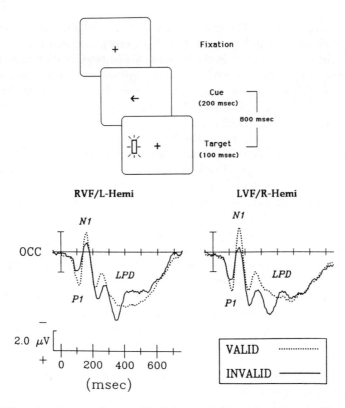

Fig. 3.5 The stimulus paradigm utilized in a trial-by-trial cueing paradigm (top). An attention-directing cue (arrow) indicates the most likely location of a subsequent target stimulus (vertical bar). Timing and probabilities are indicated in the figure. The ERPs elicited by the lateralized bar stimuli are shown at bottom. ERPs to left visual field (LVF) and right visual field (RVF) are shown from scalp sites over the contralateral scalp. Overlaid are the ERPs when the evoking stimulus was validly cued (full cumes) and invalidly cued (dotted cumes). Validly cued stimuli show significant amplitude enhancements of the P1 (P110) and N1 (N170) components. (Data from Mangun and Hillyard (1991).)

Recent studies have provided a more direct link between attention-related modulations of early ERP components and perceptual sensitivity. Heinze *et al.* (1990*b*) presented sequences of bilateral pairs of patterned stimuli and cued subjects to attend to the sequence on one side in a given trial. It was shown that d' for pattern discrimination accuracy was substantially higher on the attended side, in association with an increased amplitude of the P1 component over the contralateral occipital scalp. This relationship between the augmented P1 and improved perceptual accuracy was observed in the absence of any change in decision criteria.

A study by Luck and colleagues (Luck *et al.* 1994) demonstrated a similar relationship between early ERP modulation and detection sensitivity in a threshold

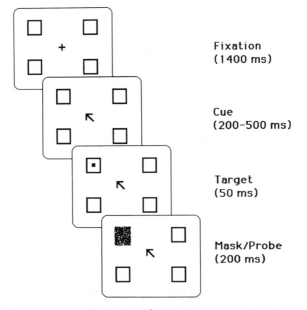

Fig. 3.6 Stimulus sequence and timing of stimulus presentations in an experiment by Luck *et al.* (1994). The trials each began with a fixation period that was followed by a centrally presented arrow cue. Following the cue a briefly flashed threshold level luminance target was presented (50 per cent of trials) and this was immediately masked by a brighter mask/probe stimulus. The ERPs were triggered by the target/mask complex.

detection task using trial-by-trial cueing. The design was patterned after that of Hawkins *et al.* (1990), and subjects were required to detect faint, masked luminance targets flashed to one of four possible target locations demarcated by continuously present outline boxes situated in each of the visual quadrants. Each trial began with an initial cue (central arrow) that pointed to the most probable location at which the target/no-target decision would be made. On 75 per cent of the trials (valid trials) the precued location was also 'post-cued' by a bright masking stimulus (with or without a preceding target), and on 25 of the trials (invalid trials) the post-cue was presented to another of the locations. The post-cue was a bright, 200 ms flash of multiple line segments that was presented only to one quadrant and also served as a mask to terminate target processing. The subject's task was to make a decision about target presence/absence only at the location where the post-cue/mask appeared; targets were presented at that post-cued location on a random 50/50 basis. The design also included a 'neutral' condition in which the initial cue consisted of four arrows and each box was equally likely to be post-cued. Stimulus timing is indicated in Fig. 3.6.

Behavioural performance measures showed that target detectability was highest on valid trials ($d' = 1.59$) and lowest on invalid trials ($d' = 1.13$), with neutral trials intermediate ($d' = 1.38$). Both attentional benefits (improvement in d' over neutral

Valid vs. Invalid

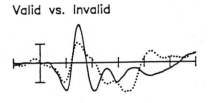

Valid vs. Neutral

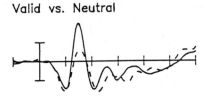

Invalid vs. Neutral

Fig. 3.7 ERPs elicited by the target/mask complex and recorded from lateral occipital scalp sites. ERPs are collapsed over left-and right-hemisphere locations and the four stimulus positions as a function of cueing. Thus, the overlaid waveforms indicate cued (valid, full curves), uncued (invalid, dotted curves) and neutrally cued (broken curves) trials, recorded over lateral occipital scalp sites contralateral to the field of the stimulus. See text for description and interpretation of effects. (Data from Luck *et al.* (1994).)

trials) and costs (reductions in d' from neutral trials) were highly reliable (both $p<0.01$). Decision criterion (beta) did not differ among the three types of trials.

To gain information about the locus of selectivity of this spatial cueing effect, ERPs were recorded from 10 scalp sites in response to the target-mask complex for each type of trial. Since the targets contained minimal stimulus energy, these ERPs were elicited by the mask post-cue and reflected the state of the sensory pathways at the post-cued location at the time of target (or non-target) occurrence. As shown in Fig. 3.7, the posterior P1 and N1 components were larger on valid trials than on invalid trials, replicating the effects of spatial attention that have been observed in previous studies using RT measures. Surprisingly, however, the neutral trials did not produce intermediate amplitudes for these components. Rather, the P1 component was approximately the same for neutral and valid trials and was suppressed on invalid trials. In contrast, the posterior N1 component was larger for valid trials and highly suppressed on both invalid and neutral trials. The P1 component therefore reflected the costs of attention, being suppressed for invalid trials relative to neutral trials, whereas the posterior N1 component reflected the benefits of attention, being enhanced for valid trials relative to neutral trials.

This experiment provides strong evidence that changes in ERP components with directed attention are closely correlated with changes in signal detectability, even in the absence of changes in decision or response criteria. Indeed, previous studies of auditory signal detection had already demonstrated that changes in decision bias were associated with alterations in the ERPs at much longer latencies than those described in the foregoing spatial attention studies (Paul and Sutton 1972; Squires *et al.* 1973). Thus, a reasonable conclusion is that the short-latency ERP modulations during spatial attention reflect an improved signal-to-noise ratio for attended inputs with a consequent improvement in perceptual sensitivity.

3.2.2 Localizing attention effects in the brain

It has been suggested that spatial cuing effects on detection sensitivity (d') provide prima facie evidence for an 'early' selection mechanism (Bashinski and Bacharach 1980; Downing 1988). This evidence by itself, however, provides little information about the stage of perceptual processing at which selection effects are manifest (cf. Müller and Humphreys 1991). The perceptual system can be divided into various processing stages based on both theoretical grounds (e.g. Sanders 1990) and physiological evidence (e.g. Felleman and Van Essen 1991). Such multistage models of perceptual processing lead one to question the idea of a simple early versus late selection dichotomy and to ask instead which of the multiple stages of input analysis are sensitive to attentional processes. To address this more complex question, converging lines of evidence must be supplied, especially with regard to the physiological bases of attentional selection.

One such line of evidence concerns the precise stage of visual processing that is reflected by the attention-sensitive P1 and N1 components described above. In order to relate these ERP attention effects to the properties of visually responsive neurons revealed in animal studies, or to PET studies in humans, it is crucial to establish their neuroanatomical site of generation. Using appropriate methods, ERP recordings can be used to help localize the anatomical sites within the visual pathways at which attention acts. The experiments reviewed above indicate that spatial attention affects evoked neural activity over the occipital cortex as early as 70–80 ms after stimulus delivery, but did not identify the precise visual areas involved.

Knowing the level at which ERP attention effects are generated in the visual processing hierarchy would help to constrain theoretical models of attentional selection. For example, if the P1 component were generated in regions of the visual pathways known to code only elementary features of stimuli (e.g. the thalamus or early visual cortical areas), then the evidence for some form of early selection would be compelling. However, if the P1 component were to arise instead from the visual association cortex at levels that contained object representations (e.g. the inferior temporal lobe), then the concept of 'early selection' as defined in psychological theories (e.g. Allport 1989) might require refinement to make clearer distinctions between sensory, perceptual, and categorical stages of encoding and selection. That is, early selection might not be possible within stages of processing that represent simple stimulus features, but might yet occur prior to categorical representation (e.g. Allport *et al.* 1985).

Localizing the neural generators of a surface-recorded brain potential such as the P1 component is not a straightforward exercise (see Chapter 1). A number of assumptions must be made in order to infer the sources of the brain currents that contribute to a voltage change on the scalp — this is the so-called 'inverse problem'. Moreover, comparisons between animal and human are problematic in that significant differences exist between the anatomical organization of, for example, monkey and human brains. None the less, inferences about the neural generators of various ERPs have been made. This has been particularly successful in the auditory system where the generators of the auditory ERPs are now fairly well understood (see Fig 3.3). A combination of evidence from lesion studies in humans and animals, scalp topographic mapping, and dipole modelling, and convergent evidence from technologies such as magnetoencephalography have been required to reach our current level of understanding of auditory ERP generators (to be discussed later). In contrast, our knowledge about the generators of visual ERPs is relatively incomplete (e.g. Regan 1989). This is attributable to the complexity of the visual system in mammals, and particularly in primates. However, as we shall see, there are ways to approach the problem of the brain site of generation of particular visual ERP components.

We sought to determine the site of generation of the early attention-sensitive P1 component through a combination of experimental manipulation and source modelling (Mangun *et al.* 1993). The scalp distribution of the P1 component shows an occipital maximum, and thus is consistent with a generator in the visual cortex. However, from its scalp distribution alone it is difficult to determine whether the P1 originates in striate or extrastriate cortical areas. This is because scalp-recorded ERPs do not only reflect the activity of the brain regions immediately underlying the recording electrode. Due to the spread of electrical currents in the conducting media of the head, skull, and scalp, a potential recorded maximally at a given scalp site might actually be generated at a more distant brain site. There are several important biophysical properties that contribute to this phenomenon, one of the most important of which is the three-dimensional orientation of the active brain tissue; in conjunction with the physical properties of the tissue, the orientation of the active brain region determines the distribution and current density of the electric fields surrounding active nerve cells. This principle may be exploited as a tool for localizing neural generators of surface-recorded ERPs, as described below.

In the striate cortex of humans a unique anatomical mapping of the visual fields exists such that upper- and lower-field stimuli will generally excite striate neurons that have opposite spatial orientations (Fig. 3.8). This arrangement predicts significant changes in the polarity and scalp distribution of visual evoked potentials recorded on the scalp, and has been used by several researchers to investigate their sites of generation. Jeffreys and Axford (1972) reported that upper versus lower-field stimuli elicited occipital scalp ERPs of opposite polarity, and several subsequent reports have confirmed this general finding, leading to the conclusion

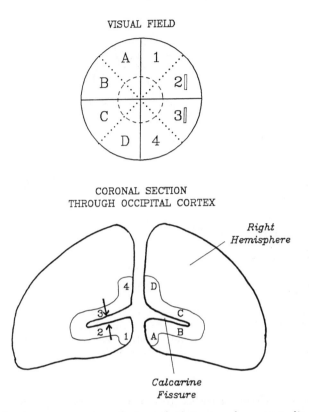

Fig. 3.8 Schematic representation of visual field (top) and corresponding mapping of visual field locations onto the striate cortex in the depths of the calcarine fissure in humans (bottom). The figure shows an idealized view of the calcarine visual region in coronal section. Of importance is the projection of upper-field location onto the lower banks of the calcarine fissure, while the lower field projects to the upper banks of the fissure. Thus, stimuli located, for example, at positions 2 and 3 in the right visual half-field would project to opposing banks of the calcarine visual fissure of the left hemisphere. This model is greatly simplified since the anatomy of the normal human striate cortex within the calcarine region is quite complex showing numerous alterations of orientation and a significant difference between the two hemispheres. None the less, for stimuli in certain visual field locations, and on average across individuals, this 'cruciform model' proves to be quite satisfactory. (Reprinted with permission from Mangun *et al.* (1993).)

that some early occipital scalp ERP components are generated in the striate cortex while other, longer-latency peaks are generated in the extrastriate cortex.

Due to significant differences in stimulus and recording parameters between those basic sensory studies and ERP studies of selective attention, it has been difficult to relate the findings from the two types of studies. However, this can be done experimentally by combining an attention task with manipulations of stimulus location in the visual field. The logic is straightforward — if the attention-sensitive P1 component is generated in the striate cortex, then it should

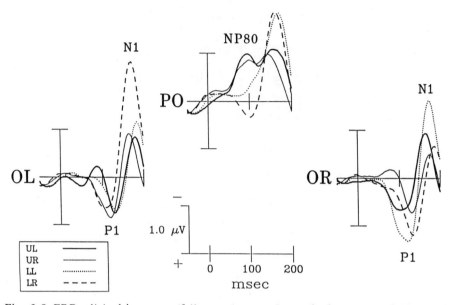

Fig. 3.9 ERPs elicited by upper (full curves) versus lower (broken curves) field stimuli when unattended. The P1 component at lateral occipital scalp sites did not show changes in polarity as a function of upper versus lower-field stimuli, but the earlier parieto-occipital (PO) NP80 component did show polarity inversions.

invert in polarity for stimuli flashed to upper versus lower portions of the visual field. We found that, in fact, the attention-sensitive P1 component did not invert in polarity, but rather a shorter-latency component (that is, NP80) did show a polarity inversion as would be expected of an ERP generated in the striate cortex (Fig. 3.9). The relative latencies of these two components were also consistent with this interpretation in that the NP80 had an onset latency of 50–60 ms whereas the P1 onset latency was between 80 and 90 ms. Moreover, in this experiment the NP80 was not affected by selective spatial attention, whereas the P1 was amplitude modulated with attention.

Multichannel mapping, current-source density analysis, and inverse dipole modelling indicated that the attention-sensitive P1 component is generated in the ventro-lateral extrastriate cortex (Brodmann's areas 18 and/or 19) (Gomez *et al.* in press; Mangun *et al.* 1993). Thus, it may be inferred that visual–spatial attention first affects stimulus processing in the extrastriate cortex. Our failure to find attention effects for the earlier striate component does not of course prove that attention cannot affect earlier structures in the visual pathways than the extrastriate cortex. Indeed, there have been reports of modulations of short-latency visual responses during spatial attention (Oakley and Eason 1990), although these effects have proved difficult to replicate. The finding that the extrastriate but not the striate cortex (or earlier structures) is affected by spatial attention is consistent with most of the findings from studies in monkeys. In such studies, visual area

V4 is typically the earliest stage of the geniculo-striate pathway in which attention-sensitive neurones have been identified by single-cell recording (e.g. Fischer and Boch 1985; Moran and Desimone 1985; Spitzer *et al.* 1988). A recent report by Motter (1993), however, has presented evidence for possible striate modulations with selective attention, and thus future work will be required to determine whether, and under which circumstances, visual structures prior to the extrastriate cortex can be affected by selective attention.

The source of the later attention-sensitive N1 component over posterior scalp areas remains unclear. However, the scalp distribution, dipole models, and latency of the peak would be consistent with either a deep occipito-temporal generator site or a relatively more broadly distributed parietal site of generation (Gomez *et al.* in press; Mangun *et al.* 1993). It is worth noting that 'the visual N1' is believed to reflect the activity of several underlying brain processes whose electrical signals overlap temporally and spatially on the scalp. One piece of evidence in support of this idea is that the peaks of the N1 component(s) have longer latencies as one proceeds from anterior scalp regions toward more occipital areas.

Mangun and Hillyard (1990*a*) suggested that the occipital P1 and occipitol-parietal N1 components in the human visual ERP might reflect processing in the two main cortical visual projection systems identified in monkeys (e.g. Desimone and Ungerleider 1989; Ungerleider and Mishkin 1982). In particular they proposed that the P1 component is generated in the ventral stream projecting to the inferior temporal lobe involved in object discrimination. In contrast, the N1 was hypothesized to represent activity in the dorsal stream, projecting from the striate cortex to the posterior parietal lobe and involved in encoding spatial aspects of visual information. In line with this idea, Johannes *et al* (1992) found that at occipital-temporal scalp regions, the 'N1 component' had a peak latency that was affected by stimulus luminance, and that this ERP could be dissociated from a parietal N1 peak whose latency was not affected by stimulus luminance (see also Gomez *et al.* in press; Mangun *et al.* 1993). In the light of these data it is reasonable to propose that the occipital-temporal projection pathway might be reflected in the human ERPs by the occipital P1 and occipital-temporal N1 components, whereas activity in the occipital-parietal projection might be reflected by a parietal N1 component.

3.2.3 Selectivity during spatial attention

In the previous section we reviewed the evidence that spatial attention first modulates processing at extrastriate cortical levels. Although this indicates that selection takes place within perceptual processing stages, it is important to note that these effects are not evident at the earliest, subcortical levels of visual processing (that is, the retina, thalamus, or thalamo-cortical projection), nor do they occur within the earliest cortical visual processing stage (that is the striate cortex). In the traditional formulations of Broadbent (1958, 1970) and Treisman (1969), an early selection mechanism should affect processing at levels in which elementary stimulus features are represented, whereas late selection would influence higher-level stimulus representations such as patterns, objects, and learned configurations. Thus, these spatial attention effects would qualify as 'early selection' in that they appear to occur prior to complete perceptual analysis.

Given that the extrastriate cortex represents both features and objects, and that it is difficult to specify precisely where in the extrastriate cortex the early ERP effects are generated, it is useful to consider additional information to verify that the spatial attention effects are indeed based on selection by location alone, and not on the basis of more complex conjunctions of stimulus features and location. To address this question, ERP recordings may be used to analyse whether all stimuli delivered to an attended location are processed equivalently, regardless of whether they share the specific features of the task-relevant stimulus class. An early selection based on location alone might be expected to facilitate the processing (and hence the early ERPs) of *all* stimuli at the attended location, whereas a late selection process would be capable of discriminating between relevant and irrelevant stimuli at the attended location. An efficient early selection process should also be capable of rejecting irrelevant-location stimuli from further processing, indexed by a reduction or suppression of both early and late ERP components to these stimuli.

These questions have been addressed in several ERP studies that investigated attention to conjunctions of location and other stimulus features. Hillyard and Münte (1984) compared the ERPs to stimuli of different colours at the attended and unattended locations in a sustained attention task. Target stimuli (requiring detection and response) were of one colour (e.g. red) and non-targets (requiring no response) were of another colour (e.g. blue). Stimuli having target and non-target colours were presented in an unpredictable order at both attended and unattended locations. It was found that spatial attention enhanced the early P1 and N1 components to both the stimuli of the target colour and the non-target colour at the attended location. Differences between the target and non-target stimuli did not appear until 150–200 ms latency in the ERPs, approximately 70 ms later than the first effects of spatial attention.

Further evidence comes from a study by Heinze *et al.* (1990a) in which relevant and irrelevant stimuli were presented at both attended and unattended locations, and task-irrelevant probes were intermixed with task-relevant stimuli. In this study, subjects attended to a location in one visual half-field (ignoring the other) with the task of detecting matches between pair of letters flashed at that location. Infrequently and unpredictably a non-letter probe stimulus was flashed at the same location (Fig. 3.10, top). The irrelevant probe stimulus was a filled square and thus differed in total luminance, spatial frequency, local contrast, and linguistic content from the task-relevant stimuli. None the less, Heinze *et al.* found that the probe stimulus also showed an attention effect upon the early P1 component, as did the task-relevant letter stimuli (Fig. 3.10, bottom). These findings indicate that the early P1 attention effect reflects attention-related changes in the processing of incoming signals as a function spatial location *per se*, which corresponds with a mechanism of early selection as defined by Broadbent (1970) and Treisman (1969).

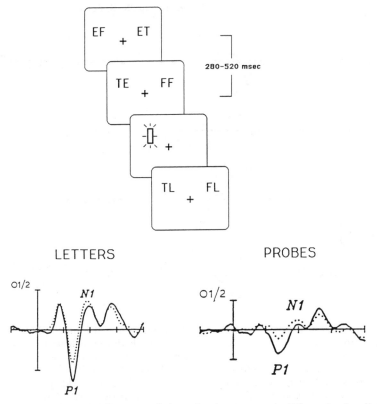

Fig. 3.10 (Top) Schematic diagram of the stimulus sequence. Bilateral stimuli (letter pairs) were flashed to left- and right-field locations. Randomly interspersed in the sequences of letters were irrelevant 'probe' stimuli (bars) that could occur in the left- or right-field locations. (Bottom left) ERPs elicited by bilateral letter arrays over the lateral occipital scalp. Note the P1 component over the hemisphere contralateral to the attended hemifield (full trace) is enlarged relative to that over the ipsilateral hemisphere (dotted trace). (Bottom right) ERPs elicited by the irrelevant bar stimuli when in the attended visual field (full trace) and irrelevant field (dotted trace). When in the attended field, the bars elicited ERPs with significant amplitude enhancements of the occipital P1 component and the anterior N1 component. (Data from Heinze *et al.* (1990*a*).)

How effective is spatial selective attention in gating the processing of stimulus features at unattended visual field locations? This question can be addressed by examining the attention effects on stimuli that do and do not share stimulus attributes with the attended, task-relevant stimulus. For example, in the studies of spatial and colour attention by Hillyard and Münte (1984) it was shown that the selection of stimuli based upon colour was hierarchically dependent upon prior selection for location, when the to-be-attended stimuli were defined by a conjunction of location and colour. Attention effects on ERPs were greatly reduced for stimuli at the unattended location, even though some of those stimuli shared a feature (that is, colour) with those defined as targets (Fig. 3.11). If indeed all

COLOR ATTENTION EFFECTS

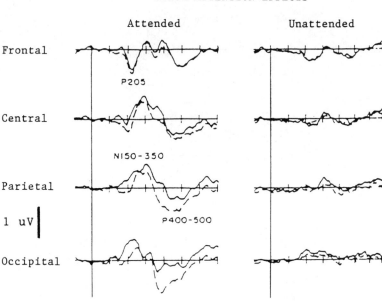

Fig. 3.11 Colour attention difference waves from Hillyard and Münte (1984). The wave-forms are difference waves obtained by subtracting the ERP to the unattended colour from the ERP to the attended colour when they were elicited by stimuli at the attended location (left column) or the unattended location (right column). The effects of colour selection are reduced for stimuli at the unattended location. Recordings were collapsed over left and right-hemisphere frontal (F3/F4), central (C3/C4), parietal (P3/P4), and occipital (O1/O2) scalp sites contralateral (full curves) and ipsilateral (broken curves) to the visual hemifield of the stimulus. Stimulus onset is at the vertical line at the left of each set of tracings, tick marks indicate 100 ms intervals, and positive polarity is plotted downward. (Reprinted with permission from Hillyard and Münte (1984).)

the elementary features of the stimuli had been evaluated prior to selection, one would expect some effect of the colour cue even at unattended locations. This evidence further supports the idea of an early selection of perceptual information during spatial attention (e.g. Johnston and Dark 1986).

Similarly, longer-latency ERPs related to stimulus processing can be partially or completely gated by spatial attention in a manner that supports early selection models of attention. In particular the N2 and P300 components have been shown to be reduced to stimuli at unattended spatial locations. The N2 component in the visual modality has been considered to be an index of both automatic and controlled stimulus evaluation and classification processes (e.g. Ritter *et al.* 1983). In cases where the separation between attended and unattended locations in the visual fields was very small (e.g. Wijers *et al.* 1987), the N2 component was largest for the attended-location targets (single letters), smaller, but present for letters of the target set at unattended locations, and absent for unattended/

irrelevant letters. Thus, in this situation there was evidence of higher-level processing of the letters that were located in nearby unattended locations, thereby indicating an incomplete selection of stimuli (see also Hillyard and Münte 1984).

In contrast, in studies where the spatial separation between attended and unattended stimulus locations was greater, and/or the target/non-target distinction was made more difficult, no N2 components were elicited by unattended-location stimuli that shared features with the target stimuli. For example, Heinze *et al.* (1990*a*) found that the N2 component was absent or greatly suppressed in response to stimuli sharing all the defining features of the target stimuli, but that occurred at the unattended location (Fig. 3.12). Neither Wijers and colleagues (1987) nor Heinze and colleagues (1990*a*) observed any evidence of a P300 (P3) component (see Chapter 1) in response to stimuli at unattended locations that shared features with the task-relevant target stimuli. Under such conditions the P300 is widely considered to reflect the final decision and identification processes related to the detection of the task-relevant stimuli. Although the selectivity in the N2 and/or P300 components reflect, in part, the activity of 'late selection' processes, these data suggest that early selection mechanisms based on elementary stimulus features may also contribute to the selectivity of higher centres by altering the inputs they receive.

3.2.4 Common mechanisms for search and spatial selection?

Much of the current theoretical and experimental work in visual attention has involved visual search tasks. Visual search is usually studied by presenting a large array of items to an observer who is required to detect a target stimulus among irrelevant distractor stimuli. Under such conditions the time to detect a target stimulus increases linearly with increasing numbers of distractors if the target shares stimulus attributes with the distractor stimuli. That is, when a target cannot be distinguished from distractors by a unique feature, a serial search processes is required. This process has been hypothesized to require focal attention (e.g. Treisman and Gelade 1980). The essential aspect of Treisman's hypothesis is that focal attention acts as a 'glue' that permits independent stimulus features (such as colour, shape, etc.) to be properly conjoined to yield a stimulus object. This conjoining makes use of spatial information to co-register feature information that has been previously analysed in separate 'feature analysis maps'.

There has been considerable interest among attention researchers in the relationship between the process of focal attention during visual search and the early sensory gain control achieved during the voluntary allocation of attention of spatial attention. This relationship has been evaluated using reaction time methods in studies that examined the effects of spatial cueing of attention to targets that were and were not defined by a conjunction of stimulus features (e.g. Briand and Klein 1987; Prinzmetal *et al.* 1986). The logic of these studies was as follows: if the so-called attentional 'spotlight' and the feature-conjoining 'glue' were aspects of the same attentional process, then targets defined by conjunctions of simple

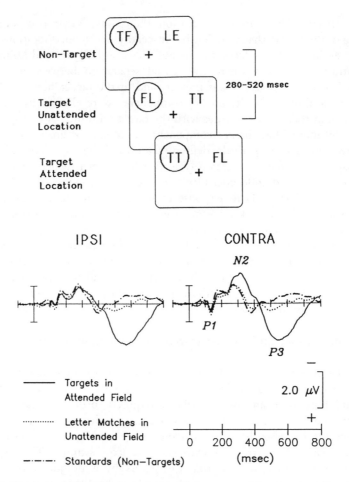

Fig. 3.12 (Top) Sequence of bilateral stimulus arrays with attention directed to one hemifield at a time (attention indicated by circles). (Bottom) ERPs from posterior sites contralateral (right) and ipsilateral (left) to the attended hemifield. Overlaid are ERPs to matching letters at the attended location (targets; full curves), matching letters at the unattended location (dotted curves), and attended non-target stimuli. A significant contralateral N2 component was elicited to the attended letter matches. (Data from Heinze *et al.* (1990*a*).)

features should be selected, detected, and responded to with greater facility when spatial attention was previously allocated to their location. In fact, cueing attention to spatial locations was found to produce greater cueing effects on reaction times for targets defined by feature conjunctions. This result suggests that the attentional process that is invoked during spatial cueing involves similar mechanisms to that involved in visual search. That is, following Briand's and Klein's (1987) provocative title, Posner's 'beam' is related to Treisman's 'glue'. However, behavioural evidence of this type does not reveal the specific levels of visual processing that are common to the two attentional processes.

The question of where in the visual hierarchy spatial attention in search and spatial selection share common mechanisms was addressed more directly by Luck *et al.* (1993). They combined a search design with a sensory probe method to ask whether during visual search for conjunction targets there was facilitation of early cortical-sensory processing at the location being searched. The design involved presentation of an array of coloured stimuli that contained targets defined by both colour and form attributes. Subjects were instructed to report with a choice response whether or not a letter 'T' in the designated colour was upright or inverted. Following the array onset by 250 or 400 ms, a 50 ms 'probe' stimulus was briefly flashed to either the target or distractor locations.

The comparison of the ERPs to the probe stimuli at target versus distractor locations provides a measure of whether spatial attention — as manifested in modulation of probe-evoked sensory responses — was involved in visual conjunction search. For example, if local spatial attention was actually allocated to the locations of the target stimuli in order to discriminate their features, then it should be the case that the ERPs to the probes would be enhanced at target versus distractor locations. That is, one should observe the same ERP attention effects on the probe stimuli as are reliably obtained in voluntary spatial attention tasks (modulation of P1, N1, N2, etc.). In contrast, if the ERPs to probes presented at target and distractor locations differed only in their longer-latency components, this would imply a qualitative difference between the mechanisms involved in the voluntary allocation of spatial attention and those required for conjoining stimulus features during visual search.

Luck *et al.* found that the ERPs to the probe stimuli at target locations showed enlarged occipital P1 and N1 components compared with those evoked at distractor locations, an effect similar to that obtained during studies of spatial selective attention (e.g. Mangun and Hillyard 1987; Mangun *et al.* 1993). These results suggest that visual search and spatial selective attention share common attentional mechanisms. Such findings are also in line with previous conclusions based on behavioural methods (e.g. Briand and Klein 1987; Prinzmetal *et al.* 1986) but extend these findings to identify the precise stage of visual processing that is involved. Thus, we conclude that during visual search for conjunction targets there is an early modulation of visual transmission within the extrastriate cortex that permits enhanced analysis of stimulus features at target locations. This improvement in feature analysis may aid in conjoining stimulus features into a coherent percept.

3.3 VISUAL FEATURE SELECTION

Attentional selection can also be readily achieved on the basis of non-spatial stimulus attributes. Selective attention to elementary stimulus features such as colour, orientation, spatial frequency, or conjunctions of such features also results in significant alterations of the ERP for attended versus unattended items (Harter *et al.* 1982; Hillyard and Münte 1984; Mangun *et al.* in press; Wijers *et al.*, 1989*a,b,c*). These attention effects, however, are not manifest as amplitude modulations of the P1 or N1 components described above. Rather, they appear as longer-latency positive- or negative-going waveforms that seem to be superimposed upon the sensory-evoked ERPs. The attention-related negative ERPs are sometimes referred to as 'selection negativities' (SN).

3.3.1 The neural specificity model

In their 'neural specificity' model of attention Harter and Aine (1984) suggested that many of the ERP changes elicited during selective attention reflected alterations of processing within the visual cortical areas encoding the elementary stimulus features that were used as the selection cue(s). Essentially, this formulation is similar, if not identical, to the proposal that attention modulates sensory/ perceptual processing by means of sensory gating or filtering of inputs (e.g. Eason 1981; Hillyard *et al.* 1973). However, in their 1984 formulation, Harter and Aine appeared to accept virtually any attention-related change in the ERP as a sign of the attentional modulation of activity in the feature-specific analysers of visual cortex. As a result, many of the details of the neural specificity model were criticized. In particular, it was argued that the most clear-cut evidence for modulation of feature-specific 'channels' with attention would be to observe amplitude changes in identifiable sensory-evoked components in the ERP, instead of slow positive or negative fluctuations added to the ERP waveform (Hillyard and Mangun 1987; Näätänen 1987).

Although these criticisms of the neural specificity model are reasonable, it remains unclear whether or not attention effects on sensory-perceptual processing must in all cases take the form of amplitude increases or decreases in well-defined ERP components. For example, we know that any given ERP deflection can, in principle, result from either a single brain process or from the summation at the scalp of the activity of several underlying brain processes (e.g. Näätänen 1992). Given this, if attention were to modulate one these subcomponent processes but not the others, the effects on the surface-recorded waveform would be the complex summation of the activity from the attentionally modulated process plus those subcomponent processes not affected by attention (cf. Woods *et al.* 1994). Thus, in order to determine whether attention has modulated a distinct neural generator or instead recruited new neuronal populations, it will sometimes be necessary to separate overlapping scalp-recorded electrical activity. Some methods have been proposed to permit such waveform decomposition (e.g. Hansen 1983; Woldorff 1992), but at present no simple method exists that performs this analysis reliably.

3.3.2 Hierarchical selection of visual inputs

Despite the ambiguities noted above, the ERP literature on attention has provided clear evidence of differences in the timing of selection processes based upon spatial versus non-spatial cues. For example, it has become clear that spatial attention affects an earlier stage of processing than does selection by other types of cues. Harter and Aine (1984) suggested that selection priority for different cues proceeds in the following order of pre-eminence: spatial location, colour, spatial frequency, and conjunctions of these features. Spatial attention is manifest as the early P1 effect (70–100 ms), whereas selection based upon other features begins later, in the latency range of 150–200 ms. Hillyard and Münte (1984) also noted that the difficulty of the between-channel discrimination affected the latency at which selective processes were evident in the ERP. Thus, colour selection could actually precede spatial selection in the ERPs if the attended and unattended locations were very close together. In this case, however, the ERP manifestations of spatial selection took the form of longer-latency negativities rather than modulations of the P1 or N1 peaks. That is, the early selection mechanisms described earlier for spatial attention were not engaged in this task situation.

Several studies have now reported that the earliest non-spatial attention effect over the posterior scalp was an increased negativity to attended features. In addition, Wijers and colleagues (e.g. Wijers *et al.* 1989) and Hillyard and Münte (1984) identified a longer-latency frontal P200 effect. However, Mangun *et al.* (in press) showed that selection on the basis of colour was also associated with an early positive occipital ERP component when the colour selection was not dependent upon selection of other stimulus features. In this study, the distribution of colour attention effects in the ERPs were investigated by means of multichannel voltage and current source density analyses (CSD). Twelve subjects were presented with purple and blue squares flashed in rapid random sequence to a single location above fixation. The task was to attend to one colour while ignoring the other, and each colour was attended in counterbalanced order in different blocks of trials. The subjects responded with a rapid manual button press to shorter-duration targets of the to-be-attended colour.

The earliest attention effect noted was a posterior scalp positivity with an onset of 100 ms latency and peak amplitude of 160 ms latency; this effect has not previously been reported in the ERP literature. Scalp topographic mapping indicated that this early effect was maximal over the occipital scalp of the right hemisphere (Fig. 3.13). Longer-latency ERP attention effects similar to those previously reported were observed, including a frontal positivity that peaked at 214 ms latency (P200), and a posterior negativity peaking at 298 ms latency (selection negativity). The early (100–160 ms) colour attention effect could be related to modulations of activity in colour-specific feature analysers, as suggested by both the neural specificity model of Harter and Aine (1984) and by recent evidence from positron emission tomography (PET) studies by Corbetta *et al.* (1991).

Taken together, the data from spatial and non-spatial attention studies using ERPs indicate that selection by location takes place at an earlier level and involves a qualitatively different mechanism from selection by other stimulus attributes. Nonetheless, it is also now apparent that selection of other stimulus features such as colour may also take place at relatively early levels of cortical processing. Future

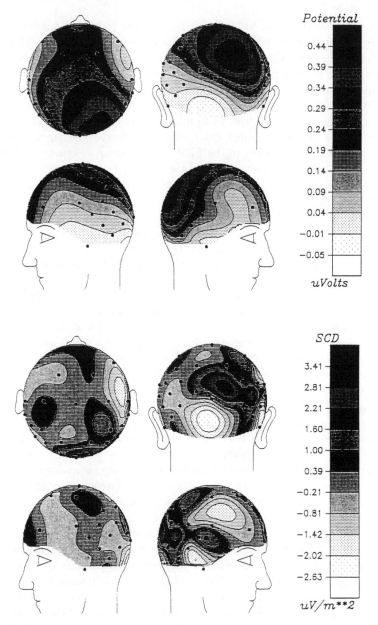

Fig. 3.13 Maps of scalp voltage (top) and current-source density (bottom) of the early positive colour attention effect. The attention difference waves are mapped (attended minus unattended waveforms at a latency of 160 ms). Voltage topographies show a maximal amplitude of the attention effect over the posterior occipito-parietal scalp regions of the right hemisphere (black shades). The current density plots provide a reference-independent map of current flow perpendicular to the skull and scalp, and thus provide a better localization of electrical activity on the scalp; the current density indicates a narrow occipital maximum for this effect. (Data from Mangun *et al.* (in press).)

studies must define the limits of early selection mechanisms for elementary stimulus features, and through information from convergent approaches establish the precise brain structures and stages of visual information processing within which early attentional selection may operate.

3.4 EXECUTIVE PROCESSES OF VISUAL ATTENTION

In addition to elucidating the stages of input processing that are affected by selective attention, it is important to delineate the executive neural systems that participate in the control of stimulus selection in the sensory pathways.

3.4.1 Brain systems controlling sensory selection

Studies using PET and brain lesion analysis methods in humans have identified several brain areas that participate in attentional control (e.g. Posner and Petersen 1990; LaBerge 1990). In order to investigate the dynamics of attentional control, however, methods with high temporal resolution such as ERP recordings must also be used.

In trial-by-trial spatial cueing paradigms like those described earlier (e.g. Mangun and Hillyard 1991), ERPs can be separately recorded for both the cue and to the target stimulus itself. Hence, an index of post-cue but pretarget processing is also obtained that presumably reflects brain processes related to executive control of attention. Harter and co-workers (Harter and Anllo-Vento 1991; Harter *et al.* 1989*a,b*) utilized this approach in order to examine the executive and preparatory processes that underlie the shifting of attention from one location to another, as well as the modulation of sensory processes that ensued. These studies used a centrally located arrow cue to direct attention to the right or left visual field on each trial. ERPs recorded in response to the onset of the left- and right-pointing arrow cues were found to differ over the two hemispheres at a latency of 200–400 ms post-cue. A negative ERP over the parietal scalp of the hemisphere contralateral to the direction of the arrow cue was larger than over the hemisphere ipsilateral to the cue direction. An example of these effects is presented in Fig. 3.14 from a study by Mangun (1994). Thus, there was a left-hemisphere negative shift following right-arrow cues, and a right-hemisphere negative shift following left-pointing arrow cues. This pattern can be interpreted as an index of the attentional control process that shifts attention to the cued location and produces an increased cortical excitability in the hemisphere contralateral to the direction of the required attention shift.

At slightly longer latencies (400–700 ms after cue onset) a different effect was observed. The posterior scalp regions were more positive over the right hemisphere for left-pointing arrows, whereas right-pointing arrows resulted in greater positivity over the left posterior scalp. Harter *et al.* suggested that this posterior contralateral positivity was a reflection of the modulation of cortical excitability in the sensory cortical areas in preparation for differential attentional processing of the forthcoming target stimulus.

Spatial Cuing

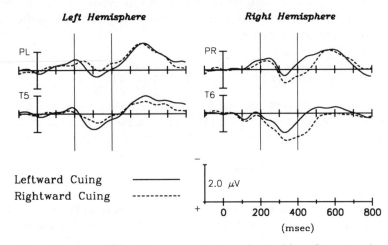

Fig. 3.14 Grand average difference waves to the cues obtained by subtracting the neutral cue traces from the left (full curve) and right (broken curves) cue ERPs. Recordings are from parietal (PL and PR) and posterior temporal (T5 and T6) scalp regions of the left and right hemispheres. The thin vertical lines through both traces indicate the time range from 200–400 ms where the effects of lateralized orienting are maximal, and are inverted in polarity for the two hemispheres as a function of cue direction. (Data from Mangun (1994).)

These ERP data help to identify processes that are involved in the executive control over attention and provide information about the time-course of such mechanisms in humans. Whether these control processes involve only cortico-cortical projections (e.g. the frontal or parietal cortex influencing the visual cortex) or are mediated via input from subcortical structures under the control of higher centres (e.g. the frontal or parietal cortex utilizing the pulvinar of the thalamus to influence the visual cortex), remains unknown. Ongoing studies in animals (e.g. Desimone *et al.* 1990) and humans (e.g. LaBerge 1990) are actively invest-igating this type of question.

3.5 AUDITORY SELECTIVE ATTENTION

In addition to the visual studies reviewed above, there has been extensive research on the ERP indices of selective attention in both auditory and somatosensory modalities. A basic question is whether or not the principles derived from studies in the visual modality also apply in the other sensory systems. To consider this question we will review studies of auditory selective attention that have employed ERP and magnetoencephalographic (MEG) recordings.

3.5.1 Subcortical gating and early selection in the auditory cortex

Early behavioural studies of auditory selective attention focused on the 'cocktail party effect' to illustrate the problem of how a human listener can attend to a single conversation in a distracting, noisy environment. For example, the work of Cherry (1953) used dichotic listening to examine the ability of listeners to select a relevant message (such as sounds, speech, etc.) in one ear while ignoring irrelevant information presented to the other ear. Cherry noted significant performance decrements when the subjects attempted to attend to both input channels simultaneously in comparison to selecting only one for analysis, thereby implying that attentional resources were limited. Related studies showed that high-priority information in an unattended input channel was also processed to the extent that it could 'break through' the attentional barrier; for example one's own name can often elicit orienting of attention to an ignored input channel (Moray 1959). This early literature set the stage for investigations of the physiological mechanisms of selective auditory attention.

The methods utilized in studies of auditory attention are essentially the same as those described earlier for visual studies and involve comparison of ERPs elicited by auditory inputs when attended, with the ERPs for those same physical stimuli when they are ignored. Studies of this type using dichotic listening paradigms have found that attention affects very early stages of auditory processing. For example, the auditory ERP studies of Woldorff and Hillyard (1991) indicate that by 20–50 ms post-stimulus the neural processing of attended versus unattended ear information can differ significantly. In these studies, subjects attended to tones of one frequency delivered to one ear (via headphones), while simultaneously ignoring tones of another frequency entering the other ear; the tones were presented at high rates (about six per second) and in random sequence. This attention effect took the form of a greater positive-polarity voltage deflection in the ERP waveform to the attended-ear tones in the mid-latency range of 20–50 ms (Fig. 3.15). Because of its very short latency (20 ms after stimulus onset), this 'P20–50 effect' was interpreted as evidence in favour of early selection of auditory signals.

In order to identify the locus at which the P20–50 attention effect was generated in the ascending auditory pathways, topographic mapping based on ERP and MEG recordings has been utilized. The MEG approach records the magnetic fields associated with intracellular current flow in active neuronal populations (e.g. Williamson *et al.* 1991). MEG recordings compliment recordings of electric fields (that is, ERPs) and can improve the localization of cortical activity (Scherg 1992). Using combined ERP and MEG recording, Woldorff *et al.* (1993) were able to provide strong evidence that the P20–50 attention effect was generated in the auditory cortex, perhaps as early as the primary sensory receiving area.

Although the P20–50 attention effect appears to be generated in the first stages of auditory cortical processing, it is possible that these effects reflect stimulus

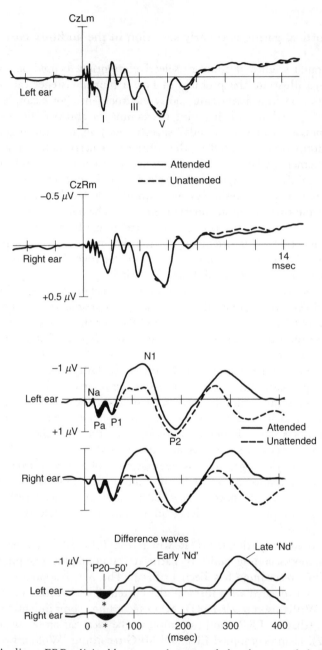

Fig. 3.15 Auditory ERPs elicited by tones when attended and unattended. (Top) Absence of attentional modulation of the brainstem-evoked responses in dichotic listening paradigm. (Bottom) Significant attentional modulations of early auditory processing at the midlatency potentials (P20–50 effect; shaded area), and the later amplitude enhancement of the N1 component to attended-ear tones. (Reprinted with permission from Woldorff *et al.* (1987).)

selection that is passed along from earlier (that is, subcortical) processing stages. Indeed, given the efferent neural projections of the olivocochlear bundle to the cochlea, modulations of processing as early as the auditory receptors themselves are possible, at least in theory. Note that no corresponding efferent projections have been demonstrated in the human visual system between the thalamus or other subcortical structures and the retina in humans (for a review see Mangun *et al.* 1986).

There have been reports of attentional modulations of very early brainstem-evoked components of the auditory ERPs (Lukas 1980, 1981). However, numerous studies have failed to replicate these effects (e.g. Hirschorn and Michie 1990; Näätänen 1990; Picton and Hillyard 1974; Woldorff and Hillyard 1991; Woods and Hillyard 1978), suggesting that their reliability is questionable. The possibility that subcortical systems are involved in auditory selective attention is not completely ruled out by these negative findings (cf. Hackley and Graham 1983; Hackley *et al.* 1987), but it appears unlikely that substantial modulations of incoming signals take place within the early subcortical pathways. In any case, the ERP and MEG evidence for attentional selection of auditory signals at early stages of cortical auditory processing provides compelling evidence in favour of early selection models of attention (e.g. Johnston and Dark 1986).

3.5.2 Long-latency attention effects in the auditory cortex

While the recently discovered P20–50 effect reflects the earliest level of the ascending auditory pathways to be reliably affected by selective attention, attentional modulations of longer-latency ERPs were reported over 20 years ago. Specifically, numerous studies have described attention effects on the sensory-evoked N1 component (80–100 ms latency) of the auditory ERP (e.g. Hillyard *et al.* 1973). Indeed, the N1 attention effect was the first demonstration of auditory selective attention in an appropriately controlled design (see Section 3.2). Previous studies had suggested that attention may alter auditory ERPs (e.g. Spong *et al.* 1965), but those earlier studies suffered from design flaws that did not rule out the possibility of non-specific (e.g. non-selective) effects influencing the ERPs (see Karlin 1970; Näätänen 1967).

The mechanism suggested by Hillyard and colleagues (e.g. Hillyard *et al.* 1973; Hillyard and Picton 1979; Schwent and Hillyard 1975; Woldorff and Hillyard 1991) to account for the N1 attention effect was a selective filtering of auditory inputs that produced amplitude modulations of the brain generators of the N1 component. Thus, the proposed mechanism is essentially the same as that suggested for the visual P1 and N1 peaks reviewed earlier, the idea being that the neural generators of these sensory-evoked potentials are influenced by descending neural systems in a selective fashion such that those neurons that encode the properties of the attended stimulus are relatively facilitated in comparison to those neurons that encode the features of the unattended stimuli.

Identifying the stage of auditory processing represented by the N1 component is important for describing the mechanisms of auditory selection. Woldorff *et al.*

Attended   **Unattended**   **Attention Effect**

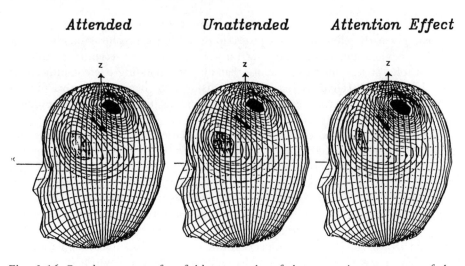

Fig. 3.16 Grand average surface field topography of the magnetic counterpart of the auditory N1 component (latency 100 ms). The three maps indicate the attended field pattern (left), the unattended pattern (centre), and the difference field for the attended–unattended maps (right). The equivalent current dipole that accounted for the obtained magnetic field patterns was situated in the superior temporal plane in auditory cortex. (From Woldorff *et al.* 1993.)

(1993) reported that the magnetic counterpart to the N1 was generated in the superior temporal plane in auditory cortex (Fig. 3.16), as was the P20–50 attention effect. The relative timing of the P20–50 and the N1 (80–100 ms) indicates that the N1 component reflects a subsequent stage of processing, and there is evidence that these attention effects may be correlated (Woldorff and Hillyard 1991). Hence, it is reasonable to propose that neural activity reflected by the P20–50 and the N1 form a serial, hierarchical network for cortical auditory information processing, although it cannot be ruled out at present that they represent activity in parallel but interrelated cortical streams.

The N1 attention effect is usually accompanied by a more prolonged negative deflection in the auditory ERPs to attended stimuli. This longer-lasting negativity can be observed most clearly by subtracting the ERP to the unattended signal from the ERP to that signal when attended. Because the effect was observed most clearly in the subtracted difference waveform, it was referred to as the 'negative difference wave' (Nd). The Nd was described in a series of attention studies by Näätänen and colleagues (Näätänen *et al.* 1978; Näätänen and Michie 1979; Näätänen 1982) and Hansen and Hillyard (1980, 1983). Näätänen (1982) considered the Nd to be a consequence of an enlarged endogenous component termed the 'processing negativity' (PN) elicited by attended-channel stimuli.

An extended controversy has ensued concerning the relationship of the PN to the N1 attention effect. The central question is whether the so-called N1 enhancement might result from the temporal and spatial overlap of the sensory-evoked N1 component and the endogenous PN (e.g. Näätänen *et al.* 1978). Such an overlap might create the appearance of an enhancement of N1 amplitude with attention. Näätänen (1982) proposed that the PN wave represented the activity of neurons specifically engaged in processing the attended stimuli, which were separate from those neurons that generated the sensory-evoked N1 peak. Thus, it was argued, the apparent enhancement of the amplitude of the N1 peak with attention does not actually reflect a larger response of the N1 generator itself but the addition of a separate PN component.

The idea that the early auditory Nd attention effect includes a true modulation of the sensory-evoked N1 wave has received mixed support. Hansen and Hillyard (1980) reported that both an early amplitude modulation of the N1 peak and a longer-lasting endogenous negativity could be observed during selective auditory attention. Subsequently, Woldorff and Hillyard (1991) presented evidence that the sensory-evoked N1 peak was indeed amplitude modulated during selective listening and found this effect to be correlated with the amplitude of the preceding P20–50 attention effect. These findings support the proposal that the early Nd attention effect represents a true amplitude modulation of sensory-evoked N1 activity. Woldorff and Hillyard concluded that a clear distinction should be made between the N1 attention effect, the P2 attention effect (120–150 ms), and a longer-latency negativity (late Nd or PN).

Recently, Näätänen and colleagues (see Näätänen 1992) have attempted to reinforce their supposition that the early Nd attention effect results from an endogenous negativity (that is, PN) that overlaps the N1 wave, rather than from a modulation of the sensory-evoked N1 itself. They compared ERP attention effects to low-frequency tones (300 Hz) that produced large N1 peaks in the unattended channels with those to high tones (6000 Hz) that produced much reduced N1 peaks. A substantial Nd attention effect was found for both high and low tones in the latency range of the N1 peak, although for the high tones the N1 peak itself was greatly reduced in the unattended channel. The authors' conclusion that the Nd did not represent an enhanced N1 component was based on the assumption that, '. . . one would expect the attention effect to be at least roughly proportional to the strength of the generator response elicited in the absence of attention . . .' (Näätänen 1992, p. 279).

Although Näätänen *et al.*'s results are impressive, their interpretation does not take into account possible interactions between sensory signal strength and attention (Hawkins *et al.* 1988). For example, it may be the case that weaker sensory signals receive a greater 'boost' with attention; this view has intuitive appeal because the weaker sensory signals would most benefit from attentional enhancement. Such a scenario could account for Näätänen *et al.*'s result. Further, if some or all of the early attention effect is a suppression of unattended signals, the unattended ERP would not represent a baseline response, but rather a condition of active suppression. Thus, the idea that the unattended ERPs represented the strength of the generator response in the absence of attention would be incorrect and there would be no logical basis to expect the attention effect to be proportional to this 'baseline' sensory response amplitude.

The question of whether the early Nd attention effect reflects a modulation of an evoked sensory response (the N1) still remains unresolved and is under active investigation (Teder *et al.* 1993; Woods *et al.* 1991, 1994). However, the well-established finding of attentional modulation of mid-latency (20–50 ms) evoked activity (e.g. Woldorff *et al.* 1993; cf. Tiitinen *et al.* 1993) strongly suggests that early selection of auditory inputs is possible within modality-specific sensory cortex.

3.6 AUDITORY FEATURE SELECTION

As with visual stimuli, one may characterize auditory signals in terms of their elementary stimulus features — consisting of qualities such as pitch, timbre, location, loudness, duration, etc. — or the conjunctions of these features that form identifiable sounds. The selection of multifeature stimuli has been investigated for complex auditory sounds, including speech. Theoretical treatments of how multifeature stimuli are selected fall into two general classes. Some early selection models emphasize that simple feature information is utilized at successive selection points during stimulus analysis, in a hierarchical selection process (e.g. Broadbend 1970; Treisman 1969). One implication of these models is that selection involves a self-terminating analysis such that processing of the non-selected items that lack a relevant stimulus feature is terminated as soon as the feature is identified. In contrast, late selection theories (e.g. Deutsch and Deutsch 1963; Norman 1968) propose that all stimulus features are processed completely prior to selection, thereby implying an exhaustive perceptual analysis of stimulus features (see Section 3.1.1). These models of stimulus selection have been examined in ERP studies using multidimensional visual (see Section 3.3.2) and auditory stimuli (e.g. Hansen and Hillyard 1983).

3.6.1 Hierarchical auditory selection

An ERP study by Hansen and Hillyard (1983) contrasted attentional selection models that propose exhaustive processing of all stimulus features prior to selection with those that imply a hierarchical selection process. They constructed four auditory stimulus 'channels' from pitch (600 versus 1500 Hz) and location (ear) cues: (i) high pitch/left ear, (ii) high pitch/right ear, (iii) low pitch/left ear, and (iv) low pitch/right ear. These stimuli were presented in random sequence and subjects were required to attend to a particular pitch/location channel in each block. Within this attended channel the subjects were required to distinguish rare target from frequent non-target stimuli (tone pips of 52 ms duration for non-targets, and 102 ms duration for targets).

Hansen and Hillyard made predictions about the expected patterns of attention-related ERP activity for the different models (see Fig. 3.17). If attentional selection is preceded by an exhaustive analysis of all stimulus features, an ERP pattern like that in Fig. 3.17A was predicted. In this case, the processing and

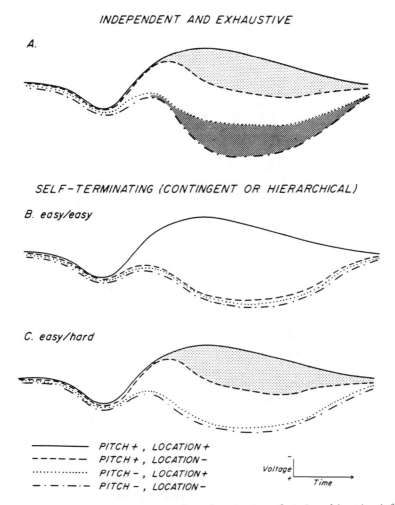

Fig. 3.17 Hypothetical ERP attention effects for selection of pitch and location information under different hypothetical models of auditory attention. See text for detailed description. (From Hansen and Hillyard 1983.)

selection of pitch and location information are not hierarchically dependent; the shaded areas indicate that the degree of location selection is the same regardless of whether or not the stimulus is in the attended pitch channel. In contrast, Figs. 3.17 B and C provide a set of hypothetical ERPs that would be expected if selection proceeded in a hierarchical manner. In B, when the inter-channel discriminability is 'easy' (that is the channels are well separated in pitch or location), the unattended stimuli receive no further processing following their rejection for lacking the relevant channel-defining features; neither location nor pitch differences are differentially processed in the unattended channels. In an additional

PITCH EASY, LOCATION EASY

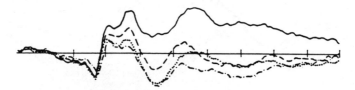

Fig. 3.18 Grand average ERPs elicited by non-target tones that matched the to-be-attended target in: (i) both pitch and location (full curve); (ii) pitch but not location (broken curve); (iii) location but not pitch (dotted curve); (iv) neither pitch or location (dot-dashed curve). Tick marks represent 100 ms intervals; the first tick is at time zero (stimulus onset). Recordings are from the frontal midline scalp site Fz. (From Hansen and Hillyard 1983.)

manipulation, Hansen and Hillyard varied the discriminability of the features that defined the channels by varying the frequency or location separation of the stimuli. Figure 3.17 C shows one possible ERP pattern that would be consistent with hierarchical processing models.

The ERP data obtained by Hansen and Hillyard (1983) strongly supported hierarchical selection models. For easy channel separations, the ERPs indicated both an early selection of attended stimuli and a suppression of feature processing for the unattended stimuli. The ERP results shown in Fig. 3.18 closely parallel those of the hypothetical waveforms of Figs. 3.17 B and C. When pitch and location cues were easily discriminable, there was a large and sustained Nd component elicited by the attended pitch–location conjunction, with only a small, transient processing afforded to the stimulus of the to-be-*attended* pitch at the to-be-*ignored* location. These results are in line with the central tenet of early selection theory — that irrelevant stimuli are rejected rapidly after an analysis of their salient features. The results are not consistent with late selection models that posit exhaustive feature analyses.

3.6.2 Stages of auditory feature selection

Woods *et al.* (1991, 1994) investigated the processing of auditory features and their conjunctions in a design similar to that of Hansen and Hillyard (1983). Stimuli consisted of randomized sequences of tone pips that varied in pitch and location to form six different stimulus classes; the tones could be either long (50 ms; non-targets) or short (30 ms; targets) in duration. The aim was to identify ERP indices that tracked the time-course of stimulus selection processes at different levels including stages of feature selection, conjunction selection, and target identification and response.

In this study, subjects attended to one of the pitch–location conjunctions during each block of trials, and to each possible combination over the course of the experiment. Their task was to monitor the attended channel for the shorter-duration target stimuli. Analysis of the scalp topographies of the sensory-evoked N1 component (70–90 ms) elicited in response to unattended stimuli showed that it varied systematically with stimulus frequency. This finding is consistent with the tonotopic representation of frequency known to exist in the auditory cortex of the superior temporal plane based on recordings in animals (e.g. Merzenich *et al.* 1979), studies in humans using MEG (Romani *et al.* 1982) and functional imaging (e.g. Lauter *et al.* 1985). Channel-selective attention produced a modulation of the rising phase of the N1 and the related P90 component. This effect also showed tonotopic organization, thereby supporting an early sensory modulation mechanism for auditory attention.

In contrast to the findings for the sensory-evoked N1 component, other attention effects reflected in the 'early Nd' component showed no tonotopic organization, and could be dissociated on the basis of latency and scalp distribution from the sensory-evoked N1 (cf. Giard *et al.* 1988). Accordingly, Woods *et al.* (1991, 1994) suggested that the early Nd component reflects feature processing in higher, non-tonotopic auditory fields. By examining the Nd components associated with processing the pitch and location cues, Woods *et al.* were able to identify three successive stages of attentional selection. The first stage spanned the interval from 80–120 ms after stimulus onset, during which the frequency and location attributes of the attended stimuli were selected in parallel and independently. In a subsequent stage of analysis (120–400 ms), it was found that attention effects (later Nd components) were evident to the conjunction of features, as well as to the individual features. After 400 ms, only those stimuli that contained the proper to-be-attended conjunction of frequency and location continued to elicit an Nd. Woods *et al.* interpreted these findings as evidence for those models that propose parallel analyses and selection of feature information. The key aspect of these results was that the selection of individual feature information continued even after the selection for conjunction information had begun.

3.6.3 Auditory sensory memory and the mismatch response

In addition to the selective processing of specific features under attentional control, processes of automatic feature analysis also play an important role in auditory perception (Hawkins and Presson 1986). An ERP component termed the 'mismatch negativity' (MMN) has been identified as an index of automatic feature analysis in the auditory cortex (Näätänen 1990). The MMN is specifically triggered (with a latency of 150–200 ms) by physically deviant sounds in a repetitive sequence, including deviations in pitch, intensity, duration, location, timing, and phoneme characteristics (see Näätänen (1992) for a review). Because the MMN may be elicited by auditory deviants even when the subject's attention is diverted from the sounds (e.g. during reading), it has been suggested that it represents an automatic form of sensory analysis. In particular, studies of the MMN provide evidence that the brain automatically forms a short-term memory trace of auditory features that can be compared against the incoming stream of sensory information for the purpose of detecting changes in the auditory milieu. Studies of the electrical and magnetic MMN indicate that the short-term memory trace for auditory stimuli, the echoic trace, may persist for 6–10 s (e.g. Sams *et al.* 1993), and that the MMN is generated primarily in the auditory cortex (Sams *et al.* 1991).

3.6.4 Attentional modulation of automatic processes

Studies by Näätänen and colleagues (reviewed in Näätänen 1992) have supported the view that MMN is not affected by selective auditory attention. These studies led to the proposal that all physical features of auditory inputs are analysed automatically and stored in short-term memory regardless of whether they are attended or ignored. Thus, in the view of Näätänen and colleagues, unattended channel inputs are processed in the auditory system at least until the level of feature analysis and the mismatch process reflected by MMN. Such a view has important implications for theories about the level of auditory processing at which selective attention can operate.

Despite these claims, recent evidence suggests that under conditions of highly focused attention during dichotic listening, the MMN is in fact sensitive to attentional factors (Woldorff *et al.* 1991). In these experiments, selective auditory attention resulted in early amplitude modulation of the P20–50 and N1 components, and a suppression of the MMN elicited by deviant tones (of lower intensity) in the unattended channel (Fig. 3.19). Thus, under conditions which maximize early

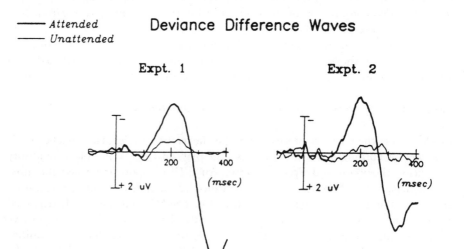

Fig. 3.19 Mismatch negativity (MMN) to deviant tones when in the attended channel (thick full curve) and unattended channel (thin full curve). Tracings are difference waves in which the ERP to the standard tones was subtracted from the ERP to deviant tones. The MMN (negative peak at 200 ms) is significantly reduced in amplitude in the unattended channel responses.

selection the MMN is gated along with other early sensory-cortical ERPs to unattended inputs. These findings, as well as more recent evidence (Woods *et al.* 1992) indicates that information processing in the auditory pathway is under the control of attentional processes at very early levels, including those processes generally considered to be automatic in nature, that are reflected in the MMN. There is still some question, however, as to whether channel-selective attention can suppress the MMN to all types of auditory deviants (Näätänen 1992).

3.7 CONCLUSIONS AND SUMMARY

Mechanisms of selective attention have been studied extensively in humans using approaches that combine behavioural methods with the non-invasive recording of ERPs and MEGs. The central question of whether attentional selection of sensory inputs can occur at a stage of processing prior to complete feature analysis has been convincingly answered by these studies: attention can indeed modulate early sensory and perceptual processing. Moreover, the ERP and MEG data indicate the level(s) of the sensory pathways at which attentional selection occurs in humans, by providing high-resolution temporal information not available using other neuro-imaging techniques. These studies have shown that selective attention modifies sensory information transmission at early cortical levels for both the auditory and visual modalities. This attentional selection mechanism acts (at least in part) as a sensory gain control that differentially modulates the amplitude of evoked activity in the cortical sensory pathways for attended versus unattended inputs. Thus, these physiological recordings are strongly supportive of early selection theories of attention.

It is still unresolved, however, whether the auditory and visual modalities differ in the cortical level at which earliest selection takes place. For visual attention, there has been no convincing evidence from ERP recordings (or from other neuro-imaging techniques) for any stimulus selection at, or prior to, the level of the primary visual cortex. Rather, the initial effects of visual–spatial attention appear to modulate information transmission between the primary cortex and visual association areas of the occipital lobe. For auditory attention, however, the short latency of the earliest attention effect (20–50 ms) and its localization in the superior temporal lobe are consistent with sensory modulation in either primary or secondary auditory cortex. If evoked activity in the primary cortex were affected by attention, this would open up the possibility of a selective input control at the level of the thalamus or the thalamo-cortical projections. Despite these possible differences in the level of selection, ERP recordings have demonstrated many fundamental similarities between auditory and visual selective attention. These include a mechanism of early sensory gain control, and a hierarchical organization that is characterized by an initial stage of parallel feature selection followed by a stage of conjunction (object) selection.

The consequences of these early selection mechanisms are that the inputs to higher perceptual and cognitive processes are altered, and thus these powerful brain mechanisms of selective attention influence our perception and awareness of the world around us. This occurs in a manner that is consistent with the strategic necessities established by our moment-to-moment intentions and expectations, and as required by evolutionary, biological constraints. Future theoretical models must take into account this compelling physiological evidence in order to arrive at a complete understanding of the mechanisms of selective attention and perception in humans (e.g. Allport 1993).

ACKNOWLEDGEMENTS

The authors thank Dr Jonathan Hansen, Dr Hans–Jochen Heinze, Dr Thomas Münte, Dr Marty Woldorff, Dr Sönke Johannes, Dr Vince Clark, and Dr Steven Luck for their important contributions to the work reviewed here, and Dr Michael Gazzaniga and Dr David Woods, Todd Handy, and Clif Kussmaul for helpful comments and support. Thanks also to Dr Peter Hagoort, Dr Colin Brown, and Tamara Swaab and the Max–Planck Institute for Psycholinguistics, Nijmegen, Netherlands for assistance during the preparation of this chapter. Supported by grants from NIMH, NINDS, the Office of Naval Research, the Human Frontier Science Program Organization, and the McDonnell–Pew Foundation.

REFERENCES

Allport, A. (1989). Visual attention. In *Foundations of cognitive science* (ed M. I. Posner), pp. 631–82. Cambridge MA, MIT Press.

Allport, A. (1993). Attention and control: have we been asking the wrong questions? A critical review of 25 years. *Attention and performance XIV* (ed. D. Meyer and S. Kornblum), pp. 183–218. Cambridge, MA, MIT Press.

Allport, A., Tipper, S. P., and Chmiel, N. (1985). Perceptual integration and post-categorical filtering. In *Attention and performance XI* (ed. M. I. Posner and O. S. Marin), pp. 107–32. Erlbaum, Hillsdale, NJ.

Bashinski, H. S. and Bacharach, V. R. (1980). Enhancement of perceptual sensitivity as the result of selectively attending to spatial locations. *Perception and Psychophysics*, **28**, 241–8.

Briand, K. A. and Klein, R. M. (1987). Is Posner's 'Beam' the same as Treisman's 'Glue'?: on the relationship between visual orienting and feature integration theory. *Journal of Experimental Psychology: Human Perception and Performance.* 13, 228–41.

Broadbent, D. A. (1958). *Perception and communication*. New York, Pergamon.

Broadbent, D. E. (1970). Stimulus set and response set: two kinds of selective attention. In *Attention: contemporary theory and analysis* (ed. D. I. Mostofsky), pp. 51–60. Appleton-Century-Crofts, New York.

Cherry, E. C. (1953). Some experiments on the recognition of speech with one and with two ears. *Journal of the Acoustical Society of America*, **25**, 975–9.

Colby, C. L. (1991). The neuroanatomy and neurophysiology of attention. *Journal of Child Neurology*, **6**, 90–118.

Corbetta, M., Miezin, F. M., Dobmeyer, S., Shulman, G. L., and Petersen, S. E. (1991).

Selective and divided attention during visual discriminations of shape, color and speed: functional anatomy by positron emission tomography. *Journal of Neuroscience*, 11, 2383–402.

Desimone, R. and Ungerleider, L. (1989). Neural mechanisms of visual processing in monkey. In *Handbook of neuropsychology* (ed. F. Boller and J. Grafman), pp. 267.

Desimone, R., Wessinger, M., Thomas, L., and Schneider, W. (1990). Attentional control of visual perception: cortical and subcortical mechanisms. In *Cold Spring Harbor Symposium*, pp. 963–71. Cold Spring Harbor Press, New York.

Deutsch, J.A and Deutsch, D. (1963). Attention: some theoretical considerations. *Psychological Review*, 70, 80–90.

Downing, C. J. (1988). Expectancy and visual-spatial attention: effects on perceptual quality. *Journal of Experimental Psychology: Human Perception and Performance*, 14, 188–202.

Eason, R. G. (1981). Visual evoked potential correlates of early neural filtering during selective attention. *Bulletin of the Psychonomic Society*, 18, 203–6.

Eason, R. G., Harter, M., and White, C. (1969). Effects of attention and arousal on visually evoked cortical potentials. *Physiology and Behavior*, 4, 283–9.

Eriksen, C. W. and Yeh, Y. Y. (1985). Allocation of attention in the visual field. *Journal of Experimental Psychology: Human Perception and Performance*, 11, 583–97.

Felleman, D. J. and Van Essen, D. C. (1991). Distributed hierarchical processing in the primate cerebral cortex. *Cerebral Cortex*, 1, 1–47.

Fischer, B. and Boch, R. (1985). Peripheral attention versus central fixation: Modulation of visual activity of prelunate cortical cells of the rhesus monkey. *Brain Research*, 345, 111–23.

Giard, M., Perrin, F., Pernier, J., and Peronnet, F. (1988). Several attention-related waveforms in auditory areas: a topographic study. *Electroencephalography and Clinical Neurophysiology*, 69, 371–84.

Gomez Gonzalez, C. M., Clark, V. P., Fan, S., Luck, S. J., and Hillyard, S. A. Sources of attention-sensitive visual event-related potentials. *Brain Topography*. (In press.)

Hackley, S. A. and Graham, F. K. (1983). Early selective attention effects on cutaneous and acoustic blink reflexes. *Physiological Psychology*, 11, 235–42.

Hackley, S. A., Woldorff, M., and Hillyard, S. A. (1987). Combined use of microreflexes and ERPs as measures of auditory selective attention. *Psychophysiology*, 24, 632–47.

Hansen, J. C. (1983). Separation of overlapping waveforms having known temporal distributions. *Journal of Neuroscience Methods*, 9, 127–39.

Hansen, J. C. and Hillyard, S. A. (1980). Endogenous brain potentials associated with selective auditory attention. *Electroencephalography and Clinical Neurophysiology*. 49, 277–90.

Hansen, J. C. and Hillyard, S. A. (1983). Selective attention to multidimensional auditory stimuli. *Journal of Experimental Psychology: Human Perception and Performance*, 9, 1–19.

Harter, M. R. and Aine, C. J. (1984). Brain mechanisms of visual selective attention. In *Varieties of attention* (ed. R Parasuraman and D. R. Davies), pp. 293–321. Academic, London.

Harter, M. R. and Anllo-Vento, L. (1991). Visual-spatial attention: preparation and selection in children and adults. In *Event-related potentials of the brain* (ed. C. H. M. Brunia, G. Mulder, and M. N. Verbaten), pp. 183–94. Elsevier, Amsterdam.

Harter, M.R, Aine, C., and Schroeder, C. (1982). Hemispheric differences in the neural processing of stimulus location and type: effects of selective attention on visual evoked potentials. *Neuropsychologia*, 20, 421–38.

Harter, M. R., Anllo-Vento, L., and Wood, F. B. (1989*a*). Event-related potentials, spatial orienting, and reading disabilities. *Psychophysiology*, 26, 404–21.

Harter, M. R., Miller, S. L., Price, N. J., LaLonde, M. E., and Keyes, A. L. (1989*b*). Neural processes involved in directing attention. *Journal of Cognitive Neuroscience*, 1, 223–37.

Hawkins, H. L. and Presson, J. (1986). Auditory information processing. In *Handbook of perception and human performance*, Vol. 2., (ed. K. R. Boff, L. Kaufman, and J. P. Thomas), pp. 1–64. Wiley, New York.

Hawkins, H. L., Hillyard, S. A., Luck, S. J., Mouloua, M., Downing, C. J., and Woodward, D. P. (1990). Visual attention modulates signal detectability. *Journal of Experimental Psychology: Human Perception and Performance*, 16, 802–11.

Hawkins, H. S., Shafto, M. G., and Richardson K. (1988). Effects of target luminance and cue validity on the latency of visual detection. *Perception and Psychophysics*, 44, 484–92

Heinze, H. J., Luck, S. J., Mangun, G. R., and Hillyard, S. A. (1990*a*). Lateralized visual ERPs index focused attention to bilateral stimulus arrays: I. Evidence for early selection. *Electroencephalography and Clinical Neurophysiology*, 75, 511–27.

Heinze, H. J., Mangun, G. R., and Hillyard, S. A. (1990*b*). Visual event-related potentials index perceptual accuracy during spatial attention to bilateral stimuli. In *Event-related potentials of the brain* (ed. C. H. M. Brunia, G. Mulder, and M. N. Verbaten), pp. 196–202. Elsevier, Amsterdam.

Hillyard, S. A. (1993). Electrical and magnetic brain recordings: contributions to cognitive neuroscience. *Current Opinions in Neurobiology*, 3, 217–24.

Hillyard, S. A. and Mangun, G. R. (1987). Sensory gating as a physiological mechanism for visual selective attention. In *Current trends in event-related potential research* (ed. R. Johnson, R. Parasuraman, and J. W. Rohrbaugh), pp. 61–7. Elsevier, Amsterdam.

Hillyard, S. A. and Münte, T. F. (1984). Selective attention to color and locational cues: an analysis with event-related brain potentials. *Perception and Psychophysics*, 36, 185–98.

Hillyard, S. A. and Picton, T. W. (1979). Event-related potentials and selective information processing in man. In *Cognitive components in cerebral event-related potentials and selective attention. Progress in clinical neurophysiology* 6 (ed. J. Desmedt), pp. 1–52. Karger, Basel.

Hillyard, S. A., Hink, R. F., Schwent, V. L., and Picton, T. W. (1973). Electrical signs of selective attention in the human brain. *Science*, 182, 177–80.

Hirschorn, T. N. and Michie, P. T. (1990). Brainstem auditory evoked potentials (BAEPS) and selective listening revisited. *Psychophysiology*, 27, 495–512.

Hoffman, J. E. and Nelson, B. (1981). Spatial selectivity in visual search. *Perception and Psychophysics*, 30, 283–90.

Jeffreys, D. A. and Axford, J. G. (1972). Source location of pattern-specific components of human visual evoked potentials. *Experimental Brain Research*, 16, 1–21.

Johannes, S., Hughes, H. C., and Mangun, G. R. (1992). Attention to locations in space: the neurophysiology of early selection. *Society for Neuroscience Abstracts*, 18.

Johnston, W. A. and Dark, V. J. (1986). Selective attention. *Annual Review of Psychology*, 37, 43–75.

Jonides, J. (1981). Voluntary versus automatic control over the mind's eye's movement. In *Attention and performance IX* (ed. J. Long and A. Baddeley), pp. 187–203. Erlbaum, Hillsdale, NJ.

Karlin, L. (1970). Cognition, preparation and sensory-evoked potentials. *Psychological Bulletin*, 73, 122–36.

Klein, R. M., Kingstone, A., and Pontefract, A. (1992). Orienting of visual attention.

In *Eye movements and visual cognition: scene perception and reading* (ed. K. Raynor), pp. 46–65. Springer, New York.

LaBerge, D. (1990). Thalamic and cortical mechanisms of attention suggested by recent positron emission tomographic experiments. *Journal of Cognitive Neuroscience*, 2, 358–72.

Lauter, J. L., Herschovitsch, P., Formby, C., and Raichle, M. E. (1985). Tonotopic organization in the human auditory cortex revealed by positron emission tomography. *Hearing Research*, 20, 199–205.

Luck, S., Fan, S., and Hillyard, S. A. (1993). Attention-related modulation of sensory-evoked brain activity in a visual search task. *Journal of Cognitive Neuroscience*, 5, 188–95.

Luck, S. J., Hillyard, S. A., Mouloua, M., Woldorff, M. G., Clark, V. P., and Hawkins, H. L. (1994). Effects of spatial cuing on luminance detectability: psychophysical and electrophysiological evidence for early selection. *Journal of Experimental Psychology: Human Perception and Performance* 20, 887–904.

Lukas, J. H. (1980). Human auditory attention: the olivocochlear bundle may function as a peripheral filter. *Psychophysiology*, 17, 444–52.

Lukas, J. H. (1981). The role of efferent inhibition in human auditory attention. An examination of the auditory brainstem potentials. *International Journal of Neuroscience*, 12, 137–45.

Mangun, G. R. (1994). Orienting attention in the visual fields: an electrophysiological analysis. In *Cognitive electrophysiology* (ed. H. J. Heinze, T. F. Münte, and G.R Mangun), pp. 81–101. Birkhaüser, Boston.

Mangun, G. R. and Hillyard, S. A. (1987). The spatial allocation of visual attention as indexed by event-related brain potentials. *Human Factors*, 29, 195–212.

Mangun, G. R. and Hillyard, S. A. (1988). Spatial gradients of visual attention: behavioral and electrophysiological evidence. *Electroencephalography and Clinical Neurophysiology*, 70, 417–28.

Mangun, G. R. and Hillyard, S. A. (1990a). Electrophysiological studies of visual selective attention in humans. In *The neurobiological foundations of higher cognitive function* (ed. A. B. Scheibel and A. Wechsler). Guilford, New York.

Mangun, G. R. and Hillyard, S. A. (1990b). Allocation of visual attention to spatial locations: tradeoff functions for event-related brain potentials and detection performance. *Perception and Psychophysics*, 47, 532–50.

Mangun, G. R. and Hillyard, S. A. (1991). Modulation of sensory-evoked brain potentials provide evidence for changes in perceptual processing during visual–spatial priming. *Journal of Experimental Psychology: Human Perception and Performance*, 17, 1057–74.

Mangun, G. R., Hansen, J. C., and Hillyard, S. A. (1986). Electroretinograms reveal no evidence for centrifugal modulation of retinal inputs during selective attention in man. *Psychophysiology*, 23, 156–65.

Mangun, G. R., Hansen, J. C., and Hillyard, S. A. (1987). The spatial orienting of attention: sensory facilitation or response bias? In *Current trends in event-related potential research* (ed. R. Johnson, J. W. Rohrbaugh, and R. Parasuaman), pp. 118–24. Elsevier, Amsterdam.

Mangun, G. R., Hillyard, S. A., and Luck, S. L. (1993). Electrocortical substrates of visual selective attention. In *Attention and performance XIV* (ed. D. Meyer and S. Kornblum), pp. 219–43. MIT Press, Cambridge, MA.

Mangun, K. S., Mangun, G. R., and Hillyard, S. A. Feature selection in the human brain: Electrophysiological analyses of attention to color. *Journal of Cognitive Neuroscience*. (In press.)

Merzenich, M. M., Andersen, R. R., and Middlebrooks, J. C. (1979). Functional and topographic organization of the auditory cortex. *Experimental Brain Research Supplement*, 2, 61–75.

Moran, J. and Desimone, R. (1985). Selective attention gates visual processing in the extrastriate cortex. *Science*, 229, 782–4.

Moray, N. (1959). Attention in dichotic listening: effective cues and the influence of instructions. *Quarterly Journal of Experimental Psychology*, 9, 56–600.

Motter, B. C. (1993). Focal attention produces spatial selective processing in visual cortical areas V1, V2 and V4 in the presence of competing stimuli. *Journal of Neurophysiology*, 70, 909–19.

Müller, H. J. and Findlay, J. M. (1987). Sensitivity and criterion effects in the spatial cuing of visual attention. *Perception and Psychophysics*, 42, 383–99.

Müller, H. J. and Humphreys, G. W. (1991). Luminance increment detection: capacity limited or not? *Journal of Experimental Psychology: Human Perception and Performance*, 17, 107–24.

Näätänen, R. (1967). Selective attention and evoked potentials. *Annales Academiae Scientiarum Fennicae B*, 151, 1–226.

Näätänen, R. (1982). Processing negativity: an evoked potential reflection of selective attention. *Psychological Bulletin*. 92, 605–40.

Näätänen, R. (1987). Event-related brain potentials in research of cognitive processes — a classification of components. In *Knowledge aided information processing* (ed. E. van der Meer and J. Hoffmann), pp. 241–73. Elsevier, Amsterdam.

Näätänen, R. (1990). The role of attention in auditory information processing as revealed by event-related potentials and other brain measures of cognitive function. *Behavioral and Brain Sciences*, 13, 201–88.

Näätänen, R. (1992). *Attention and brain function*. Erlbaum, Hillsdale, NJ.

Näätänen, R. and Michie, P. T. (1979). Early selective attention effects on the evoked potential: a critical review and reinterpretation. *Biological Psychology*, 8, 81–136.

Näätänen, R., Gaillard, A. W. K., and Mantysalo, S. (1978). Early selective attention effect on evoked potential reinterpreted. *Acta Psychologica*, 42, 313–29.

Neville, H. J. and Lawson, D. (1987). Attention to central and peripheral visual space in a movement detection task: an event-related potential and behavioral study. I. Normal hearing adults. *Brain Research*, 405, 253–67.

Norman, D. A. (1968). Toward a theory of memory and attention. *Psychological Review*, 75, 522–36.

Oakley, M. T. and Eason, R. G. (1990). The conjoint influence of spatial selective attention and motor set on very short latency VERs. *Neuropsychologia*, 28, 487–97.

Paul, D. D. and Sutton, S. (1972). Evoked potential correlates of response criterion in auditory signal detection. *Science*, 177, 362–4.

Picton, T. W. and Hillyard, S. A. (1974). Human auditory evoked potentials. II. Effects of attention. *Electroencephalography and Clinical Neurophysiology*, 36, 191–200.

Posner, M. I. (1980). Orienting of attention. *Quarterly Journal of Experimental Psychology*, 32, 3–25.

Posner, M. I. and Petersen, S. E. (1990). The attention system of the human brain. *Annual Review of Neuroscience*, 13, 25–42.

Posner, M. I., Nissen, M. J., and Ogden, W. C. (1978). Attended and unattended processing modes: The role of set for spatial location. In *Modes of perceiving and processing information* (ed. H. L. Pick and I. J. Saltzman), pp. 137–57. Erlbaum, Hillsdale, N. J.

Posner, M. I., Snyder, C. R. R., and Davidson, B. J. (1980). Attention and the detection of signals. *Journal of Experimental Psychology: General*, 109, 160–174.

Prinzmetal, W., Presti, D. E., and Posner, M. I. (1986). Does attention affect visual feature integration? *Journal of Experimental Psychology: Human Perception and Performance*, 12, 361–9.

Regan, D. (1989). *Human brain electrophysiology*. Elsevier, New York.

Reinitz, M. T. (1990). The effects of spatially directed attention on visual encoding. *Perception and Psychophysics*, 47, 497–505.

Ritter, W., Simson, R., and Vaughan, H. G., jun. (1983). Event-related potential correlates of two stages of information processing in physical and semantic discrimination tasks. *Psychophysiology*, 20, 168–79.

Romani, G. L., Williamson, S. J., and Kaufman, L. (1982). Tonotopic organization of the human auditory cortex. *Science*, 216, 1339–40.

Rugg, M. D., Milner, A. D., Lines, C. R., and Phalp, R. (1987). Modulation of visual event-related potentials by spatial and non-spatial visual selective attention. *Neuropsychologia*. 25, 85–96.

Sams, M., Kaukoranta, M., Hamalainen, M., and Näätänen, R. (1991). Cortical activity elicited by changes in auditory stimuli: different sources for the magnetic N100m and mismatch response. *Psychophysiology*, 28, 21–9.

Sams, M., Hari, R., Rif, J., and Knuutila, J. (1993). The human auditory sensory memory trace persists about 10 sec: neuromagnetic evidence. *Journal of Cognitive Neuroscience*, 5, 363–70.

Sanders, A. F. (1990). Issues and trends in the debate on discrete versus continuous processing of information. *Acta Psychologica*, 74, 123–67.

Scherg, M. (1992). Functional imaging and localization of electromagnetic brain activity. *Brain Topography*, 5, 103–11.

Schwent, V. L. and Hillyard, S. A. (1975). Evoked potential correlates of selective attention with multichannel auditory inputs. *Electroencephalography and Clinical Neurophysiology*, 38, 131–8.

Shaw, M. L. (1984). Division of attention among spatial locations: a fundamental difference between detection of letters and detection of luminance increments. In *Attention and performance X: control of language processes* (ed. H. Bouma and D. G. Bouwhuis), pp. 109–21. Erlbaum, Hillsdale, NJ.

Sperling, G. (1984). A unified theory of attention and signal detection. In *Varieties of attention* (ed. R. Parasuraman and D. R. Davies), pp. 103–81. Academic, Orlando, FL.

Sperling, G., and Dosher, B. A. (1986). Strategy and optimization in human information processing. In *Handbook of perception and performance* Vol. 1, (ed. K. Boff, L. Kaufman, and J. Thomas), pp. 2.1–2.65. Wiley, New York.

Spitzer, H., Desimone, R., and Moran, J. (1988). Increased attention enhances both behavioral and neuronal performance. *Science*, 240, 338–40.

Spong, P., Haider, M., and Lindsley, D. B. (1965). Selective attentiveness and cortical evoked responses to visual and auditory stimuli. *Science*, 148, 395–7.

Squires, K. C., Hillyard, S. A., and Lindsay, P. H. (1973). Vertex potentials evoked during auditory signal detection: relation to decision criteria. *Perception and Psychophysics*, 14, 265–72.

Teder, W., Alho, K., Reinikainen, K., and Näätänen, R. (1993). Inter-stimulus interval and the selective attention effect on auditory ERPs: N1 enhancement versus processing negativity. *Psychophysiology*, 30, 71–81.

Tiitinen, H., Sinkkonen, J., Reinikainen, K., Alho, K., Lavikainea, J., and Näätänen, R. (1993). Selective attention enhances the auditory 40–Hz transient responses in humans. *Nature*, 364, 59–60.

Treisman, A. (1969). Strategies and models of selective attention. *Psychological Review*, 76, 282–99.

Treisman, A. (1988). Features and objects: the fourteenth Bartlett Memorial Lecture. *Quarterly Journal of Experimental Psychology*. 40, 201–37.

Treisman, A. and Gelade, G. (1980). A feature-integration theory of attention. *Cognitive Psychology*, 12, 97–136.

Ungerleider, L. G. and Mishkin, M. (1982). Two cortical visual systems. In *Analysis of visual behavior* (ed. D. J. Ingle, M. A. Goodale, and R. J. W. Mansfield), pp. 549–86. MIT Press, Cambridge, MA.

Van Voorhis, S. T. and Hillyard, S. A. (1977). Visual evoked potentials and selective attention to points in space. *Perception and Psychophysics*, 22, 54–62.

Wijers, A. A., Okita, T., Mulder, G., Mulder, L. J. M., Lorist, M. M., Poiesz, R., and Scheffers, K. M. (1987). Visual search and spatial attention: ERPs in focused and divided attention conditions. *Biological Psychology*, 25, 33–60.

Wijers, A. A., Lamain, W., Slopsema, S., Mulder, G., and Mulder, L. J. M. (1989a) An electrophysiological investigation of the spatial distribution of attention to colored stimuli in focused and divided attention condition. *Biological Psychology*, 29, 213–45.

Wijers, A. A., Mulder, G., Okita, T., and Mulder, L. J. M. (1989b). An ERP study on memory search and selective attention to letter size and conjunction of letter size and color. *Psychophysiology*, 26, 529–47.

Wijers, A. A., Mulder, G., Okita, T., Mulder, L. J. M., and Scheffers, M. K. (1989c). Attention to color: an ERP analysis of selective attention, controlled search and motor activation. *Psychophysiology*, 26, 89–109.

Williamson, S. J., Lu, Z. L., Karron, D., and Kaufman, L. (1991). Advantages and limitations of magnetic source imaging. *Brain Topography*, 4, 169–80.

Woldorff, M. G. (1992). Distortion of ERP averages due to overlap from temporally adjacent ERPs: analysis and correction. *Psychophysiology*, 30, 98–119.

Woldorff, M. G. and Hillyard, S. A. (1991). Modulation of early auditory processing during selective listening to rapidly presented tones. *Electroencephalography and Clinical Neurophysiology*, 79, 170–91.

Woldorff, M., Hansen, J., and Hillyard, S. A. (1987). Evidence for effects of selective attentions in the midlatency range of the human auditory event-related brain potential. In *Current trends in event-related potential research* (ed. R. Johnson, R. Parasuraman, and J. W. Rohrbaugh), pp. 146–54. Elsevier, Amsterdam.

Woldorff, M. G., Hackley, S. A., and Hillyard, S. A. (1991). The effects of channel-selective attention on the mismatch negativity wave elicited by deviant tones. *Psychophysiology*, 28, 30–42.

Woldorff, M. G., Gallen, C. C., Hampson, S. R., Hillyard, S. A., Pantev, C., Sobel, D., and Bloom, F. E. (1993). Modulations of early sensory processing in human auditory cortex during auditory selective attention. *Proceedings of the National Academy of Sciences of the USA*, 90, 8722–6.

Woods, D. L. and Hillyard, S. A. (1978). Attention at the cocktail party: brainstem evoked responses reveal no peripheral gating. In *Multidisciplinary perspectives in event-related potential research* (ed. D. A. Otto), pp. 230–3. US Government Printing Office, Washington, DC.

Woods, D. L., Alho, K., and Algazi, A. (1991). Brain potential signs of feature processing during auditory selective attention. *NeuroReport*, 2, 189–92.

Woods, D. L., Alho, K., and Algazi, A. (1992). Intermodal selective attention I. Effects on event-related potentials to lateralized auditory and visual stimuli. *Electroencephalography and Clinical Neurophysiology*, **82**, 341–55.

Woods, D. L., Alho, K., and Algazi, A. (1994). Stages of auditory feature conjunction: an event-related brain potential study. *Journal of Experimental Psychology: Human Perception and Performance*, **20**, 81–94.

4   Mental chronometry and the study of human information processing

Michael G. H. Coles, Henderikus G. O. M. Smid, Marten K. Scheffers, and Leun J. Otten

4.1 INTRODUCTION

In this chapter, we shall focus on the use of event-related potentials (ERPs) in the study of human information processing. We shall emphasize the nature and time-course of the mental events that occur between the presentation of a stimulus and the execution of a response. The utility of ERPs as markers for the timing of mental events was anticipated by Woodworth in his classic text, *Experimental psychology*, published in 1938:[1]

Time as a dimension of every mental or behavioral process lends itself to measurement, and can be used as an indicator of the complexity of the performance or of the subject's readiness to perform. A technical difficulty at once suggests itself. 'The speed of thought,' we say; but as soon as we set about measuring the time occupied by a thought we find that the beginning and end of any measurable time must be external events. We may be able in the future to use 'brain waves' as indicators of the beginning and end of a mental process, and even now muscle currents enable us to penetrate the organism a little way with our timing apparatus; but in general it has seemed necessary to let the timed process start with a sensory stimulus and terminate in a muscular response. (Woodworth 1938; p. 298)

We shall illustrate in this chapter how brain waves (or ERPs) can be used in just the way that Woodworth anticipated. We begin by reviewing the approach to the study of human information processing that uses measures of the timing of overt behaviour (that is reaction time). Next we consider the 'chronopsycho-physiological' approach that emphasizes the utility of psychophysiological measures as well as measures of overt behaviour. We show how this approach has been used to determine how particular experimental manipulations affect the processing system and to make discoveries about its structure and function.

4.2 MENTAL CHRONOMETRY

The term 'mental chronometry' was coined by Posner (1978) to describe an approach to cognitive psychology that emphasizes the utility of measures of

---

[1] This quotation was also noted by Kutas *et al.* (1977).

reaction time in providing insights into the human information processing system. The approach is not restricted to an analysis of the duration of particular mental processes. Rather, measures of reaction time are used to make inferences about both the dynamics of information processing *and* the architecture of the processing system. Thus, for example, Meyer *et al.* (1988*b*) discuss the approach in terms of the discovery of processing entities, the description of the transformations they perform, the specification of their temporal properties, and the description of their patterns of communication.

To satisfy this interest, the chronometrician has been compelled to devise procedures that allow one to make inferences about mental processes from measures of reaction time (and accuracy). It is easy to speculate about the kinds of processes that must comprise the processing system, at least when we consider relatively simple tasks. For example, there must be processes that analyse the external world ('stimulus encoding') and there must be processes that deal with action on that world ('response selection and execution'). However, considerable ingenuity has been required to devise procedures and analytic techniques that allow the investigator to answer more detailed questions about the structure and function of a covert system from measures of overt behaviour. We now turn to a review of these procedures and techniques.

4.2.1 The Donders subtraction method

This method was designed to provide an estimate of the time required for a particular mental operation. In the original application of the method, the left or right foot of human subjects were electrically stimulated and subjects were told to respond with the hand that was on the same side of the body as the foot that was stimulated (Donders 1868/1969). In a simple reaction time condition, the side of stimulation was constant for a block of trials and, therefore, the side of response was known before stimulus presentation. In a choice reaction time condition, the side of stimulation varied from trial to trial, and therefore the side of response could not be known until after stimulus presentation. By subtracting the simple reaction time from the choice reaction time, Donders reasoned that 'the time required for deciding which side had been stimulated and for establishing the action of the will on the right or left side' (Donders 1868/1969, p. 418) would be revealed. In current terminology, these two processes would be described as 'stimulus discrimination' and 'response selection'.

Donders also used a go/no-go task condition, with multiple stimuli but only one possible response, to provide a situation that required stimulus discrimination but not response selection ('the action of the will'). The reaction time for this condition, and for the simple and choice reaction time conditions, could then be used to determine the times required for stimulus discrimination and response selection.

The simple elegance of the Donders subtraction method hides some strong assumptions, the validity of which is crucial to the legitimate application of the method (see, for example, Meyer *et al.* (1988*b*) and Sternberg (1969)). First, there is the basic idea that the durations of component mental processes combine additively to yield the overall reaction time. Second, there is the idea that the only difference between one condition and another is in the 'pure insertion' of a processing stage. For example, the only difference between a go/no-go task and a choice reaction time task is in the insertion of the response selection stage. All other processes that are involved in the go/no-go task are assumed to remain the same.

As noted originally by Külpe (1909) (see also Meyer *et al.* 1988*b*; van der Molen *et al.* 1991), the assumption of pure insertion is probably invalid. When task conditions change, not only is a new mental operation inserted or deleted but the existing operations may also change. Although Ashby (1982) and Gottsdanker and Shragg (1985) have provided some support for the validity of the principle of pure insertion under certain limited circumstances, chronometricians have tended to look to other procedures for help in the analysis of human information processing.

4.2.2 The Sternberg additive factors method

One such procedure is the additive factors method (AFM) of Sternberg (1969). The most critical feature of the AFM is that it does not require the assumption that conditions differ only with respect to the insertion or deletion of a mental process or operation. Rather, it is assumed that conditions can vary with respect to the duration of one or more of the processing stages.[2] Differences in the duration of processing stages are assumed to be related to the levels of experimental manipulations or 'factors'. For example, the duration of the stimulus encoding stage is assumed to be related to manipulations of stimulus quality, with shorter durations for intact versus degraded stimuli, but it should not be influenced by manipulations of, say, stimulus-response compatibility. Variations in stimulus-response compatibility should influence the duration of response-related processes like response translation and organization (see Sternberg 1969).

Sternberg not only provided a novel conception of the way in which experimental manipulations might influence human information processing, he also showed how application of the analysis of variance model to the kind of factorial experiment described above could aid in the 'discovery of processing stages'. In particular, for a factorial experiment with stimulus quality and stimulus-response compatibility factors, there should be main effects on reaction time of both stimulus quality and stimulus-response compatibility, but these effects should be additive with no interaction — the two factors affect different stages of processing. On the other hand, a factor such as number of response alternatives, which might influence response-related processes like response translation and organization, should interact with the stimulus-response compatibility factor — the interaction revealing that both factors influence the duration of the same processing stage.

This kind of factorial experiment can serve two purposes. First, it can reveal

---

[2] In this section, we follow the terminology of Sternberg (1969) and use 'stage' to refer to a process, or collection of processes, that operates on an input to produce an output *and contributes an additive component to RT*.

something about the number of processing stages and their organization. Thus, Sanders (1990) has recently claimed on the basis of numerous AFM experiments that there are seven different processing stages. The ordering of the stages and their description in terms of a functional label is, however, dependent on the basis of conceptual rather than empirical analysis. For example, the description 'stimulus encoding' seems to be appropriate for a processing stage that is affected by stimulus quality, and this stage should precede the response translation and organization stage. The lack of firm empirical bases for the functional labelling and the ordering of processing stages is a weakness of the AFM. When we review the psychophysiological approach, we shall see how psychophysiological measures can provide some empirical support. Second, the factorial experiment can also help to localize the effects of a new experimental factor in terms of an already established set of processing stages, by examining the effects of the new factor in conjunction with other factors whose effects are known.

As has been noted by several investigators, including Sternberg (1969) himself, several assumptions underlie the use of the AFM and these assumptions are not always valid. Most notable of these are the assumptions of *selective influence* and *constant output*. Just as a change of condition may involve more than an insertion of a stage, so it may also involve more than a change in the duration of a particular stage. It might affect the functioning of other stages and it might also influence the quality of the output of the stage. In addition, appropriate use of the AFM is critically dependent on the presence of a single, all-or-none, discrete instance of information transmission between stages of processing. The idea of discrete transmission is also associated with an additional assumption that each stage of processing is active in series and that no two stages are active in parallel. Deviations from these conditions of discrete transmission and serial ordering of processing can render the application of the AFM invalid.[3]

Recent mathematical investigations of additive factors logic have provided insights into what happens when the discrete transmission and seriality conditions are relaxed. McClelland (1979) and Ashby (1982) have shown that in some cases continuous transmission of constant output between temporally overlapping processes can produce the same RT effects as discrete transmission between serially organized processes. In particular, when two factors influence two distinct processes the effects on RT are additive; if they influence the same process the result is an interaction. On the one hand this demonstration suggests that the AFM is applicable in a more varied and less restricted set of experimental situations. On the other hand it makes clear that finding additive effects or interactions does not inform us about the nature of transmission between processes, nor about their temporal organization.

[3] It is not our intention to imply that proponents of the AFM have been insensitive to the problems that may accompany its use. Indeed, in the original AFM paper, Sternberg was very forthright in stating explicitly the assumptions underlying the method. Similarly, Sanders (1990) has recently provided a very clear statement of the relative importance of these assumptions and has stressed the criticality of the 'stage robustness' test. The idea behind this test is that the stage structure revealed by a particular factorial experiment should not change when the experiment is repeated with an additional factor.

Townsend (1974) evaluated the predicted effects on RT when two factors influence two distinct processes that are organized in parallel but transmit discrete output. He found that the factors would produce a negative interaction (that is, underadditivity). Schweickert and Townsend (1989) confirmed this finding and showed further that if two factors influence two distinct processes arranged in series, a positive RT interaction (that is, overadditivity) would occur when the two processes occur in parallel with a third one. On the other hand, Schweickert (1993) argues that additive effects will always occur if the set of processes performing a task is divided by a 'cutpoint' and the two factors influence processes on different sides of it. Similar arguments were made by Miller (1993). This author proposed a 'queue-series model' of RT, which provides a general mathematical framework for comparing continuous, single-discrete, and multiple-discrete transmission between information processes. Multiple-discrete transmission (and therefore temporal overlap) in this model only produces additive RT effects under certain restricted conditions, otherwise it results in underadditivity, as with the parallel processes studied by Townsend (1974) and Schweickert and Townsend (1989) (see also Stanovich and Pachella 1977).

These studies all involved an analysis of the effects on the additive factors logic of relaxing assumptions about the discreteness of the output and the temporal organization of the processes. In all cases, however, assumption of constant output was maintained. Indeed, it seems clear that the most important restrictions governing the use of the AFM involve the requirement that the output of a process be invariant. Unfortunately, it seems that there are, indeed, circumstances under which the conditions of constant output are not met, and these conditions require the development of new procedures to which we shall now turn.

4.2.3 Other methods: primes and probes

Meyer and his colleagues (for a review see Meyer *et al.* (1988*b*)) have devised two new methods to address the discrete–continuous issue. The first method, the *varied-priming method*, was designed to determine whether there could be graded *levels* of response preparation (Meyer *et al.* 1985). The critical question addressed by this method was whether response preparation occurs in a discrete or continuous fashion — that is, is it possible to be in states that are intermediate between being completely prepared and completely unprepared? The experimental situation involves the typical choice reaction time task. The major feature of the method is that a prime is presented just before the imperative choice stimulus is presented. The prime informs the subject of the forthcoming response and is presented at varying times before the imperative stimulus. If graded levels of response preparation are possible, then the reaction time to the imperative stimulus should show this graded benefit as an inverse function of the prime to imperative stimulus interval. In fact, the reaction time data are evaluated to determine whether this graded benefit represents a truly graded level of response preparation (that is, preparation is continuous) or whether it can be explained by differing mixtures of completely prepared and completely unprepared states (that is, preparation is discrete). On the basis of a variety of experiments, Meyer *et al.* (1988*b*) report that the method sometimes provides evidence for continuous and sometimes for discrete preparation.

The second method, *speed-accuracy decomposition*, builds on a phenomenon that was described many years ago by Woodworth (1899), the speed-accuracy trade-off. While Woodworth was interested in the relationship between the speed and accuracy of movements, Pachella (1974), Wicklegren (1977), and others have drawn attention to the importance of this trade-off in choice reaction time tasks. Since subjects can trade off accuracy for response speed, an apparent difference between two experimental conditions in reaction time may be attributed to a difference in the speed-accuracy trade-off. Of course, such trade-offs are an anathema to the AFM, because they imply that responses can be executed on the basis of fully processed output, partially processed output, or even no output from immediately preceding processes — that is, not on the basis of constant output. Indeed, although Schweickert (1985) has shown how the logic of the AFM can be applied to error data, proponents of the AFM generally require that subjects maintain a high, constant level of accuracy (Sanders 1990) and do not trade speed for accuracy.

The form of the speed-accuracy trade-off, with gradually increasing accuracy as a function of gradually decreasing response speed, suggests that information about the stimulus is accumulated gradually and that this information is passed on continuously to the response system. Thus, the speed-accuracy trade-off function seems to support a continuous view of information transmission. However, the gradually increasing function is misleading, since it could be generated by a completely discrete transmission. As Meyer *et al.* (1988*b*) argue, if transmission is discrete, with two states of either no information or complete information, then response accuracy would either be at the level of guessing or it would be maximal. If the time at which the transition from no information to complete information varies from trial to trial (that is, there is jitter in the time of transition), then averaging across trials to generate the speed-accuracy trade-off would necessarily result in a gradual function although the underlying transmission is discrete (see also Miller 1988).

The speed-accuracy decomposition procedure was designed to deal with this problem (see Meyer *et al.* 1988*a*). Subjects perform the regular choice reaction time task with an imperative stimulus that requires a choice response. On some trials, a second stimulus occurs (the 'signal') sometime after the imperative stimulus. Subjects are instructed to respond (on the basis of an analysis of the imperative stimulus) as soon as the signal occurs on signal trials. If they have not analysed the imperative stimulus when the signal occurs, they should base their response on a best guess of what that stimulus might be. The idea is that if partial information about the imperative stimulus is available (that is, if there is more than simple discrete information transmission), these best guesses will have a level of accuracy that is above chance. Comparison of responses for these signal trials (with the signal presented at different times after the imperative stimulus) with those for regular trials when no signal was presented, provides a way of dealing with the jitter problem that occurs with the usual speed-accuracy trade-off functions. Meyer *et al.* (1988*b*) indicate that data for at least in some tasks (e.g. yes-no lexical decision-making) provide support for the idea of partial information transmission.

Note that any evidence against a single discrete transmission constitutes evidence for parallel rather than serial processing. For example, if partial information about a stimulus is used to activate responses, then the response system is active while the stimulus evaluation system is still processing the stimulus (e.g. see Miller 1988; Ratcliff 1978).

The developments in methodology and analysis described above have made substantial contributions to the study of human information processing — specifically by allowing the investigator to explore the critical questions of discrete versus continuous transmission and parallel versus serial activation. However, it is important to note that these new methods are also based on several assumptions. For example, the speed-accuracy decomposition procedure requires one to assume that those processes involved in the performance of the reaction time task are unaffected by the presentation of the signal or the possible presentation of the signal. De Jong (1991) has recently argued that this assumption is not valid and, therefore, that the procedure cannot be used to address the continuous/discrete issue. Whether or not De Jong's argument extends to all instances in which the procedure is applied, the introduction of any extra stimulus into the reaction time task has the potential to complicate the understanding of the processes associated with that task. This is also the case with the traditional probe task characteristic of studies of resources and workload (e.g. Posner and Boies 1971). As van der Molen *et al.* (1991, p. 147) have argued:

With each addition of an independent variable to an information processing task, the nature of the task and the processes it engages may be transformed in subtle but important ways. That is, the task may change and with it information processing demands may change as well. These changes may be sufficient, although subtle, to subvert the assumptions of a theoretical model and to invalidate the method derived to test it. It follows from this that the most powerful procedures for evaluating chronometric processes will not involve intrusions into the information processing sequence to infer how that sequence is structured.

One hallmark of the psychophysiological approach is that it does not involve these kinds of intrusions and, therefore, it at least has the potential to address the questions of mental chronometry without the problems introduced by these intrusions.

4.3 CHRONOPSYCHOPHYSIOLOGY

As we have seen, the chronometrician's approach to the analysis of the covert information processing system has been based on one of several methods that permit one to infer something about the system from measures of overt behaviour.

We have also seen that the validity of these methods depends critically on various assumptions, and that if these assumptions are violated the inferences are invalid. Furthermore, there is good reason to believe that the assumptions are violated on at least some occasions. Thus, there is a need for alternative or at least complementary inferential procedures.

Chronopsychophysiology is a term coined by van der Molen *et al.* (1991) to describe an inferential strategy that uses psychophysiological measures to address the kinds of questions faced by the chronometrician. As with other examples discussed in this book, psychophysiological measures are seen as augmenting rather than replacing the traditional measures of response speed and accuracy. However, it is important to note that the assumptions that underlie chronopsychophysiology are not equivalent to those that underlie the use of the traditional measures. For example, discrete transmission of constant output between stages, a feature of the additive factors approach, is not assumed by the psychophysiological approach. The presence of non-overlapping sets of assumptions means that the two approaches should be seen as providing somewhat different paths to obtaining answers to the basic questions of mental chronometry.

4.3.1 Selective influence versus selective sensitivity

One way to characterize the difference between chronometric and psychophysiological approaches is to compare the emphasis given to the independent and dependent variables (see Gehring *et al.* (1992) for a detailed review of this distinction). In this regard, it is possible to discern two basic approaches, *selective influence* and *selective sensitivity*, that differ in terms of the emphasis given to the independent and dependent variables. In the case of selective influence, the investigator stresses the fact that different elements of the processing system are influenced by the manipulation of different independent variables. In the case of selective sensitivity, the claim is that different dependent variables are sensitive to the activities of different elements of the system.

Consider the Stroop task, where subjects must respond on the basis of one stimulus attribute while ignoring another, conflicting, attribute. For example, subjects must say the word 'red' to the word 'blue', written in red ink (that is, the word name and the word colour are said to be 'incompatible'). In this situation, reaction time is longer than when the word name and the word colour are the same (that is, compatible). The question is why? What is the locus of this compatibility effect? Where is processing slowed such that reaction time is prolonged?

According to the 'selective influence' approach, one would choose a number of manipulations (factors A and B) that are 'known' to influence particular elements of the processing system and then observe the pattern of main effects and inter-actions of these factors with the compatibility factor. If a significant interaction is obtained with one factor (say, A) one would infer that compatibility exerts its effect on the same part of the processing system as factor A. Of course, no positive conclusions about the locus of the effect can be made in the absence of significant interactions, and the number of possible loci is limited by the number of factors that are manipulated. Furthermore, which processing loci will be identified will depend on which variables are manipulated.

According to the 'selective sensitivity' approach one measures a dependent variable that is sensitive to the activity of that part of the system that is believed to be affected by compatibility *but insensitive to the activities of other parts of the system*. Then one determines whether the dependent variable is affected by the compatibility manipulation. For example, if the latency of a particular ERP component is longer for incompatible than for compatible stimuli, and this latency difference is equal to the difference in reaction time between the conditions, then one would infer that the compatibility effect has its locus no later than the process reflected by that ERP component. Note that problems of interpretation arise if the ERP latency effect and the reaction time effect are not the same (see Meyer *et al.* (1988*b*, pp. 53–6) for an extended discussion of this point). We shall return to this issue later.

Both selective influence and selective sensitivity approaches depend on demonstrations of validity — that is, there must be some reason to believe that a particular experimental manipulation selectively affects a particular part of the processing system, and there must be evidence that supports the selective mapping of a particular aspect of the ERP and the activity of a particular part of the system. Much effort has gone into the latter kind of mapping exercise (e.g. see Coles 1989; Donchin 1979; Donchin and Coles 1988*a,b*), and we shall review some of these efforts below for the P300 and lateralized readiness potential components.

Given this background, the major contributions of work using ERPs can be seen in two related domains. First, there has been an interest in specifying the locus of effects of particular experimental variables. For example, in the context of the Stroop effect one might ask whether the locus of the conflict that gives rise to a delay in reaction time is at the level of response selection and execution or at the level of stimulus analysis. Second, there has been an interest in specifying how the system works — that is, in describing how modules in the system communicate with each other, or in defining how the system must be configured to produce a particular behavioural consequence. As we shall see, this interest has taken us into areas concerned with executive control.

4.3.2 ERP components and mental chronometry

A variety of ERP components have been studied in the context of mental chronometry. In this chapter we shall focus on two of these components, the P300 and the lateralized readiness potential (LRP), although we shall refer to other components from time-to-time. Examples of these other components are the N_A and the complex of components referred to by the umbrella 'N2' label. These components have been linked to the timing of early processes related to sensory discrimination a review of which is beyond the scope of this chapter. The interested reader is referred to the work of Näätänen, Renault, and Ritter for a review of these components (e.g. Näätänen 1992; Renault *et al.* 1982; Ritter *et al.* 1979).

4.3.2.1 P300

The P300 is a positive component characterized by a parietally maximal scalp distribution, and a latency between 300 and 800 ms. The P300 is the most frequently measured ERP component, and, in part, this popularity can be traced to the ease with which it is measured. The component is relatively large (as much as 40 μV) and can be detected in the background EEG on individual trials. The most common way to elicit a P300 is in the 'oddball' paradigm, in which two stimuli, or classes of stimuli, occur in a Bernouilli sequence. The probability of one stimulus is generally less than that for the other and the subject's task is typically to count the rarer of the two stimuli. A larger P300 is elicited in response to the rare, counted, stimulus. One notable feature of the P300 is that it can be elicited by a variety of stimuli or events. The only requirement is that the events have distinct onsets, and that they are classifiable into two or more categories.

There have been many overviews of research on the P300 (see, for example, Donchin 1981; Donchin and Coles 1988*a*, *b*; Johnson 1988; Pritchard 1981), so we will only highlight the main findings here. Much of what follows is based on the review by Coles *et al.* (1990).

The P300 was formally discovered in 1965 by Sutton and his colleagues (Sutton *et al.* 1965) and this was followed by a series of studies that attempted to identify those conditions that influenced the amplitude and latency of the component. For *amplitude*, critical variables were the subjective probability of the eliciting event (e.g. Duncan-Johnson and Donchin 1977; Squires *et al.* 1976), and the relevance or utility of the event in the context of the goals of the task as appraised by the subject (e.g. Duncan-Johnson and Donchin 1977; Gratton *et al.* 1990; Johnson and Donchin 1978).

Research on P300 *latency* has focused on trying to identify those processes that must have elapsed prior to the elicitation of P300. In this respect, the sensitivity of the P300 amplitude to event probability implies that, at the time the P300 is elicited, those processes required to categorize the eliciting event must have transpired (e.g. Donchin 1979). Of course, further processing may have occurred, but the latency of the P300 places an upper limit on categorization or stimulus evaluation time. This idea is supported by the observation that as categorization becomes more difficult, P300 latency increases (e.g. Kutas *et al.* 1977).

In most studies involving P300 latency, it is traditional to measure the latency of the peak — that is, one finds the maximum amplitude of the waveform in a certain time-window and P300 latency is defined as the latency of that maximum. This tradition probably derives from the fact that the peak is the easiest feature of the component to identify. However, it should be noted that it is somewhat arbitrary to choose the peak rather than some other feature of the component (see Chapter 1 and Meyer *et al.* 1988*b*). Indeed, given the idea that the probability-sensitive process manifested by the P300 begins after the stimulus has been evaluated, it would seem to make more sense to focus on the latency of the onset of the P300 rather than the latency of its peak. Nevertheless, because of technical problems (see Chapter 1) few attempts have been made to measure the onset latency of the P300. Rather, investigators have continued to measure peak latency under the (usually implicit) assumption that the peak latency provides a good estimate of the relative time at which the P300 process occurs. An exception to this is the study by Scheffers and colleagues (Scheffers *et al.* 1991), who examined the relationship between estimates of peak and onset latencies of P300 derived in a choice reaction time task in which stimulus quality was manipulated. They found that, in fact, variation in peak latency did correspond closely to variation in onset latency. This finding, together with the relationships between the peak latency measure and other measures described in the next paragraph, have been taken as *de facto* evidence in favour of the assumption that the peak latency provides a good estimate of the timing of the P300 process.

Since the accuracy of responses must depend on the availability of sufficient information about the stimulus, one would expect to find a relationship between response accuracy and the timing of the response relative to the P300. Indeed, Coles *et al.* (1985) found such a relationship. Measures of reaction time, accuracy, and P300 latency were derived for every trial of a choice reaction time task. For trials with a given reaction time, accuracy was higher when P300 latency was short than when it was long. This finding is explained in terms of the proposal that when P300 latency is short, the evaluation process has proceeded quickly. Thus, when a motor response of a given latency is executed, more of the evaluation process has occurred than when P300 latency is long, and there is therefore more information available to guide the motor response. Hence, there is a dependency of response accuracy on P300 latency. In a related vein, Kutas *et al.* (1977) found that the correlation between P300 latency and reaction time is higher when subjects are given accuracy rather than speed instructions. Both these findings suggest an association between the accuracy and latency of reaction time responses and the latency of the P300.

While the demonstrations of the sensitivity of P300 latency to manipulations of stimulus evaluation are critical, the insensitivity of P300 to manipulations of other variables is equally important. Among these other variables are those that should affect response-related processes such as stimulus-response incompatibility (e.g. Sanders 1990). While manipulations of stimulus-response incompatibility have a large effect on reaction time, they have little if any effect on P300 latency (McCarthy and Donchin 1981; Magliero *et al.* 1984; Ragot 1984). Figure 4.1 shows data from McCarthy and Donchin (1981) who examined the effects of both stimulus discriminability and stimulus-response compatibility on the latency of P300. As the figure shows, reaction time was influenced by both manipulations, but P300 latency was only significantly influenced by stimulus discriminability.

Results from two other studies strongly support the claim that P300 latency is insensitive to response selection requirements. Smid *et al.* (1992) found that an increase in response selection difficulty failed to influence P300 latency, while it

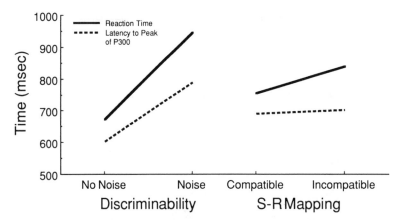

Fig. 4.1 The effects of stimulus discriminability and stimulus–response compatibility on measures of reaction time and P300 latency. The effect of discriminability is evident on both measures but the effect of compatibility is only significant for the reaction time measure. (From McCarthy and Donchin (1981). *Science*, 211, 77–80. Copyright © 1981 by the AAAS, reprinted with permission.)

resulted in an increase of about 70 ms in reaction time. On the other hand, when the difficulty of stimulus identification was increased, P300 latency increased by about 70 ms, and the latencies of the response-related measures increased by the same amount. Similar results were obtained by De Jong *et al.* (1988).

Taken together, these data suggest that the P300 is emitted after the completion of those processes that are needed for the evaluation of the stimulus, but that the timing of the P300 is independent of the processes associated with response selection and execution. The dependence of the *amplitude* of the P300 on event probability in the oddball task is important in establishing the fact that the processes that precede the P300 must include stimulus evaluation. However, from the perspective of mental chronometry, it is the latency of the P300 that is more interesting. P300 latency can be used to provide a measure of the relative timing of the evaluation process — 'relative' because of course we do not know about the duration of any additional processing that might occur after the completion of evaluation but before the emission of the P300.

4.3.2.2 *The lateralized readiness potential (LRP)*

As we noted earlier (in Chapter 1), one can record movement-related potentials from the scalp, especially over motor areas of the cortex. These potentials occur before the movement itself and they show an asymmetrical distribution across the scalp. They are generally larger over scalp sites that are contralateral to the side of the body that is to be moved. These attributes suggest that the potentials may be useful in monitoring covert aspects of motor preparation (Kutas and Donchin 1980).

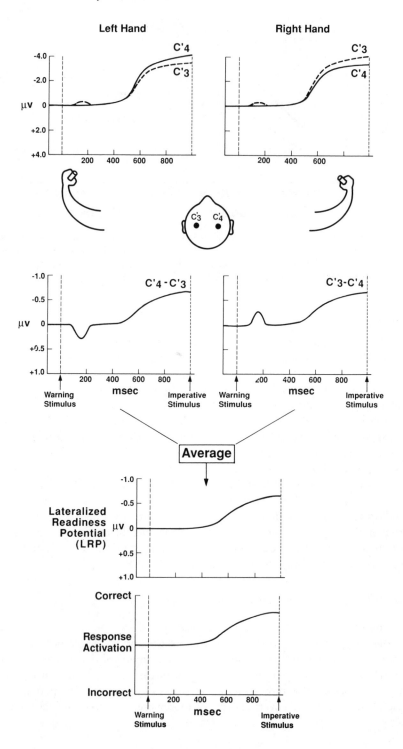

Fig. 4.2 The derivation of the lateralized readiness potential. The top panel shows idealized scalp-recorded brain potentials from left (C′₃) and right (C′₄) scalp sites in a warned reaction time task when subjects know in advance of the imperative stimulus the hand to be used to execute a correct response. Potentials associated with left-hand movements are shown on the left; those associated with right-hand movements are shown on the right. As subjects prepare to execute a movement, a negativity develops that is maximum at scalp sites contralateral to the responding hand. The asymmetry in these potentials is illustrated by subtracting the potential recorded at the scalp site ipsilateral to the movement from that recorded contralateral to the movement (second panel). Then, the difference potentials for left- and right-hand movements are averaged to yield the lateralized readiness potential (third panel). Note that this procedure eliminates the negative deflection following the warning stimulus that occurs consistently at C′₃ irrespective of the side of movement. We propose that the lateralized readiness potential reflects response activation (lower panel). When these procedures are performed with reference to the correct response hand on each of a group of trials, deviations of the trace in the upward (negative) direction reflect preferential activation of the correct response, whereas downward deflections indicate preferential activation of the incorrect response. The formula for deriving the lateralized readiness potential (LRP) is as follows:

$$\text{LRP} = [\text{Mean}(C4'\text{-}C3')_{\text{left-hand movement}} + \text{Mean }(C3'\text{-}C4')_{\text{right-hand movement}}]/2$$

(From Coles 1989). Copyright © 1989 Society for Psychophysiological Research. Reprinted with permission of Cambridge University Press.)

Of course, not all asymmetrical brain activity is related to motor function. The two hemispheres are differentially engaged in a variety of functions. Consequently, it is necessary to isolate the asymmetrical brain activity that can be attributed solely to movement. This can be accomplished in two stages (see Fig. 4.2). First, we compute the asymmetrical activity separately for left- and right-side movements by subtracting the activity over the hemisphere ipsilateral to the movement from that over the hemisphere contralateral to the movement. Second, we average the asymmetry across the two kinds of movements (see Coles (1989) and Fig. 4.2, for a complete description of this procedure). This procedure eliminates all those asymmetries that remain constant when the side of movement changes — that is, it removes all non-motoric asymmetries. The resulting measure, the *lateralized readiness potential*, is believed to reflect the relative activation of left and right motor responses.

As we have reviewed elsewhere (Coles 1989), there is considerable evidence to suggest that lateralized readiness potentials are generated in the motor cortex. This evidence includes intracranial recordings in animals (e.g. Miller *et al.* 1992; Requin *et al.* 1988) as well as magnetoencephalographic recordings (Okada *et al.* 1982). In addition, the relationship between the lateralized readiness potentials and various experimental manipulations supports the claim that the measure is related to the selection and preparation of motor responses. For example, the provision of a warning stimulus and the validity of a warning cue, both of which should affect motor preparation, affect the LRP during the foreperiods of reaction time tasks (Gehring *et al.* 1992; Gratton *et al.* 1990). Additionally, measures of the subject's behaviour are related to the LRP in just the manner one would expect of a measure of preparation. Reaction times are faster when the subject shows lateralized activity in the foreperiod (in the appropriate direction), and the reaction time response itself is released when the LRP achieves a particular amplitude or threshold level (Gratton *et al.* 1988).

All of these data, as well as the logic of the procedure used to derive the LRP, support the association between the LRP and the relative activation of selected motor responses. From the perspective of mental chronometry, the dependence of the LRP on response selection is very important because this implies that the LRP can indicate whether and when a motor response is selected.

4.4 THE LOCUS OF EXPERIMENTAL EFFECTS

4.4.1 Stroop and related conflict tasks

As is evident from MacLeod's (1991) recent review, the Stroop paradigm has generated considerable interest ever since its discovery in 1935 (Stroop 1935). When subjects must name the colour of the ink in which a word is written, their reaction times are influenced by the congruence between the colour of the word and the identity of the word. In particular, reaction times are longer when word colour and word identity are different.

From the ERP perspective, the paradigm provides a fertile testing ground because of the controversy concerning the locus of interference in this paradigm. Indeed, there are now two classes of ERP data that could impinge on this issue. It was shown several years ago that incongruence between the colour of the word and the name of the word was *not* associated with a delay in the P300, even though reaction time was delayed (Duncan-Johnson and Kopell 1981). If indeed P300 latency is a marker of stimulus evaluation time, then this result would suggest that the interference occurs somewhere downstream from the system responsible for stimulus evaluation. Of course, a good candidate is the system responsible for response selection and execution, whose activities are manifested in the LRP. However, as of the present time, no one has successfully used the LRP to investigate the locus of Stroop interference.

In a number of other paradigms involving Stroop-like conflict, where incongruence is associated with a delayed overt response, the LRP has been used to localize the interference effect. In each case, the LRP suggested that the incorrect response was activated before the correct response on some kinds of incongruent trials. For example, when subjects must judge whether a digit is odd or even or whether it is low or high, then the digit's magnitude can interfere with odd–even judgements (Otten *et al.* submitted). The response that is mapped to the digit's magnitude is activated and this activation can then interfere with the activation of the correct response that should follow an analysis of whether the digit is odd or even. Similarly, when the phonology of a word conflicts with its orthography, and the subject must make an orthographic judgement, the locus of this effect seems to be in the response system (see Coles *et al.* 1988). It is important to note that in each case the pattern of conflict is not symmetrical. For example, there is less evidence of interference at the level of the overt response when subjects must judge digit magnitude in the presence of possibly conflicting parity information, or when phonological judgments are made in the presence of possibly conflicting orthography.

All these instances of Stroop-like conflict suggest that some kinds of stimulus information have more privileged, or at least faster, access to the response system than other kinds of stimulus information. Thus, the lateralized readiness potential measure appears to be sensitive to the temporal aspects of the evaluation process and to suggest that the results of a partial analysis of the stimulus can affect the response system. As we shall see (Section 4.5.1), such an effect is consistent with continuous models of information processing but inconsistent with simple discrete models.

4.4.2 Eriksen noise/compatibility paradigm

Attention is not perfect. Even though subjects know precisely about the spatial location of a forthcoming target stimulus in a visual display, they appear to be unable to resist processing non-target stimuli that occur in other locations in the display, at least when the non-target stimuli are close to the target. This instance of spatial confusion appears to have effects that are similar to those described above in connection with the Stroop task: however, in the Eriksen case, the concern is with stimuli in multiple spatial locations rather than with an individual stimulus with multiple attributes but in a single location.

The classic paradigm used to investigate this phenomenon is the Eriksen flankers task (Eriksen and Eriksen 1974; Eriksen and Hoffman 1973). Subjects perform a choice reaction time task in which the presentation of one letter (H) is associated with one hand (left), while another letter (S) is associated with the other hand (right). On any trial an array of letters is presented. The array contains a target letter, located in the centre of the array, and distractor or non-target letters that are presented to the left and right of the target. The subject is required to respond to the centre target letter of the display. Sometimes the non-target, distractor letters that surround the target are repetitions of the same letter (e.g. HHHHH) in which case the array is said to be compatible. Sometimes the other distractors are repetitions of the other letter (e.g. SSHSS), in which case the array is said to be incompatible. A consistent finding has been that responses to 'incompatible' arrays are longer than those to 'compatible' arrays.

As in the case of the Stroop task, the concern is with the locus of the interference effect. Is it the case that the H is somehow less discernible when it is surrounded by distractor Ss — or is it the case that the distractors lead to an activation of the incorrect right-hand response? That is, is the locus in the evaluation 'stage' or a response 'stage'?

There have now been several experiments that converge in suggesting both an evaluation and a response locus for this Eriksen effect. First, we have shown that incompatible arrays are associated with longer P300 latencies than compatible arrays (Coles *et al.* 1985). The delay in P300 is about half that found in reaction time. Second, we found that the remaining delay could be attributed to response conflict. The incompatible noise letters lead to an activation of the incorrect response, evident at both central (LRP: Gratton *et al.* 1988; see Fig. 4.3) and more peripheral levels (electromyogram: Coles *et al.* 1985; Eriksen *et al.* 1985). In turn, activation of the incorrect response appears to 'compete' with activation of the correct response and, therefore, to delay the execution of the correct response (Coles *et al.* 1985).

These findings have been replicated and extended by Smid *et al.* (1990). These authors confirmed that incompatibility has an effect on both P300 latency and

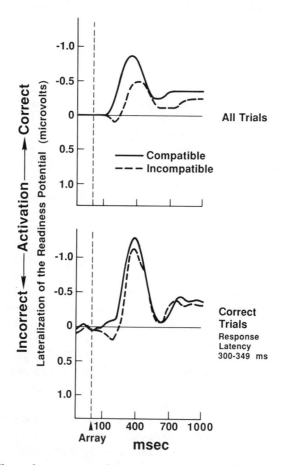

Fig. 4.3 The effects of noise compatibility on the LRP in the Eriksen task. In the upper panel we see data for all trials regardless of response speed or response accuracy. In the lower panel we see data for trials for which there was no evidence of an incorrect response (at the level of the electromyogram) and for which response latency was between 300 and 349 ms. Note the 'dip' in the lateralized potential after array onset on incompatible trials. This 'dip' reflects activation of the incorrect response, even though there were no overt signs of movement. (Fig. 4 from Gratton *et al.* (1988). Copyright © 1988 American Psychological Association, reprinted by permission.)

measures of response activation. However, Smid *et al.* (1991) obtained a different pattern of results in a situation where the non-target stimuli had no experimentally defined response, but could share features with the target stimulus. When features of the distractors were similar to the target, the stimulus was described as compatible, and when distractor features were similar to the other target stimulus (and therefore associated with the incorrect response), the stimulus was described as incompatible. As above, there was a difference in reaction time between compatible and incompatible trials. However, there was no effect on P300 latency, but only on response-related measures (the LRP). Thus, the locus of interference in this variant of the Eriksen task appears to be more like that observed in the Stroop task.

4.4.3 Spatial stimulus-response compatibility

In this section, we consider another kind of conflict situation. In this case, the conflict occurs when the spatial location of a stimulus does not correspond to the side of the body (usually the hand) that must be used to respond. Such a situation arises, for example, when subjects must respond to a stimulus presented on the left side of space with the right hand. If the side on which the stimulus is presented does not correspond to the side of the response, reaction times are longer and error rates are higher than when there is correspondence. The spatial location of the stimulus may be *relevant* to the subject's task — as when the instructions specify a response with a particular hand as a function of the spatial location of the stimulus. Alternatively, the spatial location may be *irrelevant* to the task — as when subjects must respond as a function, say, of the colour of the stimulus. In the latter case, the prolongation in reaction time for non-correspondence is referred to as the 'Simon effect' (Simon and Rudell 1967).

Several studies have examined the psychophysiological effects of both relevant and irrelevant spatial stimulus-response compatibility. In all cases, the measure of interest has been the LRP, and the analysis has focused on whether the response on the side of the body that corresponds to the spatial location of the stimulus is 'automatically' activated following stimulus presentation. This idea of automatic activation is explicit in the work of Kornblum and his colleagues (Kornblum *et al.* 1990), among others.

Osman and his colleagues (Osman *et al.* 1992) used a paradigm in which the subject had to choose between left- and right-hand responses as a function of the location of a stimulus on a screen — that is, the spatial location was a relevant stimulus attribute. Subjects had to execute a response if the stimulus was a letter, but to withhold the response if the stimulus was a digit. The stimulus could appear to the left or right of fixation. Under compatible conditions, a letter on the left designated a response with the left hand, and a stimulus on the right required a response with the right hand. In incompatible conditions, the mapping was reversed. Analyses of the LRP data for the time-period immediately following the stimulus revealed a 'dip' suggesting that the incorrect response was initially activated when the spatial location of the stimulus was opposite to the side of the correct response (see Coles *et al.* (1992) for a description of this analysis).

Similar results have been obtained by a variety of other researchers. For example, Smulders (1993, Ch. 3, Experiment 1) found a dip in the LRP when subjects were instructed to respond with the hand contralateral to the side of stimulus presentation. However, in many of these conditions (including the Osman experiment), the interpretation of the LRP is compromised by a serious confound. As Smulders (1993, Ch. 3, Experiment 2) points out (see also De Jong *et al.* 1994), this confound involves the fact that the spatial location of the stimulus covaries with the side of the response (of course this is the essence of the spatial compatibility effect). However, there is a class of event-related brain potentials whose asymmetries are determined by the spatial location of the stimulus, when the stimulus is presented laterally (e.g. Rugg *et al.* 1987). The covariation between stimulus and response locations means that asymmetries due to stimulus location will not be removed when the subtraction procedure is used to compute the LRP. As a result, the dip in the LRP that can be seen in the data of Osman *et al.* might be attributable to brain activity associated with the perception of a lateralized stimulus rather than activity associated with the response.

To deal with this problem, De Jong *et al.* (1994) recently looked at the LRP in a Simon task using a compatibility manipulation that involved conflict in the vertical rather than horizontal dimension. Thus, the stimuli were presented either above or below fixation and the responding hands were similarly arranged with one hand above the other. Furthermore, the relative position of the hands was changed from trial block to trial block. This vertical arrangement of both stimuli and responses resulted in a preservation of the usual compatibility effects while, at the same time, permitting the computation of the LRP to proceed without the problem of the differential engagement of the two hemispheres associated with lateral presentation (De Jong *et al.* 1994). In fact, the LRP revealed a clear early activation of the response hand that shared the spatial position of the stimulus (above or below), supporting the idea that at least some of the spatial compatibility effect can be attributed to the early activation of the spatially compatible response.

The De Jong *et al.* (1994) study went further than the usual Simon effect experiment and examined the paradoxical 'reverse Simon effect'. This effect is evident when the (irrelevant) spatial position of the stimulus does not correspond to the position of the response *and* some other (relevant) attribute of the stimulus (colour) is incompatible with the response (colour of the response key). When the relevant attributes of stimulus and response are incompatible, reaction times are paradoxically faster under conditions of spatial non-correspondence (Hedge and Marsh 1975). To explain this effect, De Jong *et al.* (1994) provide a dual process account in which there is both an automatic activation of the spatially corresponding response *and* a slower, conditionally automatic activation. This latter process results from a generalization of any transformation that must be performed on relevant task attributes so that the transformation is also performed on irrelevant task attributes. For example, when subjects are required to respond by pressing a response button that has the opposite colour to the stimulus (e.g. a red stimulus requires the green response button to be pressed), it is assumed that a reverse transformation must be performed. It is proposed that this transformation process is generalized so that the spatial location of the stimulus (although irrelevant to the subject's task) is also transformed (left becomes right and vice versa). When the subject must perform the colour transformation and the spatial location of the stimulus does *not* correspond to the side of the correct response, responses are actually faster than when the spatial location does correspond to the side of the correct response. In the former case, the generalization of the transformation leads to the activation of the correct response, while in the latter case the incorrect response becomes activated. Consistent with this interpretation, De Jong *et al.* (1994) found that, in the latter condition, the LRP reflected initial activation of the correct response, followed by activation of the incorrect response (because of the application of the transformation), and finally activation of the correct response (see Fig. 4.4). In this case, the LRPs provided critical confirmatory evidence for both aspects of this dual-process account.

As we have seen, accounts of the effects of the compatibility between the spatial position of the stimulus and the response have implicated response activation as a critical variable in leading to the costs and benefits of (in)compatibility. Psycho-

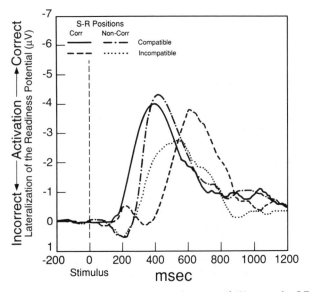

Fig. 4.4 The effects of spatial correspondence and compatibility on the LRP in the task used by De Jong *et al.* (1994). Note the early 'dip' in the direction of incorrect response activation for the non-correspondence conditions suggesting an early automatic activation of the incorrect response. Note also the triphasic shape of the LRP for the incompatible correspondence condition. This suggests an initial automatic activation of the correct response (because of spatial correspondence), followed by activation of the incorrect response (because of the generalization of the colour transformation to the irrelevant spatial dimension), followed finally by correct response activation. (Fig. 9 from De Jong *et al.* (1994). Copyright © 1994 American Psychological Association, reprinted by permission.)

physiological evidence (especially derived from measures of the LRP) has been critical in providing support for these kinds of accounts[4].

4.4.4 The Sternberg task

Over the past 25 years, the Sternberg memory task has been widely used to explore human memory processes. This popularity is due both to the elegance of the task itself as well as to the fact that the task has been analysed by one of the most popular chronometric methods, Sternberg's additive factors method (see Section 4.2.2).

In this task, as originally described by Sternberg (1966), each trial started with the presentation of one or more digits (0 through 9) which had to be memorized (memory set). The set-size varied from one to six items which were presented sequentially. After the last memory set item, a warning stimulus was given which was followed by the test digit (probe). The subject's task was to give one of two responses when the probe matched one of the digits in the memory set (positive response) and to give the other response when it did not match (negative response). Probes associated with a positive response are sometimes called targets, while those associated with a negative response are called non-targets.

The memory search paradigm produces a characteristic pattern of performance results. Reaction times increase linearly with increasing set-size, and the slopes of the linear regression functions relating reaction time to set-size are similar for targets and non-targets (about 38 ms). Reaction times for non-targets are longer than for targets and this is reflected in a higher intercept of the regression line. Sternberg (1969, 1975) proposed at least four stages to account for performance in this task: stimulus encoding, memory search, binary decision, and response selection and organization. The stimulus encoding stage, whose duration is affected by such factors as stimulus quality (intact, degraded), prepares an internal representation from the stimulus input. The output code of this first stage is transmitted to the memory comparison stage where the code is used in a scanning process with the items stored in memory. The duration of this comparison stage is influenced by set-size. Given the linear increase in mean reaction time with increasing set-size, Sternberg (1975) suggested that all memory set items are retrieved from memory and compared with the probe one at a time (serial search).

---

[4] Alternative accounts of the effects of *irrelevant* spatial incompatibility have been proposed by Stoffels *et al.* (1989) and by Hasbroucq and Guiard (1991). Relying on reaction time measures, these authors have proposed that the locus of conflict is perceptual rather than motoric. This proposal can be evaluated by studies of the effects of compatibility on P300 latency, a measure that is claimed to be related to stimulus evaluation time and to be immune to effects of response conflict (see above). Early work by Ragot and Renault (1981) found that P300 latency was influenced by incongruity between the *irrelevant* spatial position of a light and the side of the response indicated by the light. More recent work by Smulders (1993, Ch. 3, Experiment 1) found no effects on P300 latency of incongruity between the relevant spatial position of a visual stimulus and the response side. Thus, although recent behavioural accounts of the Simon effect have rejected a perceptual locus (e.g. De Jong *et al.* 1994), psychophysiological data suggest that this possibility is still worthy of investigation. As we saw in the case of the Eriksen task, it may be that the effect has both a perceptual and a response locus.

Since reaction times for targets and non-targets increase at the same rate with increasing set-size, the search was assumed to be exhaustive. The binary decision stage, which is affected by response type (positive, negative), receives the outcome of the search process and determines whether a positive or negative response is made. When the response decision is made, the response selection and organization stage prepares and executes the motor response.

The nature of the memory search process has been the subject of extensive debate, and several alternative models have been proposed to account for the basic phenomena (Townsend and Ashby 1983). Among these is the memory retrieval model of Ratcliff (1978), that can account for both the basic average reaction time data and for data relating to reaction time distributions and accuracy. According to this model, the probe is compared simultaneously with each item stored in memory (parallel search). The comparison process resembles a continuous random walk driven by the relatedness, or amount of similarity, between the probe and the memory set items, and is terminated as soon as a match is found (self-terminating).

As with other paradigms reviewed in this section, the main purpose of using ERPs is to try to understand the nature of processing in the Sternberg paradigm. In most cases, the measure of interest has been the latency of the P300, and the principal issue has been to localize the set-size effect by examining the relationship between the timing of the evaluation process (the latency of the P300) and the timing of the overt response (the reaction time).

All ERP studies using a single probe replicated the pattern of reaction time and accuracy data reported by Sternberg (1969, 1975). Reaction times increase directly with increasing set-size for positive and negative responses while error rates are usually low (less than 5 per cent). Like reaction time, P300 latency increases directly with increasing set-size and this effect was similar for target and non-target stimuli. The effects of set-size on average P300 latency and reaction time are in the same direction, but the magnitude of the effects are consistently smaller for P300 latency than for reaction time. In particular, as Fig. 4.5 shows, the slopes of the regression lines are about half as steep for P300 latency as for reaction time (Ford *et al.* 1979; Gomer *et al.* 1976; Pratt *et al.* 1989).

Adding visual search to the Sternberg task by presenting the probe with distractors (increased display load) also increases P300 latency (Brookhuis *et al.* 1983). However, P300 latency is not affected when the probes do not have the designated relevant attribute (Wijers *et al.* 1989*a*) or are presented in to-be-ignored locations (Okita *et al.* 1985). On the other hand, as with single-item displays, P300 latency for relevant probes is directly related to the size of the memory set, with the slope of regression of P300 latency on set-size being about half that for reaction time.

Of course, interpretation of this partial dissociation between P300 and reaction time depends on the model of the processes involved in the task and on the theory of P300. As we discussed earlier, it has been proposed that P300 is not emitted until the stimulus has been fully categorized. In the context of the memory search paradigm, 'evaluation' has been held to include all processes up to the end of the

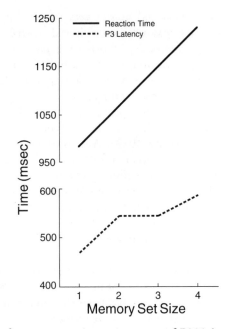

Fig. 4.5 The effects of memory set-size on measures of P300 latency and reaction time in the Sternberg task. Note that the slope of the P300 latency function is less than that for reaction time. (From Ford *et al.* (1979). Copyright © 1979 Elsevier Science Ireland, Ltd., reprinted by permission.)

memory comparison process (e.g. Ford *et al.* 1979). Thus if (as Sternberg proposed) the effect of set-size is to increase only the duration of the memory comparison process, while subsequent decision and response-related processes are left unaffected, one would have expected P300 latency and reaction time to be perfectly associated. Thus the fact that the reaction time/set-size function has a slope that is about twice that for P300 latency points to a need to reconsider Sternberg's account of the effect. First, set-size could affect the binary decision, response selection, or response execution stage, stages that follow the memory comparison process (Ford *et al.* 1979). Second, and relatedly, Ford *et al.* (1979) suggested that subjects may recheck the outcome of the memory comparison stage before a response decision is made, thus introducing an additional stage to Sternberg's original model. This proposal is consistent with the idea that the decrease in P300 *amplitude* with increasing set-size is directly related to the subject's equivocation about having identified the stimulus correctly. Reduced P300 amplitudes, together with increases in P300 latencies, reaction times and error rates, are found whenever stimulus discriminability, and thus the subject's equivocation, is increased (Johnson and Donchin 1978, 1985; Parasuraman and Beatty 1980; Ruchkin and Sutton 1978). Third, the quality of the information transmitted from the memory search stage to the decision stage might be reduced as set-size increases. In this case, the duration of the decision stage may increase proportionally. Fourth, responses could be activated in parallel with ongoing stimulus evaluation (McClelland 1979). Increasing set-size could increase the probability that both responses are activated because there would be an increase in the probability that the probe would share features with both target and non-target sets. This would lead to more competition between the responses, and thus a greater delay in execution of the correct response, as set-size increases.

Of these alternatives, only the first and last have received empirical examination. Wijers *et al.* (1989*b*) using a go/no-go variation of the Sternberg paradigm showed that the dynamics of response execution (that is, the interval between the onset of the electromyogram and reaction time for go stimuli) was not affected by set-size. These findings argue against the idea of response competition, although limited to a go/no-go situation, and also provide converging evidence for the idea that response execution is unaffected by set-size.

While the first two accounts are consistent with the original processing model of Sternberg, although of course not with his account of the set-size effect, the last two accounts are antithetical to the ideas underlying serial, discrete-stage models. This is because, for these models, the only property of a stage that can vary is duration (and not the quality of the output), and the only way for stages to be organized is serially.

Of course, the need for a reinterpretation of the locus of the set-size effect is unnecessary if, in fact, the peak of the P300 is not so closely time-locked to termination of the memory search process. Several other investigators have taken this view (e.g. Meyer *et al.* 1988*b*). In this regard, it is important to note that it is not unusual to observe a partial dissociation between P300 latency and reaction time. Experimental variables that affect perceptual processing, such as stimulus quality or stimulus discriminability (see Fig. 4.1), also influence reaction time to a greater degree than P300 latency. To explain this general class of dissociations, Meyer *et al.* (1988*b*) argued that there is no a priori reason to assume that the criterion for the generation of the P300 is set at the end of the stimulus evaluation stage when activation is maximal. The criterion for generation of the P300 could be lower than the criterion for the transmission of information from evaluative to response stages. In this situation, if the evaluation process proceeds at different rates for experimental conditions, then the effects on reaction time would exceed the effects on P300 latency, because it would take relatively more time to cross the upper criterion for information transmission than the lower criterion for elicitation of P300. On this basis, Meyer *et al.* (1988*b*) argued that the dissociation between P300 latency and reaction time as a function of set-size does not have to imply that set-size affects response-related stages after memory search has been completed. Also, it may be unnecessary to assume an additional stage that rechecks the outcome of the memory comparison stage when the subject's equivocation increases.

The dissociation between P300 latency and reaction times is also quite consistent with the parallel search model proposed by Ratcliff (1978). This model assumes that memory comparison is a diffusion process driven by the relatedness of the probe and the memory set items. The latency of the reaction time response is directly related to the time at which the diffusion process crosses a boundary. If the boundary for the P300 process is lower than that for reaction time, then decreases in the drift rate of the diffusion process will be associated with smaller changes in P300 latency than in reaction time. If increases in set-size decrease relatedness and reduce the activation rate of the comparison process, the resulting increases in P300 latency would be less than those in reaction time.

4.4.5 Summary

In this section we have illustrated how ERPs might be used to establish the locus of experimental effects. Because of the logic of its derivation, the LRP measure has enabled the most definitive attributions of experimental effects to loci within the processing system. Thus, in a variety of different kinds of conflict situations, it is apparent that at least part of the conflict reaches the level of the response system where it acts so as to delay the overt response. With other effects, such as the memory set-size effect in the Sternberg task, attempts at localization have proved to be more controversial. In part, this controversy arises from the difficulty in specifying exactly when (and where) in the process of stimulus evaluation the P300 component is emitted. Nevertheless, taken together, the results reviewed in this section clearly illustrate that data from ERPs can contribute to the resolution of theoretical disputes about the way in which the system responds to experimental challenges. In the next section we consider how ERPs can be used to address more 'metatheoretical' issues.

4.5   STRUCTURE AND FUNCTION OF THE INFORMATION PROCESSING SYSTEM

In the preceding section we saw how ERP measures can be used to investigate the locus of the effect of a particular experimental manipulation on the processing system. In this section we review evidence about fundamental properties of the system. We ask questions about the nature of interactions among the elements of the system and about the operation of higher-level (control) systems that exert an influence on the more basic elements of information processing.

4.5.1 The nature of transmission

A central issue in mental chronometry has been the question of transmission of information between elements of the processing system (e.g. Eriksen and Schultz 1979; Grice *et al.* 1982; McClelland 1979; Miller 1988; Sanders 1990). Is it discrete or is it continuous? The answer to this question is critical because discrete transmission of constant output is assumed by the additive factors method, one of the methods for exploring human information processing (see above). As Miller (1988) has pointed out, it is possible to recast this question in terms of the grain size of information that is transmitted. Discrete transmission involves the transmission of information in a single chunk, while continuous transmission involves transmission in an infinite number of small grains. Note that, according to this conception, transmission can be neither fully continuous nor fully discrete. Looked at in this way, the discrete–continuous issue can be recast in terms of whether communication is anything less than fully discrete — and the critical question concerns whether there is a transfer of partial information about a stimulus to the response system before that stimulus has been completely evaluated. Of course, the existence of less than discrete communication is a problem for the additive factors method. Although in our early work, some of us were more cavalier in claiming psychophysiological evidence for continuous transmission (Coles and Gratton 1986), we have become more restrained recently in arguing only that our data support the claim that, on some occasions, partial information transmission occurs.

What is the evidence for partial information transmission? At first glance it would seem to be a relatively simple matter to demonstrate that overt responses can be executed before stimulus evaluation is completed. After all, in the P300 we have a putative marker for the end of the evaluative process, and it is quite common to find that the overt response is released before the peak of the P300 (e.g. Coles *et al.* 1985). The problem with this argument is that the evidence supports the claim that the latency of the P300 can be used as a measure of the **relative** duration of the evaluation process — and not the absolute duration. The interval between the end of the evaluation process and the P300 peak is unknown.

A second, more complex argument can be made on the basis of the relationships among reaction time, response accuracy, and P300 latency. As we noted earlier, for responses with a given reaction time, the shorter the P300 latency, the higher the accuracy. Furthermore, response accuracy increases in a graded fashion as P300 latency decreases. These kinds of data suggest that, in accordance with the continuous flow idea, information about the stimulus is continuously available to guide responses — the shorter the P300 latency, the faster evaluation has proceeded, the more information will be available and the more accurate responses will be. The problem with this argument (and with corresponding arguments based on speed-accuracy trade-off data — see Meyer *et al.* (1988*b*), is that the apparent graded changes in accuracy may actually be the result of averaging a discrete process that is jittered in time. If the evaluation process has just two states, no evaluation and complete evaluation, and if the time of the transition between these two states varies from trial to trial, then accuracy will appear to increase gradually. Such a gradual increase would give the misleading impression that the underlying transition is also gradual rather than discrete.

Because of these problems we must turn to other kinds of psychophysiological data. In two earlier reviews (Coles *et al.* 1988, 1991), we distinguished between different kinds of paradigms that have been used to address the question of the transmission of partial information. For *conflict* paradigms, partial information transmission would lead to activation of the incorrect response. On the other hand, for *congruence* paradigms partial information transmission would lead to activation of the correct response, at a 'sub-threshold' level. Finally, in the related *go/no-go* paradigm, partial information transmission would lead to response activation on no-go trials.

4.5.1.1 Conflict

As we reviewed above, several psychophysiological experiments have suggested a response locus for the interference effect observed in Stroop-like tasks, in the Eriksen task, and in stimulus-response compatibility tasks. In each case the delay in correct reaction time associated with incompatible or incongruent stimuli, or stimulus configurations, was attributed to the activation of the incorrect response and the 'competition' between the incorrect and correct response. The incorrect response was apparently activated on the basis of an early, preliminary analysis of the stimulus or stimulus configuration. In the case of the Eriksen task, for example, we have argued that preliminary analysis of an incompatible array (HHSHH) would favour the incorrect response. During initial phases of stimulus analysis, the subject is unable to associate letters (features) with their locations, (and thus to know what letter is at the center target location) and all that is available is information about the identity of the letters (or of their features, see below). Because the dominant letter in the array is the letter associated with the incorrect response, the incorrect response is activated first. This means, of course, that partial information about the array is transmitted to the response system, and that information is not transmitted in a discrete, all-or-none fashion. Parallel arguments can be made for the Stroop and stimulus–response compatibility tasks described earlier, although in these cases the tasks involve stimuli with multiple attributes rather than stimulus configurations with multiple stimuli.

It is one thing to demonstrate that partial information transmission can occur, but quite another to specify how 'partial' is the information, or, in Miller's terms, to specify the grain size of the information. For example, in the Eriksen task is information passed on in two chunks, one related to the processing of the letters without regard to their locations and one related to the processing of the central target letter? Or is the evidence passed on continuously, gradually changing from location-independent to location-dependent information? Many of the psychophysiological data are unable to distinguish between these two possibilities. In this regard, it is important to note that the smooth *average* lateralized readiness potential traces we observe in these tasks may not accurately represent the form of the underlying process. As with the speed-accuracy trade-off phenomenon, one can obtain these smooth kinds of functions, suggestive of a continuous underlying process, by averaging a two-stage discrete process that is jittered in time.

What psychophysiological evidence is there, then, for the kind of continuous flow described by Eriksen and his colleagues (e.g. Eriksen and Schultz 1979) or the kind of cascading processes described by McClelland (1979)? Strong claims in this regard have recently been made by Smid and his colleagues (Smid *et al.* 1991). As was noted earlier, they used a variant of the Eriksen paradigm in which the noise letters only share features with the target letters but do not have experi-

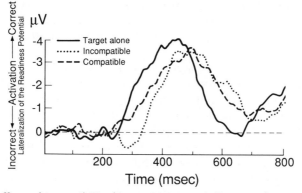

Fig. 4.6 The effects of compatibility between target and distractor features in an Eriksen-type task. Note the 'dip' in the LRP for incompatible arrays when the distractors shared features with the target letter associated with the incorrect response. (Fig. 6 amended from Smid *et al.* (1991). Copyright © 1991 American Psychological Association, reprinted by permission.)

mentally defined responses. The target appeared at an unpredictable location in a display, together with three non-targets. Therefore the subjects had to identify, on the average, 2.5 letters in the display to find the target. These display letters were rather small (0.4° of visual angle). As Fig. 4.6 shows, incorrect response activation occurred when the noise letters shared features with the target letter associated with the incorrect response. These findings suggest that shape elements of the non-target letters were used for a preliminary response choice. What was transmitted was partial information representing letter-shape features rather than information about the letters. Furthermore, because an average of 2.5 letters had to be identified to find the target, transmission seems to have occurred in an average of five steps. For each letter there was one transmission about the features signalling a response, and one transmission about the features signalling a target or a non-target, this latter transmission being equivalent to a go/no-go signal. This analysis suggests that the grain size of the transmitted partial information is relatively small, involving shape features of the non-targets. To explain these findings with discrete models, assumptions must be made, for example, about how the response system 'knows' that the initial transmissions it receives do not concern information about the target. After considering this and other discrete explanations of these findings, Smid and colleagues conclude that the continuous-flow conception offer the most parsimonious explanation, because it requires no such additional assumptions (Smid *et al.* 1991).

4.5.1.2 Congruence and go/no-go

In these paradigms the subjects must evaluate, on each trial, a single, dual-attribute stimulus. The conjunction of the values of the two attributes indicates the correct response. In congruence tasks, one of four possible responses must be selected and executed. These responses consist of the middle and index fingers of the left and right hands. In go/no-go tasks, one of two possible responses must be executed, a response with the left hand or the right hand, or no response is required.

De Jong *et al.* (1988) used a congruence task in which the letters S and N were presented in either large or small sizes, with letter size deliberately adjusted to make letter size more difficult to identify than letter shape and letter name. In one condition, the letter name indicated the response hand while size indicated the required finger. This stimulus-response assignment, in principle, makes it possible for the subject to use partial information associated with letter identity to select a response hand before the more difficult size attribute has been identified. However, De Jong *et al.* (1988) found that information about the letter and about its size were used at about the same time for the selection of responses, and they concluded that under these conditions no partial information is used for the pre-liminary selection of response hand.

Smid *et al.* (1992) further investigated the use of partial information in the congruence paradigm, by augmenting the congruence task with a go/no-go procedure. Using various stimulus-response assignments, coloured letters were assigned to the four response fingers and to a no-go response. In one condition, the colour of the letter indicated the hand to respond with (e.g. red and green), while the letter name indicated response finger (e.g. H for the middle and M for the index finger) or the no-go response (e.g. W). With this assignment, colour can be used as partial information to select the response hand before the letter is identified. If the response hand is selected and activated in this preliminary way, an LRP should be present in the no-go trials. This no-go LRP should indicate activation of the hand indicated by the colour, because at the time of response-hand activation, the letter is not yet identified and the subject would not yet know whether or not to respond. A no-go LRP was, in fact, observed in these data. In another condition, the letter name indicated the response hand, while colour indicated the response finger or the no-go response. With this assignment, letter identity can be used as partial information to activate the response hand before the colour is identified. In fact, an LRP was again found on no-go trials reflecting activation of the hand indicated by the letter.

On the basis of these results, Smid *et al.* (1992) arrived at a different conclusion from De Jong *et al.* (1988), namely, that partial information in the congruence paradigm *can* be used to select responses. However, before discussing how these contradictory conclusions can be reconciled, we first turn to other studies that have used the go/no-go paradigm.

In the go/no-go paradigm, one easily identifiable stimulus attribute indicates a left- or a right-hand response, while a difficult-to-identify attribute indicates whether or not a response is required. Miller and Hackley (1992) presented the letters S and T in two sizes, with the size attribute being more difficult to discriminate than letter identity. The letter indicated the response hand, and the size attribute whether to respond. For example, a relatively large S required a response with the left hand, but no response was required if the S was relatively small. In this situation, partial information about letter identity can be used to activate a response hand before the more difficult size attribute has been evaluated. The data revealed that on both go and no-go trials, an LRP was evident suggesting activation of the hand indicated by the letter name. On go trials (but not on no-go trials), the amplitude of the LRP developed further until it reached the level associated with a muscular and overt response. The authors concluded that letter identity was used as partial information to activate a lateral response before the size attribute had been evaluated.

Similar findings were obtained by Osman *et al.* (1992). These authors applied the go/no-go paradigm to investigate whether the location of a symbol can be used as partial information. The letter 'l' or the digit '1' were presented either to the left or right of fixation. The location indicated the response hand while the symbol indicated whether a response was required. As in the Miller and Hackley study, there was an initial LRP on both go and no-go trials, in this case being related to the location of the stimulus. Later, presumably after the symbol was identified, the LRP on no-go trials dissipated, while that on go trials increased to the threshold level associated with overt response activation. Figure 4.7 shows these effects.

Thus, in the go/no-go paradigm the results consistently show that partial information about a dual-attribute stimulus can be used to select and activate responses before the stimulus has been fully identified. In the congruence paradigm the results are not so consistent. Why would this be so? Comparison of the stimuli used by De Jong *et al.* (1988) and Smid *et al.* (1992) suggests that part

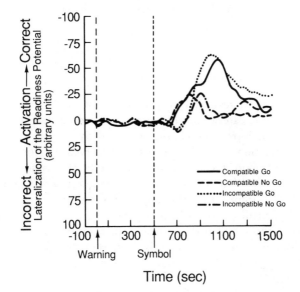

Fig. 4.7 Response activation in a go/no-go task. Note the presence of a significant LRP on no-go trials. (Fig. 5 amended from Osman *et al.* (1992). Copyright © American Psychological Association 1992, reprinted by permission.)

of the answer lies in the separability of the particular stimulus attributes that are used (Garner 1970). Recall that in the De Jong *et al.* (1988) study the stimuli consisted of letters of different sizes. The evidence indicated that the letter and its size were not used separately to activate responses. Using the same task as De Jong *et al.* (1988), Smid *et al.* (1992) found that the letter and its colour *can* be used separately to activate responses. These data suggest that the colour and letter attributes are easier to process separately than the size and letter attributes. Indeed, selective-attention studies have shown that it is more difficult to selectively process size from shape than colour from shape (Wijers *et al.* 1989*b*). Since the separability of stimulus attributes is a necessary condition for using one of the attributes as partial information, variation in separability may be responsible for the inconsistency in the evidence for the use of partial information.

Another part of the answer is suggested by a comparison of the De Jong *et al.* (1988) and Miller and Hackley (1992) studies. In both studies the same letter stimuli were used, but the tasks differed with respect to the number of responses required (four fingers versus two fingers and no-go). When response selection requirements were relatively high (four possible stimuli and four possible responses), no evidence for the use of partial information was found. When they were low, the evidence suggested that the attributes that are difficult to process separately were used as partial information. It seems, then, that whether partial information is used may depend on its utility in producing a fast and accurate response. Response selection strategies that use partial information seem to produce higher error rates than those using fully identified information (Gratton *et al.* 1992). Calculation of the utility of response selection options is a feature of control processes, which are the topic of the next section.

4.5.2 Control

4.5.2.1 *Modulation of the use of partial information*

In the previous section we reviewed the psychophysiological evidence for the claim that partial information can be transferred to the response system. While most of the data certainly supported the claim, we noted that there were situations in which partial information transmission was not observed (De Jong *et al.* 1988) — although in other circumstances, involving exactly the same, multi-attribute stimuli, there was evidence for partial information transmission (Miller and Hackley 1992). We argued that this apparent variability in the use of partial information is dependent on the task situation (that is, on 'bottom-up' influences) and on the control the subject can exert over the transmission process (that is, in a 'top-down' fashion). This section deals with the control of the transmission process, and the possibility that the information code transmitted may vary with experimental conditions.

As we noted earlier, evidence for different transmission under different conditions (levels of an experimental factor) invalidates an assumption that underlies the use of the AFM, namely that under different conditions processes transmit constant output codes to their successors. In this case, by 'constant output', we refer to the informational content of the code (e.g. values on the same stimulus dimension) rather than to its technical quality (e.g. the spatial resolution of a shape code). This constant-output assumption is important because a change in output code (e.g. a change in stimulus dimension about which information is transmitted) can affect the duration of subsequent processes. This in turn may have consequences for the selective influence assumption about the factor that changed the output code. In terms of recent mathematical research with additive factors logic (Schweickert and Townsend 1989; Miller 1993), the factor would change the 'critical path' through the discrete mental network.

To date, there have been three studies that have provided evidence to support the idea of top-down control over the transmission process. These studies have looked at the effects of instructions and of the utility of using partial information on what is actually being transmitted.

Gratton *et al.* (1992) explored this question using the Eriksen task described earlier. As noted above, processing in the task seems to involve two phases, a location-independent phase (or parallel phase) in which target and noise letters are processed together without regard to their location, and a location-dependent phase (or focused phase) in which subjects are able to identify the letter at the target location. Note that a fast and accurate response can be based on the first phase, if the array is compatible, but, for incompatible arrays, accurate responses will depend on the focused phase. Clearly, then, if the array is compatible, optimal performance (in terms of speed and accuracy) can be achieved if the results of the location-independent phase are used to activate responses (that is, if there is partial information transmission). On the other hand, optimal performance for incompatible arrays can only be achieved if the results of the location-dependent phase are used (that is, until all information is available). Based on these considerations, Gratton *et al.* (1992) reasoned that if subjects could exercise control over their processing systems, they would choose between the results of the two phases as a function of the utility of partial information transmission. Thus, if subjects 'expect' a compatible array, they would favour a strategy that uses partial information; while expectancies for the appearance of an incompatible array would lead to a choice of the complete analysis strategy.

To detect variation in the use of partial information, Gratton *et al.* (1992) looked at the compatibility effect (the difference between measures for compatible and incompatible arrays). We argued earlier that activation of the incorrect response following the presentation of an incompatible array was evidence for partial information transmission. Similarly, activation of the correct response in the same time-window following a compatible array would also suggest partial information transmission. Thus, the magnitude of difference between the activation functions for the two arrays (as is evident in the LRP measure) reflects the degree to which partial information influences the response system.

To manipulate subjects' expectancies for compatible and incompatible arrays, the probability of the different arrays was varied in three different ways. In a 'global probability' experiment, the probability of compatible/incompatible arrays was fixed within, but varied between, trial blocks. In a 'conditional probability' experiment, the probability of compatible/incompatible arrays was communicated to the subjects by a precue before each array presentation. Finally, the authors looked at sequential effects from one of the original studies using the Eriksen task in which the probabilities were 0.5/0.5. Based on work by Remington (1969) and others on trial-to-trial dependencies, Gratton *et al.* (1992) reasoned that subjects would 'expect' that the compatibility of the array on trial *n* would be the same as on trial *n*-1.

In each of these three experiments there was a larger compatibility effect when compatible arrays were more probable or expected. Reaction-time and error-rate data, along with the LRP waveforms, converged in suggesting that the noise letters exerted a greater influence over the responses under these conditions. This pointed to a larger effect of the location-independent phase of processing than when the subject expected an incompatible array. The variation in the influence of the noise letters is *not* the same as the commonly observed trade-off between speed and accuracy — subjects did not just respond more quickly when they expected a compatible array. This evidence suggests that subjects modulate the use of partial information depending on its utility for producing fast and accurate responses. The top-down origin of this modulation in the use of partial information is strongly suggested by the fact that the effect could be produced by a symbolic precue that was presented just prior to the array.

A second experiment applied the congruence paradigm to study the modulation of the use of partial information (Smid *et al.* 1992). In this study, individual coloured letters were assigned in different ways to the middle and index fingers of both hands. In one condition, the colour of the letter signalled the responding hand, while the shape of the letter signalled the responding finger. The LRP and RT data suggested that subjects first used partial information about the colour of the letter to select the response hand, and then used the letter shape/name to select the response finger. The LRPs also suggested that at the time the colour was used to select response hand, information about the letter shape was not yet available. In another condition, the shape of the letter signalled the response hand, while the colour of the letter signalled the response finger. The data in this condition implied that the subjects first used partial information concerning the letter to select the response hand, and next used the colour to select the final response. On no-go trials, LRP data indicated that at the time the letter was used to select the response hand, the colour was not yet available. Furthermore, in both instruction conditions, the data showed that using partial information to select the response hand in advance greatly reduced RT and error rate. This evidence shows that subjects can choose which partial information to use, depending on its utility for producing fast and accurate responses. The top-down origin of the strategic use of partial information in this study is strongly suggested by the fact that either the colour of the letter or its shape could be used as partial information, depending on which stimulus attribute could be used to select the hand attribute in advance of full stimulus identification.

Finally, a third experiment conducted by De Jong *et al.* (1994) suggests that the use of partial information can depend on task instructions, and therefore can be strategically modulated. In this stimulus-response compatibility experiment (see above), the use of partial information about the colour of a letter depended on the instructed correspondence between stimulus and response codes.

These findings all suggest that, in advance of stimulus presentation, a higher-order control process can 'tag' a stimulus attribute to be used as partial information. They further suggest that the higher-order process can tag different attributes depending on variations of task variables such as stimulus probability and stimulus-response compatibility. Thus there appears to be substantial empirical evidence that there is variability in the transmission process and thus that the central assumption of the additive factor methodology, the constant-output assumption, is not valid in at least some circumstances. Note that the LRP findings show that perceptual and motor-related processes are not arranged in series. In terms of Schweickert's (1993) models, this implies that the 'cutpoint' between processes that can be selectively influenced to yield additivity cannot lie between perceptual and motor processes.

4.5.2.2 Stopping

Stopping what we have started exemplifies our ability to exert control over our processing systems (see Logan (in press) for a comprehensive review). This ability to interrupt what we are doing and either do something else, or do nothing at all, has been studied experimentally using the 'stop-signal' paradigm. In this paradigm, the subject is required to perform the kind of reaction time task that we have reviewed throughout this chapter. On some trials, a stop-signal is presented and the subject must try to inhibit the reaction time response. The timing of the stop-signal is adjusted so that on 50 per cent of the trials the subject is unable to stop. In different variants of the task, the subject may be required to stop all responses, to stop one response but to make another, or to stop only one of several possible responses.

Psychophysiological measures have been used to address two basic questions about stopping: first, where is the point of no return, after which a response once started cannot be stopped, and second, what is the mechanism used to inhibit responses?

In a stopping experiment designed to investigate the locus of the point of no return, De Jong and colleagues (De Jong *et al.* 1990) used measures of electro-myographic activity and of overt response force to classify trials as a function of the degree to which the subject was successful in stopping the response. While there were some trials where the subject was totally successful in stopping, there were other trials where the subject made a partial response, exerting force on the response device at a level that was insufficient to be registered as a response. The existence of these partial responses suggests that the point of no return was very late in the chain of processes leading up to a response — and certainly after the point of response initiation.

Measures of the LRP in the same experiment provided some interesting insights into the mechanism by which this inhibition is accomplished. Recall that the amplitude of the LRP is apparently related to the production of the overt response. Gratton *et al.* (1988) showed that, regardless of reaction time and response accuracy, the electromyographic activity associated with the overt response occurred at the same LRP amplitude. This suggested that there was a threshold level of the LRP which, when crossed, was associated with a muscular response. This idea of response threshold was confirmed by De Jong *et al.* (1990) for those trials where no stop-signal was presented and the overt response proceeded in an uninhibited fashion. However, on those trials where the subjects were completely successful in inhibiting their responses (there was no electromyographic activity or squeeze activity), the amplitude of the LRP *exceeded* the threshold level normally associated with muscular activity. This observation suggested that successful inhibition was accomplished by a peripheral inhibitory mechanism that operates at a lower level (more downstream) than the system responsible for the LRP, that is, central preparatory processes implemented in motor cortex.

In a follow-up study, De Jong *et al.* (in press) examined the nature of inhibitory processes in more detail. Following Bullock and Grossberg (1988), they proposed that there were two possible inhibitory mechanisms that could be used in these kinds of tasks. First, subjects could use the *peripheral* mechanism described earlier that operates in a non-selective fashion to inhibit all ongoing behaviour even after it has been initiated. Second, subjects could use a more *central* mechanism that operates selectively to inhibit response activation processes before the issuance of central motor commands. De Jong *et al.* (in press) reasoned that, while the non-selective peripheral mechanism could be used successfully in the usual stopping paradigm where the stop-signal requires that all responses be stopped (the stop-all condition), this mechanism would be ineffective in those situations where selective inhibition is required, as when the stop-signal requires both the stopping of one response *and* the execution of another response (the stop-change condition). Less clear is which mechanism is used when the stop-signal requires the subject to inhibit responses made with one hand but not with the other (the stop-selective condition). In this case, subjects could use the central selective mechanism to inhibit the responses of one hand or they could first determine which response was to be made and then use the peripheral non-selective mechanism if the response to be executed required inhibition.

By using LRP measures along with other measures derived from application of the race model to the reaction time data (see Logan and Cowan 1984), De Jong *et al.* (in press) were able to demonstrate that, indeed, the central inhibitory mechanism was used in the stop-change condition. As Fig. 4.8 shows, on success-fully stopped trials, the level of the LRP never exceeded the threshold. However, in the stop-selective condition, the LRP data resembled those for the stop-all condition. The LRP exceeded the threshold on successfully stopped trials. These results suggested that in the stop-selective condition, the subject did *not* apply the selective inhibitory mechanism to the response that had to be stopped. Rather, after determining which response was required on a particular trial, the subject applied the non-selective mechanism as needed.

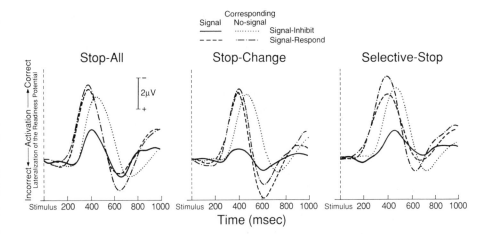

Fig. 4.8 Response activation in various stop-signal paradigms. LRPs for trials where the subjects did and did not succeed in inhibiting their responses as required by the stop signal. Note the smaller LRP for successfully stopped trials in the stop-change condition, compared with the other two conditions. (Fig. 2 from De Jong *et al.* (in press). Copyright © 1994 American Psychological Association, reprinted by permission.)

These data on stopping provide important insights into the mechanisms available to the processing system whereby it can exercise control over its output. Two mechanisms are apparently available and which one gets implemented depends on the situation.

4.5.2.3 *Error detection, correction, and compensation*

The examples of control discussed in the preceding sections all point to the fact that humans have the ability to monitor and adjust their own behaviour (Logan 1985; Shallice 1975; Stuss and Benson 1986). Modulation of the use of partial information and attempts to stop action are all conducted within a general context of monitoring and adjusting the information processing system so that as far as possible it achieves the task goals as interpreted by the subject. We now review evidence for a particular kind of control system that is involved when these task goals are not met, a system concerned with error detection, correction, and compensation.

The existence of this kind of system is axiomatic for many theories of human cognition including those concerned with action, learning, and language. Furthermore, explicit attempts to explore the nature of this system have been undertaken by Rabbitt (1966, 1968). Using the traditional chronometric approach, Rabbitt showed that errors are frequently followed by correct responses and responses are slower on trials after an error has been made. These observations are certainly consistent with an error detection/compensation system. However, as has been argued (Gehring *et al.* 1993), when a correct response follows an error, the correct response could be produced in parallel with, but more slowly than, the error. Furthermore, the slowing down observed on trials after errors could be attributed to a persistence of whatever processing problem caused the error in the first place. Thus, neither of these behavioural observations provide direct evidence for the operation of an error-detection/compensation system.

On the other hand, ERP data provide more definitive evidence that something very different happens at around the time an error is being made — and this difference seems to involve an active error-detection and compensation mechanism. Two laboratories, working independently, have described a negative component of the ERP that is evident on error trials, but not on correct trials[5] (see Falkenstein *et al.* 1990; Gehring *et al.* 1993). This component has been labelled the 'error-related negativity' (ERN) or the NE. The amplitude of the component can be as large as 10 μV, with a maximum over the front and middle of the scalp. Its onset is shortly after the onset of the EMG activity associated with the incorrect response. These features of the ERN can be seen in Fig. 4.9.

The component has been observed in a number of different tasks including Eriksen, Sternberg, and sentence verification tasks (Gehring *et al.* in press) as well as divided attention and no-go tasks (Falkenstein *et al.* in press). In these tasks, the erroneous responses appear to be attributable to the fact that the subject responds before sufficient information has been extracted from the stimulus. Thus, the responses may be classified as fast guesses or as responses based on misleading

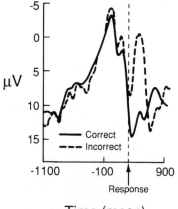

Time (msec)

Fig. 4.9 ERP waveforms (for the Cz electrode) for correct and incorrect trials in a choice reaction time task. The vertical broken line indicates the time at which electromyographic activity was detected on the responding limb. The ERP waveforms are time-locked to this response measure rather than to the onset of the stimulus. Note the negative deflection that occurs just after the response on incorrect trials. This is the error-related negativity (the ERN). (From Coles *et al.* (1992) Copyright © 1992 Elsevier Science Ltd., reprinted by permission.)

[5] However, correct trials that are subsequently 'corrected' (followed by the incorrect response), do seem to be associated with an error-related negativity.

partial information. In these tasks, extended processing of the task stimuli will generally result in correct responses.

These basic observations have led to the proposal that the component is related to a brain process associated with error-detection, error-correction, and/or error-compensation. Evidence in favour of this proposal can be derived from several sources. First, instructions and pay-offs that emphasize the relative importance of the speed or accuracy of responses influence the size of the ERN. It is larger (more negative) when accuracy is emphasized (Falkenstein *et al.* 1990; Gehring *et al.* 1993). Second, aspects of the subjects' behaviour that seem to reflect attempts to inhibit or compensate for errors are related to the size of the ERN. Thus, for example, large ERNs are associated with less forceful errors, with errors that are more likely to be corrected immediately, and with slower correct responses on trials following errors (Gehring *et al.* 1993; cf. Rabbitt 1966). The component is also delayed when errors are made to auditory stimuli under conditions of divided attention versus focused attention, that is, when auditory and visual stimuli could appear in an unpredictable sequence rather than in a predictable sequence (see Falkenstein *et al.* 1990). This suggests that the ERN system competes with attentional mechanisms for resources.

Taken together, these observations present a picture of a system that is actively involved in error-monitoring and in trying to deal with errors once they have been detected. Such a system must presumably involve a comparison between a representation of the response that is being executed and a representation of the response that should be executed (although see Schmidt and Gordon (1977) for a proposal that error-detection can involve comparison between expected and actual *stimuli* that are presented). The origin of these representations remains uncertain. However, because the onset of the component is so closely tied to the onset of the incorrect movement, it seems unlikely that proprioceptive feedback is the source of the representation of the response that is being made. Rather, it is more likely that this representation derives from some kind of corollary discharge that is generated as the (incorrect) movement is generated (Angel 1976). The source of the representation of the correct response is presumably derived from further analysis of the stimulus and application of the appropriate stimulus-response mapping.

The apparent sensitivity of the ERN to mismatches between actual and correct responses suggests a similarity between this component and other negative components including the 'mismatch negativity' (see Chapter 3) and the N400 (see Chapter 6) (see also Falkenstein *et al.* in press). These other components are also sensitive to mismatches of various kinds, and this suggests that the ERN and these other components may together comprise a family of negative, mismatch-dependent components. However, as far as the ERN is concerned, the data collected so far do not permit one to identify the component specifically with the mismatch (error) detection process. It is quite possible that the component is related to processes that are a consequence of error-detection, such as error-correction and compensation. Thus, for the present, we must remain agnostic as to whether the component we have labelled the ERN reflects the activity of an error-detection system, or some system that acts after errors have been detected.

4.5.3 Summary

In this section we have seen how ERPs have been used to make claims about the way in which the information processing system works. In contrast to traditional approaches to mental chronometry (e.g. those that use the AFM), the chrono-psychophysiological approach does not make assumptions about the way in which information is transferred in the processing system. Indeed, perhaps the most important empirical discoveries described in this section are those that suggest that partial information transmission can occur, and that the use of partial information is under strategic control.

Of course, the claims we have made must be considered in the context of the particular tasks and, most importantly, the particular stimuli we have employed. In many cases, these 'nominal' stimuli are composed of multiple functional stimuli. For example, in the Eriksen task, the flanking letters and the target letter are multiple attributes of the nominal five-letter array stimulus. Similarly, word identity and word colour are multiple attributes of the individual word stimuli used in the Stroop task. With these kinds of stimuli, the psychophysiological approach serves to provide a method of defining the relationship between the nominal stimulus and the functional stimulus. Whenever partial information transmission is observed, the nominal stimulus contains, by definition, more than one functional stimulus. Since it can be argued that the AFM is only applicable to tasks involving single functional stimuli (Sanders 1993), our psychophysiological data can be used to delineate the boundary of the range of applicability of the AFM and the associated serial discrete stage model. Note that even in cases where stimuli appear to be so elemental or simple that the nominal and functional stimulus are the same, our psychophysiological methods suggest that partial information transmission may occur (Smid *et al.* 1991). The features of a nominal letter stimulus, such as shape, can evidently operate as if they constitute multiple functional stimuli.

It is not only important to note that partial information transmission occurs — it is also important to note that the processing system is flexible and that aspects of the system are under strategic control. Thus, psychophysiological data helped us to demonstrate that there is variation in the degree to which partial information is used and that this variation seems to be determined by the principle of utility. Furthermore, we have reviewed other evidence that highlights the flexibility of the system. In particular, we have provided psychophysiological evidence for the existence of an error-monitoring or error-correction system and we have shown how different options appear to be available when actions must be inhibited. These kinds of higher-level functions are becoming more and more popular as topics for mental chronometry. We believe that the psychophysiological method will make their analysis more tractable.

4.6 CONCLUSIONS

We began this chapter with a quotation from Woodworth in which he seemed to anticipate the promise of measures of brain waves in the analysis of mental processes. We have shown how this promise has been fulfilled, at least in part, by measures of the event-related potential. Our measures have contributed to the resolution of some of the problems encountered by the traditional chronometric approach as it tries to understand covert processes by relying exclusively on measures of overt behaviour. Because of their selective sensitivity to particular mental processes, our measures provide a view of the mind that is considerably richer than that provided by the traditional approach. Note, however, that the traditional measures of response speed and accuracy are still viewed by us as critically important to the chronometric enterprise. Indeed, it is the configural pattern of data provided by these overt measures and the ERP measures that has enabled us to proceed.

As with other mental processes reviewed in this book, the challenge now is to relate what we have learned to the question of the implementation of these processes in the brain. For the principal measure discussed in this section, the LRP, there is good reason to believe that it reflects the activity of neurons in the motor cortex (for a review see Coles 1989; Miller *et al.* 1992). However, we need to go well beyond statements about measures reflecting particular brain activities if we are to achieve a precise understanding of how the cognitive system is implemented in the brain.

REFERENCES

Angel, R. W. (1976). Efference copy in the control of movement. *Neurology*, **26**, 1164–68.

Ashby, F. G. (1982). Deriving exact predictions from the cascade model. *Psychological Review*, **89**, 599–607.

Brookhuis, K. A., Mulder, G., Mulder, L. J. M., and Gloerich, A. B. M. (1983). The P3 complex as an index of information processing: the effects of response probability. *Biological Psychology*, **17**, 277–96.

Bullock, D. and Grossberg, S. (1988). Neural dynamics of planned arm movements: emergent invariants and speed accuracy properties during trajectory formation. *Psychological Review*, **95**, 49–90.

Coles, M. G. H. (1989). Modern mind-brain reading: psychophysiology, physiology and cognition. *Psychophysiology*, **26**, 251–69.

Coles, M. G. H. and Gratton, G. (1986). Cognitive psychophysiology and the study of states and processes. In *Energetics and human information processing* (ed. G. R. J. Hockey, A. W. K. Gaillard, and M. G. H. Coles), pp. 409–24. Martinus Nijhof, Dordrecht.

Coles, M. G. H., Gratton, G., Bashore, T. R., Eriksen, C. W., and Donchin, E. (1985). A psychophysiological investigation of the continuous flow model of human information processing. *Journal of Experimental Psychology: Human Perception and Performance*, **11**, 529–53.

Coles, M. G. H., Gratton, G., and Donchin, E. (1988). Detecting early communication: using measures of movement-related potentials to illuminate human information processing. *Biological Psychology*, 26, 69–89.

Coles, M. G. H., Gratton, G., and Fabiani, M. (1990). Event-related brain potentials. In *Principles of psychophysiology: physical, social and inferential elements*, (ed. J. T. Cacioppo and L. G. Tassinary), pp. 413–55. Cambridge University Press, Cambridge, UK.

Coles, M. G. H., De Jong, R., Gehring, W. J., and Gratton, G. (1991). Continuous versus discrete information processing: evidence from movement-related potentials. In *Event-related potentials of the brain*, EEG Suppl. 42, (ed. C. H. M. Brunia, G. Mulder, and M. N. Verbaten), pp. 260–9. Elsevier, Amsterdam.

Coles, M. G. H., Gehring, W. J., Gratton, G., and Donchin, E. (1992). Response activation and verification: a psychophysiological analysis. In *Tutorials in motor behaviour II* (ed. G. E. Stelmach and J. Requin), pp. 779–92. Elsevier, Amsterdam.

De Jong, R. (1991). Partial information or facilitation? Different interpretations of results from speed-accuracy decomposition. *Perception and Psychophysics*, 50, 333–50.

De Jong, R., Wierda, M., Mulder, G., and Mulder, L. J. M. (1988). Use of partial information in responding. *Journal of Experimental Psychology: Human Perception and Performance*, 14, 682–92.

De Jong, R., Coles, M. G. H., Logan, G. G., and Gratton, G. (1990). In search of the point of no return: the control of response processes. *Journal of Experimental Psychology: Human Perception and Performance*, 16, 164–82.

De Jong, R., Liang, C.-C., and Lauber, E. (1994). Conditional and unconditional automaticity: a dual-process model of effects of spatial stimulus-response correspondence. *Journal of Experimental Psychology: human Perception and Performance*, 20, 721–50.

De Jong, R., Coles, M. G. H., and Logan, G. D. Strategies and mechanisms in nonselective and selective inhibitory motor control. *Journal of Experimental Psychology: human Perception and Performance*. (In press.)

Donchin, E. (1979). Event-related brain potentials: a tool in the study of human information processing. In *Evoked potentials and behavior* (ed. H. Begleiter), pp. 13–75. Plenum, New York.

Donchin, E. (1981). Surprise! . . . Surprise? *Psychophysiology*, 18, 493–513.

Donchin, E. and Coles, M. G. H. (1988a). Is the P300 component a manifestation of context updating? *Behavioral and Brain Sciences*, 11, 355–72.

Donchin, E. and Coles, M. G. H. (1988b). On the conceptual foundations of cognitive psychophysiology. *Behavioral and Brain Sciences*, 11, 406–25.

Donders, F. C. (1868/1969). On the speed of mental processes. In *Attention and performance II* (ed. and trans. W. G. Koster), pp. 412–31. North-Holland, Amsterdam.

Duncan-Johnson, C. C. and Donchin, E. (1977). On quantifying surprise: the variation of event-related potentials with subjective probability. *Psychophysiology*, 14, 456–67.

Duncan-Johnson, C. C. and Kopell, B. S. (1981). The Stroop effect: brain potentials localize the source of interference. *Science*, 214, 938–40.

Eriksen, B. A. and Eriksen, C. W. (1974). Effects of noise letters upon the identification of target letter in visual search. *Perception and Psychophysics*, 16, 143–9.

Eriksen, C. W. and Hoffman, J. E. (1973). The extent of processing of noise elements during selective encoding from visual displays. *Perception and Psychophysics*, 14, 155–160.

Eriksen, C. W. and Schultz, D. W. (1979). Information processing in visual search: a continuous flow conception and experimental results. *Perception and Psychophysics*, 25, 249–63.

Eriksen, C. W., Coles, M. G. H., Morris, L. R., and O'Hara, W. P. (1985). An electromyographic examination of response competition. *Bulletin of the Psychonomic Society*, 23, 165–8.

Falkenstein, M., Hohnsbein, J., Hoormann, J., and Blanke, L. (1990). Effects of errors in choice reaction tasks on the ERP under focused and divided attention. In *Psychophysiological brain research* (ed. C. H. M. Brunia, A. W. K. Gaillard, and A. Kok), pp. 192–5. Elsevier, Amsterdam.

Falkenstein, M., Hohnsbein, J., and Hoormann, J. Event-related potential correlates of errors in reaction tasks. In *Proceedings of the 10th International Conference on event-related potentials of the brain*, EEG Suppl., (ed. G. Karmos). (In press.)

Ford, J. R., Roth, W. T., Mohs, R. C., Hopkins, W. F., III, and Kopell, B. S. (1979). Event-related potentials recorded from young and old adults during a memory retrieval task. *Electroencephalography and Clinical Neurophysiology*, 47, 450–9.

Garner, W. R. (1970). The stimulus in information processing. *American Psychologist*, 25, 350–8.

Gehring, W. J., Gratton, G., Coles, M. G. H., and Donchin, E. (1992). Probability effects on stimulus evaluation and response processes. *Journal of Experimental Psychology: Human Perception and Performance*, 18, 198–216.

Gehring, W. J., Goss, B., Coles, M. G. H., Meyer, D. E., and Donchin, E. (1993). A neural system for error-detection and compensation. *Psychological Science*, 4, 385–90.

Gehring, W. J., Coles, M. G. H., Meyer, D. E., and Donchin, E. A brain potential manifestation of error-related processing. (In press.)

Gomer, F. E., Spicuzza, R. J., and O'Donnell, R. D. (1976). Evoked potential correlates of visual item recognition during memory-scanning tasks. *Physiological Psychology*, 4, 61–5.

Gottsdanker, R. and Shragg, G. P. (1985). Verification of Donders' subtraction method. *Journal of Experimental Psychology: Human Perception and Performance*, 11, 765–76.

Gratton, G., Coles, M. G. H., Sirevaag, E. J., Eriksen, C. W., and Donchin, E. (1988). Pre- and post-stimulus activation of response channels: a psychophysiological analysis.

Gratton, G., Bosco, C. M., Kramer, A. F., Coles, M. G. H., Wickens, C. D., and Donchin E. (1990). Event-related brain potentials as indices of information extraction and response priming. *Electroencephalography and Clinical Neurophysiology*, 75, 419–32.

Gratton, G., Coles, M. G. H., and Donchin, E. (1992). Optimizing the use of information: strategic control of activation of responses. *Journal of Experimental Psychology: General*, 121, 480–506.

Grice, G. R., Nullmeyer, R., and Spiker, V. A. (1982). Human reaction times: toward a general theory. *Journal of Experimental Psychology: General*, 111, 135–53.

Hasbroucq, T. and Guiard, Y. (1991). Stimulus–response compatibility and the Simon effect: toward a conceptual clarification. *Journal of Experimental Psychology: Human Perception and Performance*, 17, 246–66.

Hedge, A. and Marsh, N. W. A. (1975). The effects of irrelevant spatial correspondences on two-choise response time. *Acta Psychologica*, 39, 427–39.

Johnson, R., Jr. (1988). The amplitude of the P300 component of the event-related potential: review and synthesis. In *Advances in psychophysiology*, Vol. 3, (ed. P. K. Ackles, J. R. Jennings, and M. G. H. Coles), pp. 69–138. JAI Press, Greenwich, CT.

Johnson, R., Jr. and Donchin, E. (1978). On how P300 amplitude varies with the utility of the eliciting stimuli. *Electroencephalography and Clinical Neurophysiology*, 44, 424–37.

Johnson, R., Jr. and Donchin, E. (1985). Second thoughts: multiple P300s elicited by a single stimulus. *Psychophysiology*, 22, 182–94.

Kornblum, S., Hasbroucq, T., and Osman, A. (1990). Dimensional overlap: cognitive basis for stimulus–response compatibility — a model and taxonomy. *Psychological Review*, 97, 253–70.

Külpe, O. (1909). *Outlines of psychology: based upon the results of experimental investigation*, (3rd edn.) (translation of original work published in 1893). New York, Macmillan.

Kutas, M. and Donchin, E. (1980). Preparation to respond as manifested by movement-related brain potentials. *Brain Research*, 202, 95–115.

Kutas, M., McCarthy, G., and Donchin, E. (1977). Augmenting mental chronometry: the P300 as a measure of stimulus evaluation time. *Science*, 197, 792–5.

Logan, G. D. (1985). On the ability to inhibit simple thoughts and actions: II. Stop-signal studies of repetition priming. *Journal of Experimental Psychology: Learning Memory and Cognition*, 11, 675–91.

Logan, G. D. On the ability to inhibit thought and action: a users' guide to the stop signal paradigm. In *Inhibitory processes in attention, memory, and language* (ed. D. Dagenbach and T. H. Carr). Academic P., San Diego.

Logan, G. D. and Cowan, W. B. (1984). On the ability to inhibit thought and action: a theory of an act of control. *Psychological Review*, 91, 295–327.

McCarthy, G. and Donchin, E. (1981). A metric of thought: a comparison of P300 latency and reaction time. *Science*, 211, 77–80.

McClelland, J. L. (1979). On the time relations of mental processes: an examination of systems of processes in cascade. *Psychological Review*, 86, 287–330.

MacLeod, C. M. (1991). Half a century of research on the Stroop effect: an integrated review. *Psychological Bulletin*, 109, 163–203.

Magliero, A., Bashore, T. R., Coles, M. G. H., and Donchin, E. (1984). On the dependence of P300 latency on stimulus evaluation processes. *Psychophysiology*, 21, 171–86.

Meyer, D. E., Yantis, S., Osman, A., and Smith, J. E. K. (1985). Temporal properties of human information processing: tests of discrete versus continuous models. *Cognitive Psychology*, 17, 445–518.

Meyer, D. E., Irwin, D. E., Osman, A. M., and Kounios, J. (1988*a*). The dynamics of cognition and action: mental processes inferred from speed–accuracy decomposition. *Psychological Review*, 95, 183–237.

Meyer, D. E., Osman, A. M., Irwin, D. E., and Yantis, S. (1988*b*). Modern mental chronometry. *Biological Psychology*, 26, 3–67.

Miller, J. O. (1988). Discrete and continuous models of human information processing: theoretical distinctions and empirical results. *Acta Psychologica*, 67, 191–257.

Miller, J. O. (1993). A queue-series model for reaction time, with discrete-stage and continuous-flow models as special cases. *Psychological Review*, 100, 702–15.

Miller, J. O. and Hackley, S. A. (1992). Electrophysiological evidence for temporal overlap among contingent mental processes. *Journal of Experimental Psychology: General*, 121, 195–209.

Miller, J. O., Riehle, A., and Requin, J. (1992). Effects of preliminary perceptual output on neuronal activity of the primary motor cortex. *Journal of Experimental Psychology: Human Perception and Performance*, 18, 1121–38.

Näätänen, R. (1992). *Attention and brain function*. Erlbaum, Hillsdale, NJ.

Okada, Y. C., Williamson, S. J., and Kaufman, L. (1982). Magnetic fields of the human sensory-motor cortex. *International Journal of Neurophysiology*, 17, 33–8.

Okita, T., Wijers, A. A., Mulder, G., and Mulder, L. J. M. (1985). Memory search and visual spatial attention: an event-related brain potential analysis. *Acta Psychologica*, 60, 263–92.

Osman, A., Bashore, T. R., Coles, M. G. H., Donchin, E., and Meyer, D. E. (1992). On the transmission of partial information: Inferences from movement-related brain potentials. *Journal of Experimental Psychology: Human Perception and Performance*, 18, 217–32.

Otten, L. J., Sudevan, P., and Coles, M. G. H. Magnitude versus parity in numerical judgements: event-related brain potentials implicate response conflict as the source of interference. (Submitted.)

Pachella, R. G. (1974). The interpretation of reaction time in information processing research. In *Human information: tutorials in performance and cognition* (ed. B. H. Kantowitz), pp. 41–82. Erlbaum, Hillsdale, NJ.

Parasuraman, R. and Beatty, J. (1980). Brain events underlying detection and recognition of weak sensory signals. *Science*, 210, 80–3.

Posner, M. I. (1978). *Chronometric explorations of mind*. Erlbaum, Hillsdale, NJ.

Posner, M. I. and Boies, S. J. (1971). Components of attention. *Psychological Review*, 78, 391–408.

Pratt, H., Michalewski, H. J., Barrett, G., and Starr, A. (1989). Brain potentials in a memory-scanning task. I. Modality and task effects on potentials to the probes. *Electroencephalography and Clinical Neurophysiology*, 72, 407–21.

Pritchard, W. S. (1981). Psychophysiology of P300. *Psychological Bulletin*, 89, 506–40.

Rabbitt, P. M. A. (1966). Errors and error correction in choice-response tasks. *Journal of Experimental Psychology*, 71, 264–72.

Rabbitt, P. M. A. (1968). Three kinds of error signalling responses in a serial choice task. *Quarterly Journal of Experimental Psychology*, 20, 179–88.

Ragot, R. (1984). Perceptual and motor space representation: an event-related potential study. *Psychophysiology*, 21, 159–70.

Ragot, R. and Renault, B. (1981). P300 as a function of S–R compatibility and motor programming. *Biological Psychology*, 13, 289–94.

Ratcliff, R. A. (1978). A theory of memory retrieval. *Psychological Review*, 85, 59–108.

Remington, R. J. (1969). Analysis of sequential effects in choice reaction times. *Journal of Experimental Psychology*, 82, 250–7.

Renault, B., Ragot, R., Lesèvre, N., and Rémond, A. (1982). Onset and offset of brain events as indices of mental chronometry. *Science*, 215, 1413–15.

Requin, J., Riehle, A., and Seal, J. (1988). Neuronal activity and information processing in motor control: from stages to continuous flow. *Biological Psychology*, 26, 179–98.

Ritter, W., Simson, R., Vaughan, H. G., jun., and Friedman, D. (1979). A brain event related to the making of a sensory discrimination. *Science*, 203, 1358–61.

Ruchkin, D. S. and Sutton, S. (1978). Emitted P300 potentials and temporary uncertainty. *Electroencephalography and Neurophysiology*, 45, 268–77.

Rugg, M. D., Milner, A. D., Lines, C. R., and Phalp, R. (1987). Modulation of visual event-related potentials by spatial and non-spatial visual selective attention. *Neuropsychologia*, 15, 85–96.

Sanders, A. F. (1990). Issues and trends in the debate on discrete versus continuous processing of information. *Acta Psychologica*, 74, 123–67.

Sanders, A. F. (1993). Performance theory and measurement through chronometric analysis. In *Attention and performance XIV* (ed. D. E. Meyer, and S. Kornblum), pp. 689–99. MIT Press, Cambridge, MA

Scheffers, M. K., Johnson, R., jun., and Ruchkin, D. S. (1991). P300 in patients with unilateral temporal lobectomies: the effects of reduced stimulus quality. *Psychophysiology*, 28, 274–84.

Schmidt, R. A. and Gordon, G. B. (1977). Errors in motor responding, 'rapid' corrections, and false anticipations. *Journal of Motor Behavior*, 9, 101–11.

Schweickert, R. (1985). Separable effects of factors on speed and accuracy: memory scanning, lexical decision, and choice tasks. *Psychological Bulletin*, 106, 318–28.

Schweickert, R. (1993). Information, time, and the structure of mental events: A twenty-five-year review. In *Attention and performance XIV* (ed. D. E. Meyer and S. Kornblum), pp. 535–66. MIT Press, Cambridge, MA.

Schweickert, R. and Townsend, J. T. (1989). A trichotomy: interactions of factors prolonging sequential and concurrent mental processes in stochastic discrete mental (PERT) networks. *Journal of Mathematical Psychology*, 33, 328–47.

Shallice, T. (1975). On the contents of primary memory. In *Attention and performance V* (ed. P. M. A. Rabbitt and S. Dornie), pp. 269–80. Academic, London.

Simon, J. R. and Rudell, A. P. (1967). Auditory S-R compatibility: the effect of an irrelevant cue on information processing. *Journal of Applied Psychology*, 51, 300–4.

Smid, H. G. O. M., Lamain, W., Hogeboom, M. M., Mulder, G., and Mulder, L. J. M. (1991). Psychophysiological evidence for continuous information transmission between visual search and response processes. *Journal of Experimental Psychology: Human Perception and Performance*, 17, 696–714.

Smid, H. G. O. M., Mulder, G., and Mulder, L. J. M. (1990). Selective response activation can begin before stimulus recognition is complete: a psychophysiological and error analysis of continuous flow. *Acta Psychologica*, 74, 169–201.

Smid, H. G. O. M., Mulder, G., Mulder, L. J. M., and Brands, G. J. (1992). A psychophysiological study of the use of partial information in stimulus–response translation. *Journal of Experimental Psychology: Human Perception and Performance*, 18, 1101–19.

Smulders, F. T. Y. (1993). *The selectivity of age effects on information processing: response times and electrophysiology*. Universiteit van Amsterdam, Faculteit Psychologie, Amsterdam.

Squires, K. C., Wickens, C., Squires, N. K., and Donchin, E. (1976). The effect of stimulus sequence on the waveform of the cortical event-related potential. *Science*, 193, 1142–6.

Stanovich, K. E. and Pachella, R. G. (1977). Encoding, stimulus–response compatibility, and stages of processing. *Journal of Experimental Psychology: Human Perception and Performance*, 3, 411–21.

Sternberg, S. (1966). High speed scanning in human memory. *Science*, 153, 652–4.

Sternberg, S. (1969). The discovery of processing stages: extensions of Donders' method. In *Attention and performance II* (ed. W. G. Koster), pp. 276–315. North-Holland, Amsterdam.

Sternberg, S. (1975). Memory scanning: new findings and current controversies. *Quarterly Journal of Experimental Psychology*, 27, 1–32.

Stoffels, E. J., van der Molen, M. W., and Keuss, P. J. G. (1989). An additive factors analysis of the effect(s) of location cues associated with auditory stimuli on stages of information processing. *Acta Psychologica*, 70, 161–97.

Stroop, J. R. (1935). Studies of interference in serial verbal reactions. *Journal of Experimental Psychology*, 18, 643–62.

Stuss, D. T. and Benson, D. F., (1986). *The frontal lobes*. Raven, New York.

Sutton, S. Braren, M., Zubin, J., and John, E. R. (1965). Evoked potential correlates of stimulus uncertainty. *Science*, 150, 1187–8.

Townsend, J. T. (1974). Issues and models concerning the processing of a finite number of inputs. In *Human information processing: tutorials in performance and cognition* (ed. B. H. Kantowitz), pp. 133–85. Erlbaum, Hillsdale, NJ.

Townsend, J. T. and Ashby, F. G. (1983). *Stochastic modeling of elementary psychological processes*. Cambridge University Press.

van der Molen, M. W., Bashore, T. R., Halliday, R., and Callaway, E. (1991). Chronopsychophysiology: mental chronometry augmented by psychophysiological time markers. In *Handbook of cognitive psychophysiology: central and autonomic nervous system approaches* (ed. J. R. Jennings and M. G. H. Coles), pp. 9–178. Wiley, Chichester.

Wicklegren, W. A. (1977). Speed–accuracy trade-off and information processing dynamics. *Acta Psychologica*, 41, 67–85.

Wijers, A. A., Mulder, G., Okita, T., Mulder, L. J. M., and Scheffers, M. K. (1989a). Attention to color: An analysis of selection, controlled search, and motor activation, using event-related potentials. *Psychophysiology*, 26, 89–109.

Wijers, A. A., Mulder, G., Okita, T., and Mulder, L. J. M. (1989b). Event-related potentials during memory search and selective attention to letter size and conjunction of letter size and color. *Psychophysiology*, 26, 529–47.

Woodworth, R. S. (1899). The accuracy of voluntary movement. *Psychological Review*, 3, (2, Whole No. 13).

Woodworth, R. S. (1938). *Experimental psychology*. Holt, New York.

5 ERP studies of memory[*]

Michael D. Rugg

5.1 INTRODUCTION

This chapter reviews ERP studies of human memory. In doing so, some general assumptions are made about the relationship between ERPs and cognitive processing. The most important of these are first, that there is a relationship between the amplitude and latency of an ERP effect, and the strength and timing of the activity of the neural population(s) generating it. Second, that ERP effects with qualitatively different scalp distributions reflect different patterns of neural activity in the brain. Third, that different patterns of neural activity are most probably identifiable with functionally dissociable cognitive processes (see Chapter 2).

5.1.1 Scope of chapter

As noted by Kutas (1988), many ERP phenomena are reflections of memory, broadly defined. For example, there are several ERP components that are sensitive to stimulus probability, a property that presumably depends on processes sensitive to the relative frequency of events over time, that is, on some kind of memory mechanism. Indeed, it has been proposed that one such component, the 'mismatch negativity', directly reflects the operation of a preattentive acoustic memory system (see Chapter 3).

   This chapter will not consider all possible situations in which ERPs might be related to memory processes. Its aim is to provide a selective review of ERP studies of memory encoding and retrieval relevant to present-day cognitive and neuropsychological work on human long-term memory. Thus it will not cover studies of sensory memory mentioned above, nor will it consider the extensive literature concerning 'memory-scanning' tasks, which are largely of relevance to an understanding of short-term memory.

5.1.2 Overview of relevant memory research

There is now considerable evidence that memory performance relies on multiple processes or systems, which are tapped to different extents by different memory tasks (Richardson-Klavehn and Bjork 1988; Squire *et al*, 1993). A distinction that has become especially important in recent years is that between 'explicit' ('declara-

* This chapter is a revised and extended version of a contribution to Gazzaniga, M. S. (ed.) 1994 *The cognitive neurosciences* (MIT Press).

tive' or 'conscious') and 'implicit' ('non-declarative' or 'unconscious') memory. Explicit memory is usually assessed by 'direct' memory tests, such as free or cued recall, which make specific reference to a previous learning episode and encourage subjects to reflect on the content of their memories. By contrast, evidence of implicit memory is obtained when prior experience affects behaviour in the absence of any conscious retrieval of that experience. Typically, implicit memory is assessed with 'indirect' tests, the critical feature of which is that task performance can be influenced by, but is not dependent upon, memory for the study items. For example, in 'word stem completion' subjects first encounter a list of words (e.g. MOTEL) in a study task, and subsequently are presented with word stems (e.g. MOT——), some of which belong to the studied words. The instructions are to complete each stem with the first word to come to mind. Even when unaware of the relationship between study and test items, subjects are typically biased to complete stems with studied words rather than alternatives (e.g. MOTEL rather than MOTOR). Such biases or facilitation in performance on indirect tests arising from prior experience are often referred to as 'priming' effects.

Performance on direct and indirect memory tests can be dissociated both in normal subjects and, more dramatically, in neurological populations. Dissociations are especially strong in the amnesic syndrome, when entirely normal priming can coexist with a devastating impairment on tests such as free recall (for reviews see Shimamura 1989; Squire *et al.* 1993).

Whereas the empirical evidence for dissociations between performance on different kinds of memory task is largely uncontested (though see Jernigan and Ostergaard 1993), the same cannot be said of theoretical accounts of these dissociations. A major point of contention is whether dissociations between performance on direct and indirect memory tests should be interpreted as evidence for the existence of qualitatively different memory systems, which operate according to different functional principles, or whether they instead reflect the operation of different memory processes, which function within a single, functionally homogeneous system (cf. Roediger *et al.* 1989; Squire 1992).

An important issue stemming from a multiple-component view of memory concerns the difficulties inherent in identifying different forms of memory with different types of test. It has been argued that while explicit memory may best be revealed by direct tests, and implicit memory by indirect tests, it is difficult to ensure that these two kinds of test are 'process pure', that is, that test performance does not result from a mixing of the two kinds of memory (Dunn and Kirsner 1988; Jacoby and Kelley 1992).

This issue is especially important in light of the proposal that performance on tests of recognition memory can reflect the influence of more than one memory process. According to 'dual-process' theories of recognition memory (e.g. Jacoby and Kelley 1992; Mandler 1980), recognition performance is determined both by the probability that an item is recognized as 'old' on the basis of 'recollection' — the retrieval of information about the context in which an item was last encountered — and on the basis of its 'familiarity' — the feeling that an item has recently been encountered in the absence of any specific knowledge about where and when the encounter occurred. It has been argued that the 'familiarity component' of recognition memory depends on the same processes that underlie priming, and arises because subjects are sensitive to the ease (or 'fluency'; Jacoby and Dallas 1981) with which they identify test items. Items identified relatively fluently (as in the case of those 'primed' by a recent prior presentation) will engender higher levels of familiarity, compared with a pretest baseline, than if they had not recently been encountered (that is, they will have higher levels of relative familiarity). Relative familiarity can therefore serve as a basis for judging whether an item has recently been experienced independently of the outcome of recollection.

While recollection can clearly be identified as an example of explicit memory, the place of the familiarity component of recognition within the framework provided by the explicit/implicit dichotomy is less certain. As noted above, it has been claimed that familiarity depends upon the same processes that are responsible for implicit memory phenomena such as priming. It is unclear, however, whether these processes are sufficient to permit familiarity-based responding in tests of recognition memory, as argued for example by Jacoby and Kelley (1992), or whether processes additional to those mediating priming are also necessary. An extensive discussion of this issue can be found in Mayes (1992).

This and other unresolved issues mean that the validity and generality of dual-process accounts of recognition are not without controversy, especially in regard to explanations of the relationship between recognition and recall in amnesia (cf. Haist *et al.* 1992; Verfaille and Treadwell 1993). The outcome of this debate has implications both for the theoretical understanding of memory and for the interpretation of patterns of performance by normal subjects and memory-impaired patients on tests of recognition memory.

Another important issue in memory research concerns the nature of the encoding processes that promote the formation of durable memories. One aspect of this question concerns the relationship between how an item is processed at study and its subsequent retrievability. Perhaps the most influential body of work on the role of encoding processes in memory stems from the 'levels of processing' framework (Craik and Lockhart 1972). In its original form, this framework was predicated on the assumption that the memorability of an item increases as a function of its 'depth' of processing, such that items processed to the level of their physical features are less likely to be remembered than those subjected to phonological processing, which in turn are less memorable than semantically processed items. Since its original formulation, the framework has been subjected to revision (e.g. Craik and Tulving 1975), and has been criticized for its apparent circularity (Baddeley 1978). However, the terminology introduced with the theory, and the experimental manipulations found reliably to influence memory performance, live on, and have permeated some of the ERP work discussed in the next section.

An important intellectual cousin of the levels of processing framework is the principle of 'transfer appropriate processing'. This term originated in the work of Morris *et al.* (1977), and is related to such concepts as Tulving's encoding specificity principle (Tulving 1983). The most prominent recent proponents of transfer appropriate processing as a framework for understanding the relationship between encoding and retrieval have been Roediger and his associates (e.g. Roediger *et al.* 1989).

The essence of the transfer appropriate processing principle is that the probability of retrieval is largely determined by the amount and specificity of the overlap between processing carried out at study and test. This principle has been invoked to account for levels of processing effects on tests such as recall and recognition. It has been argued that when confronted with such tests, subjects tend to adopt a 'conceptually driven' mode of processing, which leads to the use of semantic features of target items as retrieval cues (Roediger *et al.* 1989). When memory is probed in this way, 'encoding efficacy' will therefore be found to depend heavily on the amount and nature of the semantic processing that took place during study, since the greater the semantic processing at study, the greater will be the overlap with processing engaged at test. On the other hand, if tests are employed which encourage 'data-driven' processing — processing which emphasizes the operations needed to form a perceptual representation of the input — variation in conceptually driven processing at study will have little influence, and performance will be dependent on the similarity of the perceptual processing engaged at study and test. According to Roediger and colleagues, most indirect memory tests, for example word stem completion, are strongly data driven. Thus performance on these tests is highly sensitive to changes between study and test in physical format (e.g. input modality), but is largely insensitive to 'classical' levels of processing manipulations.

It remains to be seen exactly how such 'processing' accounts of dissociations of performance on different types of memory test will mesh with the commonly held notion that such dissociations reveal the operation of functionally and neurologically independent memory 'systems'. None the less, one lesson from this approach is clear: the question of what constitutes effective memory encoding makes sense only if the conditions under which the encoded information is to be retrieved are specified.

5.2 ERPs AND MEMORY

ERPs are useful in principle in memory research for several reasons. First, they have high temporal resolution. Thus they are well suited to addressing questions about the time-course of brain activity associated with memory processes, for example by providing an upperbound estimate of the time required to discriminate 'new' from 'old' items in tests of recognition memory.

Second, ERPs can be used as 'covert' measures of processing in the absence of overt behavioural responding, allowing one to investigate, for example, whether new and old items evoke differential brain activity when no discriminative response is required.

Third, comparison of the spatial distribution over the scalp of ERP effects can be used to assess whether stimuli from different experimental conditions evoke

different patterns of neural activity, and hence whether they might engage functionally distinct processes. Different patterns of activity evoked by items repeated in
indirect and direct memory tests could, for example, constitute evidence that the
two types of test engage different cognitive processes (see Chapter 2 for caveats
associated with such reasoning).

Finally, as knowledge of the functional significance and intracerebral origins of
ERPs accumulates, they will provide a method for the 'on-line' monitoring of the
neural activity underlying specific cognitive processes.

There are of course serious limitations to the use of ERPs in memory research.
Many of these arise because ERP waveforms can only be used to study processes
that are time-locked to some detectable event. For example, activities such as
rehearsal or free recall are unlikely to be suitable for study with current ERP
techniques, since there is no obvious event to which ERPs could be time-locked.

There have been sporadic reports of ERP studies of memory since the early
1970s. Until the mid-1980s, the bulk of these were conducted within the 'memory-
scanning' paradigm introduced by Sternberg (1966) (see Kutas (1988) for a
review), and had little to say about encoding or retrieval operations in long-term
memory. The past decade has seen a proliferation of ERP studies in this area. As
in the area of memory research as a whole, however, these ERP studies have
focused largely on verbal memory, and indeed have usually employed visually
presented words (see Friedman (1990*a*) and Noldy *et al.* (1990) for exceptions);
considerably more ERP work on non-verbal memory is needed to redress the
balance.

5.3 STUDIES OF MEMORY ENCODING

The general experimental approach taken by ERP researchers to the question of
memory encoding has involved variations on a single paradigm. The essence of
the paradigm is the presentation of a series of items in a study task, during which
EEG epochs time-locked to the presentation of each item are sampled and separately
stored. Subsequently, memory for these items is tested. The EEG sampled at study
is then used to form two classes of ERP, associated respectively with successfully
and unsuccessfully retrieved items. These ERPs can be inspected for differences
that led to some items apparently being encoded more effectively than others. For
ease of exposition, such ERP differences are referred to below as a 'subsequent
memory effect'. This term is preferred to the term 'Dm' (difference due to
memory), introduced by Paller *et al.* (1987*a*). Although intended by Paller *et al.*
to be purely descriptive, a label such as Dm can too easily be taken to imply the
existence of a single component or mechanism responsible for subsequent memory
effects, and worse, that this mechanism has causal role in memory encoding. As
will become clear in this section, neither of these conclusions is justified by the
available evidence, hence the preference for a more overtly neutral term.

The first study along the lines described above was by Sanquist *et al.* (1980).
Subjects performed 'same-different' judgements on sequentially presented pairs

of words on the basis of orthographic, phonological, or semantic attributes. For a few subjects only, sufficient trials existed to average ERPs evoked at study as a function of subsequent memory performance. In the phonological and semantic tasks, ERPs to studied word pairs were more positive-going when evoked by subsequently recognized rather than unrecognized words.

Interpretation of the subsequent memory effect described by Sanquist *et al.* (1980) is complicated by the fact that the two types of study ERP contained different proportions of items associated with 'same' and 'different' responses. None the less, their finding has stood the test of time; to date, all reports of subsequent memory effects have found subsequently remembered items to evoke more positive-going ERPs.

In a series of studies, Fabiani and colleagues investigated the relationship between ERPs evoked by words at study and the words' subsequent retrievability (Fabiani *et al.* 1986, 1990*a*, *b*; Karis *et al.* 1984; for review see Donchin and Fabiani 1991). In all but Fabiani *et al.* (1986), a 'Von Restorff' procedure was employed. In this procedure, a series of items is presented, one of which (the isolate) deviates in some way from the others. The Von Restorff effect refers to the better memory shown for isolates than for other members of the study list. In the experiments of Fabiani and colleagues, subjects viewed short lists of visually presented words. An isolation effect was created by presenting one of the words in letters of a different size from that of the remainder of the items on the list. The rationale for this procedure derived from two hypotheses: (i) the amplitude of the P300 component (see Chapter 1) indexes the extent to which an evoking item causes a revision of the contents of 'working memory' (or, in Donchin's (1981) terminology, to 'context updating'); and (ii) items that give rise to extensive revision will be especially memorable. Isolated words in the Von Restorff paradigm will, as a consequence of their low probability, evoke especially large P300 components, so the hypothesized relationship between context updating, P300, and memory can be addressed by comparing the amplitudes of the P300s evoked by remembered and unremembered isolated words.

In the first experiment in this series (Karis *et al.* 1984), study items were presented under intentional memory instructions. Subjects were segregated *post hoc* on the basis of whether they showed large or small Von Restorff indices (a measure of the relative recall advantage of isolated over non-isolated words). The three subjects with the highest indices reported adopting 'rote' mnemonic strategies, while the three with the smallest indices reported the use of 'elaborative' strategies (the term elaborative refers not so much to the integration or association of a target item with existing knowledge, as to the explicit use of mnemonic aids, and the construction of inter-item associations). In both rote and elaborative groups, ERPs to the isolates differed as a function of subsequent memory performance, in that they were more positive-going when evoked by subsequently recalled than unrecalled words (see Fig 5.1). However, Karis *et al.* argued that in the rote subjects this effect resulted from the modulation of a parietal-maximum P300 component, while in elaborators it was associated with changes in the amplitude of a frontal-maximum 'slow positive wave'. Karis *et al.* (1984) found that ERPs evoked by

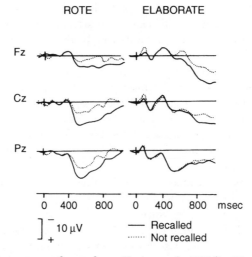

Fig. 5.1 Grand-average waveforms from Karis *et al.* (1984), illustrating ERPs from midline electrodes evoked by 'isolated' study words that were subsequently recalled or not recalled. ROTE: ERPs averaged over the three subjects using a rote strategy to remember the study items; ELABORATE; ERPs averaged over the three subjects using elaborative mnemonic strategies at study. (Adapted from Donchin and Fabiani (1991) with permission. Copyright © J. Wiley & Sons Ltd 1991.)

non-isolated words were also more positive-going for subsequently recalled as opposed to unrecalled words, although the P300s in these ERPs were smaller than for the isolated words

Fabiani *et al.* (1986) studied ERPs to recalled and unrecalled words in an incidental memory task. Subjects performed different versions of an 'oddball' task involving intermingled male and female names. The task was followed by an unanticipated memory test for the names. ERPs to words that were later recalled were once again more positive-going than those to unrecalled words, an effect that was attributed entirely to modulation of the P300 component.

Returning to the Von Restorff paradigm, Fabiani *et al.* (1990*a*) investigated the effects of manipulating mnemonic strategy directly. In separate sessions, subjects were required either to rehearse study items by rote or by 'elaboration'. Study ERPs were more positive-going for recalled than non-recalled items in both conditions. In the elaboration condition this effect was confined largely to the frontal electrode, whereas in the rote condition the effect was distributed more posteriorly, involving what Fabiani *et al.* took to be the P300 component. All effects were as evident in the ERPs evoked by non-isolated as by isolated words.

Donchin and Fabiani (1991) offered a theoretical account of the findings from this series of experiments. This account was based on the idea that 'non-elaborative' mnemonic strategies lead to a subsequent memory effect arising from modulation of the P300 component, while elaborative strategies are associated with ERP differences in a separate component, a frontal-maximum positive wave.

They suggested that this latter effect may be an index of 'extended processing' (Donchin and Fabiani 1991, p. 489), processing which overrides the mnemonic benefits of the encoding processes reflected by the P300. Donchin and Fabiani further hypothesized that the subsequent memory effect in P300 reflects variations in item 'distinctiveness'. In the absence of elaborative processing, the relative distinctiveness of the physical attributes of words is an important determinant of the efficacy of memory encoding, and underlies the recall advantage of isolated over non-isolated words in the Von Restorff paradigm. Donchin and Fabiani (1991) hypothesized that the amplitude of P300 is proportional to the 'subjective distinctiveness' (Donchin and Fabiani 1991, p. 488) of the stimulus evoking it. Hence, to the extent that performance at test reflects variations in the subjective distinctiveness of study items, there will be a relationship between P300 at study and subsequent memory performance.

It is hard to evaluate Donchin and Fabiani's claim that the 'frontal positive wave' and the P300 component are dissociated by memory strategy. The data certainly suggest that rote and elaborative strategies can be associated with subsequent memory effects that differ over posterior scalp regions, and there is no reason why this strategy-dependent difference should not include the differential involvement of the generators of the P300. It has, however, yet to be demonstrated that the subsequent memory effect in rote memorizers does not include a contribution from the 'frontal positive wave'. For example, in some of the conditions of Fabiani *et al.* (1986), the subsequent memory effect is of equal magnitude, or is larger, at the mid-frontal than the mid-parietal electrode, a scalp distribution at variance with that of the prominent, mid-parietal maximum P300 wave evident in their waveforms. And in Fabiani *et al.* (1990*a*), the subsequent memory effect attributable to the frontal slow wave was apparently of equal magnitude in the rote and elaborate conditions (as indexed by the absence of a significant strategy by memory effect interaction).

As mentioned above, Donchin and Fabiani propose that when encoding is 'non-elaborative', subsequent memory effects are attributable to the P300 component, and are mediated by variations in distinctiveness. This view has further implications for the expected scalp distribution of these effects. Specifically, they should have the same scalp distribution as the differences in the amplitude of P300s evoked by isolates and non-isolates, as these differences too are considered to reflect variations in subjective distinctiveness. These predictions about scalp distribution have yet to be subjected to formal test.

Finally, Donchin and Fabiani's (1991) hypothesis seems predicated on the assumption that variations in recall within a sample of physically distinctive items (e.g. physical isolates in the Von Restorff paradigm) is largely attributable to variation along the same dimension that makes these items, as a class, easier to remember; that is, to differences in their 'subjective distinctiveness'. Unless the concept of distinctiveness is to be operationalized in terms of recall probability, with all the problems of circularity that this would entail, the basis for this assumption is unclear (see Schmidt (1991) for a review of the concept of distinctiveness, and the problems involved in defining and measuring it). There seems no reason to assume that, *within* a sample of physically distinctive items, relative distinctiveness is the most important determinant of recall probability.

In contrast to Donchin and Fabiani (1991), other investigators have been more circumspect in ascribing subsequent memory effects to the modulation of specific ERP components, although it has been argued that these effects do not involve the generators responsible for the N400 component (Neville *et al.* 1986).

Neville *et al.* (1986) examined the relationship between study ERPs and subsequent memory for words presented in a semantic judgement task. On each trial, subjects saw a four-word phrase, followed by a fifth word that either fitted or did not fit the sense of the phrase. The task was to respond discriminatively on the basis of the appropriateness of the word. ERPs to subsequently recognized target words that fitted their context were more positive-going than those to un-recognized 'fit' words. As shown in Figure 5.2, this difference onset at around 250 ms, and persisted beyond the recording epoch of 1200 ms. Study ERPs to recognized and unrecognized 'no-fit' words showed very similar differences, also shown in Figure 5.2, with the important exception that these differences did not emerge until 400–500 ms post-stimulus. As is typical for ERPs evoked by words that are semantically unrelated to a prior context, they contained a prominent N400 component. This was of equivalent size for recognized and unrecognized words, and 'occupied' a region of the waveform that, in the ERPs evoked by 'fit' words, already showed a subsequent memory effect. Similar findings were reported by Kutas (1988), who employed a cued recall rather than a recognition memory

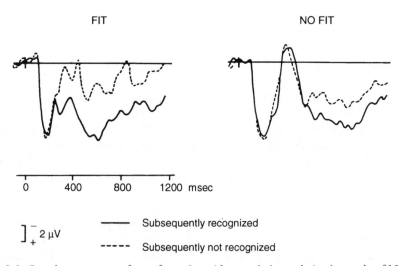

Fig. 5.2 Grand-average waveforms from the mid-central electrode in the study of Neville *et al.* (1986), evoked by words during a semantic judgement task and averaged according to whether the words were subsequently recognized. Note the prominent N400 wave in the waveforms evoked by words that did not fit their semantic context (no-fit), and the relatively late onset of the subsequent memory effect. (Adapted with permission of the authors and publisher. Copyright © Academic Press Inc. 1986.)

task, and tested memory for words that terminated sentences either congruously or incongruously.

Neville *et al.* (1986) interpreted their subsequent memory effects as reflecting differences in the 'elaborative/consolidation procedures' (Neville *et al.* 1986, p. 89) undergone by words as they are encoded into memory. They further argued that the later onset of these effects in the ERPs to the inappropriate words may have been responsible for the relatively poor memory exhibited for these items.

Paller and associates have reported several studies of ERPs and memory encoding. In the first of these studies (Paller *et al.* 1987*a*), ERPs were obtained during incidental 'same/different' tasks that varied with level of processing; two of the tasks required matching on semantic attributes, and two on non-semantic attributes. When study ERPs were averaged on the basis either of subsequent recall or recognition accuracy, they were found to be more positive-going when evoked by remembered than by forgotten items. This effect was found in all tasks, although it was larger for those requiring semantic processing, and indeed, was larger for one of the semantic tasks (edible/non-edible discriminations) than the other (living/non-living judgements). Paller *et al.* concluded that ERP subsequent memory effects did not merely reflect the extent of semantic processing accorded study words. They suggested that the effect might instead reflect the degree of 'associative' processing undergone by words once their meanings had been derived. On the basis of a number of dissociations between a late positive component they identified as the P300, and their ERP subsequent memory effect, they concluded that the effect could not be accounted for in terms of the modulation solely of the P300.

In another experiment (Paller *et al.* 1987*b*), ERPs evoked by words in an incidental study task (judgement of concreteness) were averaged as a function of performance on two direct tests (free recall and recognition) and one indirect (stem completion) test of memory. Study ERPs did not reliably differentiate subsequently recognized or recalled words, but did differentiate words that were subsequently given as stem completions from those that were not (an effect more prominent for words of high than low frequency of occurrence). These findings were interpreted as suggesting that subsequent memory effects in ERPs index some general level of 'activation' of a word's memory representation, rather than the encoding operations important for the formation of episodic memories. A subsequent study (Paller *et al.* 1988) found evidence for a difference between two direct memory tasks, recognition and recall. Subsequent memory effects were larger, and indeed were only reliable, for the recall task.

Paller (1990) returned to the question of whether ERP subsequent memory effects were specific to one form of memory. ERPs were recorded in a 'directed forgetting task', in which detection of occasional target words embedded in a list was combined with the need to remember half of the words on the list, and to 'forget' the remainder (a distinction cued by the colour of the words). Three tests of retrieval were given: half the subjects received a cued recall test, in which the three-letter stems of critical study words served as cues. The remaining subjects received a stem completion test in which the same stems were intermixed with

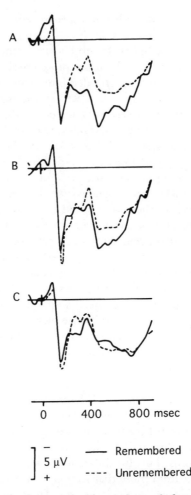

Fig. 5.3 Grand-average waveforms evoked by study words from the mid-parietal electrode in the study of Paller (1990). A, averaged according to whether words were subsequently freely recalled. B, averaged according to whether the words were successfully recalled in a cued recall task. C, averaged according to whether the words were subsequently employed to complete word stems in a stem completion task. (Adapted from Paller (1990). Copyright © the American Psychological Association 1990.)

others that could not be completed by study words. All subjects then received a test of free recall. ERP subsequent memory effects were found for both recall tests, but not for the stem completion test (see Fig. 5.3). The effects appeared to onset earlier and to be larger with free recall than cued recall, but as the effects in the different tasks were not directly compared it is unclear whether these differences were reliable.

Paller interpreted these findings as evidence that explicit and implicit memory rely on qualitatively different encoding processes. This interpretation may be premature, however, in light of the fact that in a previous study (Paller *et al*, 1987*b*), ERP subsequent memory effects *were* found for the stem completion task. The discrepancy between the studies is associated with marked differences in stem completion performance. In Paller *et al.* (1987*b*), almost 60 per cent of word stems were completed, against a baseline (guessing) level of around 12 per cent. By contrast, in the experiment of Paller (1990), only about 20 per cent of stems were correctly completed, against a baseline rate of 10 per cent.

Two possible resolutions of the discrepant ERP findings suggest themselves. First, it could be that study ERPs are indeed sensitive to the processes under-lying priming, as manifest in the stem completion task. In the Paller (1990) study, however, these differences were 'diluted' because 50 per cent or so of the trials used to form the relevant study ERPs were associated with words given as completions by chance. Paller (1990) rejected this possibility on the grounds that the scalp distributions of the ERP subsequent memory effects for the cued recall and stem completion tasks differed; a rather unsatisfactory argument in view of the fact that, according to the statistical analyses, there were no such effects in the completion task. A second way of accounting for the discrepancies between Paller *et al.* (1987*b*) and Paller (1990) is to assume that the true state of affairs is indeed as suggested by Paller (1990). By this argument, the (very high) completion performance in the previous study resulted from 'contamination' of the completion task by explicit memory, subjects treating the task as one of cued recall.

Even if this second account is correct, it is still not clear that Paller's (1990) data point to a qualitative rather than a quantitative difference in subsequent memory effects for tests tapping explicit and implicit memory. As already noted, cued recall (a putative test of explicit memory) seemingly gave rise to smaller sub-sequent memory effects than did free recall (another test of explicit memory). Until a principled account can be given for such differences between tests supposedly dependent on the same form of memory, it will not be clear what status should be given to differences between tests putatively tapping different forms of memory.

Smith (1993) reported findings consistent with the idea that different forms of recognition memory have at least some encoding processes in common. He tested recognition with a procedure designed to segregate recognized test items into those that evoked 'recollective experiences', as opposed to those judged old solely on the basis of a feeling of familiarity (see Section 5.4.2.2 for further details of this procedure and its rationale). Recollective experiences are thought to depend on the same processes responsible for explicit memory of items in other kinds of direct memory test. By contrast, non-recollective recognition judgements show many of the functional properties of implicit memory, and are held to depend on the same processes (e.g. Gardiner and Parkin 1990). Smith (1993) found, how-ever, that subsequent memory effects were equally large for items attracting either type of recognition judgement, a finding that sits uncomfortably with Paller's (1990) interpretation of his failure to find subsequent memory effects for the stem completion task.

5.3.1 ERPs and memory encoding — conclusions

The findings reviewed above offer rather limited scope for generalization. Clearly, there are circumstances in which ERPs recorded at study discriminate words on the basis of whether the words are subsequently remembered. When this effect has been found, it has invariably involved greater positivity in the ERPs evoked by the subsequently remembered items. In several studies, this positivity has taken the form of a sustained, frontal-maximum wave; in others, the effect has had an even distribution over the midline, or a posterior maximum. In at least one study in which lateral electrodes were employed (Neville *et al.*, 1986), the effect was larger over the left than the right hemisphere. Thus it is likely that multiple ERP components are involved in the effect; their number, identity, and the circumstances under which each makes its contribution remain to be ascertained.

What conclusions do these findings permit about memory encoding? Evidently, some of the processes that make a study item memorable may be active as early as 300–400 ms post-stimulus, even in intentional learning tasks when subjects are presumably engaging in mnemonic processing that extends beyond the recording epoch. The data of Neville *et al.* (1986) and Kutas (1988) further suggest that the processes associated with ERP subsequent memory effects, whatever their identity, are incompatible with certain other kinds of cognitive operation, such as those responsible for dealing with semantic incongruity. Furthermore, the differing scalp distributions of the effects, both within and across studies, suggest that they cannot all be attributed to a single non-specific variable such as the level of arousal at the time of presentation, or degree of 'effort' expended in item processing.

It is difficult to see what further generalizations about memory encoding can be made from this work at present. Thus while there seems good cause for optimism that this approach will provide an important means of studying processes that determine how effectively an item is encoded into memory, little information about the nature of these processes has yet been obtained. If progress along these lines can be made, it may be possible to use ERP subsequent memory effects as an independent measure of encoding effectiveness, thereby 'breaking the circle' created by the need to make inferences about efficacy of encoding solely on the basis of subsequent memory performance (cf. Baddeley 1978).

One way forward from the studies reviewed here might be to give more emphasis to the question of the compatibility between encoding and retrieval operations than hitherto. As discussed in Section 5.1.2, there are grounds for thinking that a critical variable influencing the likelihood of retrieval is the degree of the overlap between processing carried out at study and test. In this light, the implications for future ERP work seem clear: a better understanding of the nature of ERP subsequent memory effects will probably have to await studies in which both encoding and retrieval operations are systematically manipulated. To give one example, it would be of considerable interest to know whether, if study-test compatibility is maintained, data-driven and conceptually-driven encoding/retrieval processes give rise to similar patterns of ERP subsequent memory effect.

5.4. STUDIES OF MEMORY RETRIEVAL — REPETITION EFFECTS AND RECOGNITION MEMORY

The second principal means by which memory processing has been studied with ERPs is by comparing waveforms evoked by items presented in an experimental setting on the first or a subsequent occasion, that is, by comparing 'new' and 'old' items. Numerous such experiments have been conducted using both indirect and direct tests, and both kinds of experiment will be reviewed in this section (see Rugg and Doyle (1994) for a more detailed review of studies employing indirect tests).

5.4.1 ERP repetition effects in indirect tests

There is a sizeable literature on the modulation of ERPs by the repetition of words and other stimuli in indirect memory tests (see, for example, Bentin and Peled 1990; Besson *et al*, 1992; Hamberger and Friedman 1992; Karayanidis *et al*. 1991; Rugg 1987, 1990; Rugg *et al*. 1988; Van Petten *et al*. 1991). Several of these studies have employed a task in which subjects must respond to occasional 'target' items (e.g. non-words) against a background of repeating 'non-targets' (e.g. words), and in which repetition has been over intervals of less than a minute. In such studies, ERPs evoked by repeated items have consistently been found to be more positive-going than those to first presentations, (e.g. see Fig. 5.4). This effect — the ERP repetition effect — has been exploited to investigate such questions as the nature of the interaction between word frequency and repetition (Rugg 1990; Van Petten *et al*. 1991; Young and Rugg 1992), the effects of repeating words across rather than within sensory modalities (Rugg *et al*. 1993), and the role of selective attention in word identification (Otten *et al*. 1993). The sensitivity of ERPs to item repetition in indirect tests naturally raises the question of whether ERP repetition effects reflect the same processes that are responsible for 'repetition priming' effects on task performance.

Repetition priming refers to the facilitatory effects of prior exposure on an item's subsequent processing. It has generally been studied either in tasks requiring speeded decisions (e.g. lexical decision), when priming is indexed by faster reaction times to repeated than unrepeated items, or in tasks requiring items to be identified under degraded viewing conditions, when the benefits of repetition take the form of increased probability of correct identification (for a review see Schacter *et al*. (1993)). These tasks are examples of indirect memory tests, in that performance can be influenced by, but is not dependent upon, prior experience with the critical items. And the phenomenon of repetition priming is an example of implicit memory, in that it is relatively insensitive to many of the variables that influence explicit memory, and can be normal even in severely amnesic patients (Schacter *et al*. 1993).

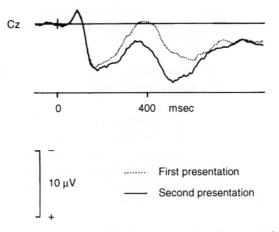

Fig. 5.4 The ERP repetition effect. Grand-average ERPs from a mid-central electrode elicited by non-target words presented for the first versus the second time (inter-item lag of six) in a task requiring button presses to infrequently occurring targets (animal names in this example).

Clearly, a repetition effect on ERPs can only occur if the brain is in some way responding differentially to repeated and unrepeated items, in other words, if it is exhibiting some form of memory. The fact that such effects can be observed when the interval between successive presentations exceeds the capacity of short-term memory (Nagy and Rugg 1989) indicates that these effects involve more than the matching of an item to a representation in short-term memory. What cannot be assumed, however, is that merely because ERP repetition effects have been observed in tasks resembling those used to demonstrate repetition priming on, say, reaction time, it follows that these effects reflect the same processes as the behavioural phenomena. Indeed, showing that an ERP effect is an expression of implicit rather than explicit memory presents formidable methodological difficulties. A convincing demonstration that an ERP effect is a reflection of implicit memory requires evidence that the effect occurs without awareness of prior experience with the test item, and that it is insensitive to experimental variables known selectively to influence explicit memory (e.g. depth of processing). In short, to establish an ERP 'correlate' of implicit memory, it is not sufficient merely to record ERPs in indirect memory tests resembling those used to study the effects of implicit memory on behaviour.

Despite the indirect nature of the tasks in which they have been studied, there are two reasons why ERP repetition effects shed little light on implicit memory. First, the nature of these studies makes it impossible to determine which, if any, aspect of these effects is independent of subjects' awareness that they are processing repeated rather than unrepeated items. Second, the repetition effects evoked by isolated words are rather short-lived, dissipating in less than 15 min (Rugg 1990). This finding stands in marked contrast to the effects of repetition on behavioural performance; a single exposure of a word can be sufficient to facilitate its sub-sequent processing in lexical decision and perceptual identification tasks hours or even days later (e.g. Jacoby 1983; Scarborough *et al.* 1977). Thus even if the ERP repetition effects described in the studies cited above should turn out to be independent of explicit memory, their fragility over time suggests that they reflect only a subset of the processes mediating implicit memory for words in behavioural tasks.

5.4.1.1 The context integration hypothesis

Rugg and Doyle (1994) rejected the notion that ERP repetition effects are associ-ated with implicit memory. The starting point for their argument was that these effects arise in large part through the modulation of the intensively researched N400 component (see Chapter 6). They proposed that the amplitude of N400 is correlated with the ease with which the evoking stimulus can be integrated or associated with the context in which it is presented (see also Halgren and Smith 1987; Rugg 1990). Thus in the now classical paradigm used to modulate the N400 — terminating a sentence with unpredictable, semantically incongruent versus predictable, semantically congruent words (Kutas and Hillyard 1980) — the larger N400 evoked by incongruent endings is held to reflect the greater difficulty of intergrating such items with the context provided by the preceding items. Rugg and Doyle (1994) argued that a similar account could be given for the sensitivity of N400 to semantic priming manipulations with isolated words (e.g. Bentin *et al.* 1985; Rugg 1985); namely, that words are easier to integrate with a preceding context that includes a semantic associate (doctor-→NURSE) as compared to an unrelated item (lecture→NURSE). Rugg and Doyle suggested that like sentential and semantic priming, repetition too can modify the ease with which an item can be integrated or assimilated with its context. They proposed that contextual integration is facilitated when an item re-occurs in the same context, leading to a smaller N400 component and a more positive-going ERP.

Rugg and Doyle went on to argue that their hypothesis extended beyond ERP repetition effects associated with words. They proposed that N400 was generated in response to any item that could be represented by a unitized code — a code that uniquely represented the item within some domain of processing. They argued that any such code (semantic, lexical, phonological, etc.) could be subjected to contextual integration, and hence would lead both to the generation of an N400, and to the attenuation of N400 with repetition. For instance, since orthographic-ally legal non-words (e.g. BLINT) can be coded phonologically, they should evoke ERP repetition effects. By contrast, orthographically illegal non-words (e.g. FKHRA) cannot easily be coded, and hence will neither generate N400s nor show large ERP repetition effects. This pattern of results was reported by Rugg and Nagy (1987). In further support of their argument, Rugg and Doyle (1994) described a study (conducted in collaboration with S. Thomas, M. Harries, and D. Perrett) of the effects of repetition on ERPs evoked by meaningful and non-meaningful pictures. As predicted, repetition of meaningful pictures led to a positive-going repetition effect, whereas no such effect was found with the meaningless stimuli.

Rugg and Doyle further argued that their context integration hypothesis was compatible with the results of two studies investigating the consequences of repeating words that formed the terminal items of short sentences (Besson *et al.* 1992; Besson and Kutas 1993). Besson *et al.* (1992) found that the repetition of sentences containing predictable, congruent endings had very little effect on the ERPs evoked by their terminal words, whereas the sizeable N400 component evoked by terminal words of incongruent sentences was markedly attenuated on repetition. In a further study, Besson and Kutas (1993) employed sentences with congruous but unpredictable terminal words. They found that the attenuation of N400 caused by the repetition of the terminal words was context-dependent: no repetition effect was observed when the same word was used to terminate two different sentences, and repetition of a preceding sentence fragment had only a small effect on the amplitude of the N400 evoked by a new terminal word.

Within the framework of Rugg and Doyle (1994), the finding that the ERPs evoked by predictable, congruent terminal words are relatively insensitive to repetition reflects the fact that such words are easy to integrate with their preceding context when presented for the first time, and hence evoke little or no N400 activity even before repetition. By contrast, unpredictable terminal words are difficult to integrate when the sentences are first presented. Repetition of such sentences reinstates the context in which the terminal word was first processed. This reinstatement facilitates the integration of the word relative to the first time the sentence was presented, and the amplitude of the N400 evoked by the word diminishes accordingly. When a word is repeated in a new context, integration must begin anew, and the N400 resembles that evoked by unrepeated words. (Despite their compatibility with the context integration hypothesis, it should be noted that the congruence between the studies of Besson *et al.* (1992) and Besson and Kutas (1993), and those in which ERP repetition effects are evoked by the repetition of isolated items in lists, might be more apparent than real. After the first presentation of the list of sentences, Besson and Kutas (1993) carried out a cued recall test in which subjects had to retrieve the terminal word of each sentence in response to the cue provided by the preceding sentence fragment. When the sentences were subsequently repeated in their entirety, ERP repetition effects were found only for terminal words that had been correctly retrieved in the intervening test of cued recall. Thus it would appear that ERP repetition effects for sentence endings are confined to items that subjects are able explicitly to predict from prior context.)

The parsimony of the context integration hypothesis of the modulation of N400 by item repetition is appealing. It is therefore unfortunate that a direct test of the hypothesis (Rugg *et al.* 1994*a*) failed to find any evidence in its favour. In this study, items were presented on each trial in pairs, on the assumption that each item would form part of the context of the processing of its partner. The critical contrast was between ERPs evoked by items repeated under two conditions.

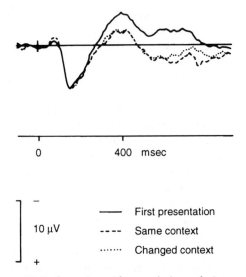

Fig. 5.5 Grand-average ERPs from the mid-central electrode in experiment 2 of Rugg *et al.* (1994*a*). First presentation-word pairs presented for first time. Same context-pairs of words repeated in same pairing as when first presented. Changed context-repeated words, re-paired between first and second presentations.

In the 'same context' condition, words were repeated in the same pairing as when first presented, whereas in the 'changed context' condition, repeated words were re-paired between first and second presentations. According to the context integration hypothesis, ERP repetition effects should have been larger for the same than for the changed-context condition. In three separate experiments, this result failed to materialize (see, for example, Fig. 5.5).

In the light of these findings, the validity of the context integration hypothesis of ERP repetition effects must be called into question. Unfortunately, no alternative hypothesis currently exists that can account for the diversity of the circumstances in which these effects are observed.

5.4.1.2 *ERP repetition effects and implicit memory*

It was mentioned earlier that the fragility of ERP repetition effects over time meant that the effects were very unlikely to reflect processes responsible for long-lasting repetition priming. This does not mean that the effects may not be associated with processes supporting more short-lived manifestations of implicit memory. The findings from two studies of ERP repetition effects in memory-impaired individuals suffering from Alzheimer's-type dementia are consistent with this possibility (Friedman *et al.* 1992; Rugg *et al.* 1994*b*). In both of these studies, Alzheimer patients exhibited ERP word repetition effects that were statistically indistinguishable from those of age-matched controls, even when several items intervened between first and second presentations of the critical items. Friedman *et al.* (1992) argued that since it is known that relatively intact implicit memory can coexist in Alzheimer's disease alongside severely impaired explicit memory, their findings were consistent with the idea that ERP repetition effects reflect some form of implicit memory.

This conclusion is premature, given the available evidence. The findings of Friedman *et al.* (1992) and Rugg *et al.* (1994*b*) show that ERP repetition effects are remarkably robust in the face of severe memory pathology, and indicate that the effects are not heavily dependent on those processes subserving explicit memory that are compromised in Alzheimer's disease. But this does not mean that ERP repetition effects are independent of those processes. In neither study was it ascertained whether Alzheimer's patients could explicitly detect the repetition of words over the interitem lags employed to evoke the ERP repetition effects, leaving open the possibility that the patients were aware of the repeating items. It therefore remains to be established whether preserved ERP repetition effects in Alzheimer's disease are wholly independent of explicit memory.

Bentin *et al.* (1992) have claimed that, even in young normal subjects, differences between ERPs evoked by repeated and unrepeated words can indeed occur in the absence of explicit memory. In their experiments, an initial incidental study task was followed by a recognition memory test, in which words from the study task had to be discriminated from new words. There then followed a lexical decision task, in which words new to the experiment were presented along with words from the two preceding tasks. In this last task, ERPs were increasingly more positive as a function of the number of prior exposures the evoking words had received, independent of whether they had been correctly classified in the recognition memory test. Bentin *et al.* (1992) took these findings as evidence that the effects of word repetition on ERPs occur independently of whether repeated words are explicitly recognized as such. They suggested that these effects reflect the general 'strength' of a word's representation in a single memory system subserving both explicit and implicit memory.

Bentin *et al.*'s interpretation is open to question. Words 'missed' in the intermediate recognition task could none the less have been recognized as having previously been presented when they were shown in the final lexical decision task. Thus ERP repetition effects may have occurred only for words which subjects were aware had been presented earlier in the experiment.

One finding from Bentin *et al.* (1992) is not susceptible to this criticism. In the recognition task, they reported that ERPs evoked by old items misclassified as new were more positive than those evoked by genuinely new words, the first (and only) report of a dissociation between overt recognition judgements and concurrently recorded ERPs. Since much evidence indicates that items that are not recognized explicitly can none the less influence memory implicitly, this finding is consistent with the idea that ERPs can reflect implicit memory. An alternative explanation is possible, however. Subjects may have adopted a criterion for choosing a 'yes' response that was so strict as to dissociate a 'continuous' measure of recognition, ERPs, from the discontinuous measure of yes/no responding. That is, some of the missed items might have been judged old under a more lenient response criterion. A replication adopting a more fine-grained behavioural measure (for example a confidence rating scale) would help resolve this question.

This brief review is sufficient to indicate that there is at present little evidence to demonstrate that ERPs reflect implicit memory. In this respect, ERP research lags behind that employing a different physiological index — electrodermal activity — as a covert measure of memory (Bauer and Verfaille 1992; Verfaille *et al.* 1991). While it may transpire that ERPs are insensitive to the processes mediating priming and other implicit memory phenomena (the neural activity associated with these processes may, for example, simply not be detectable at the scalp; see Chapter 1), this conclusion is premature on the basis of the available evidence. Two developments would rectify this state of affairs: first, studies employing more sophisticated experimental designs, permitting the systematic study of variables known to dissociate implicit and explicit memory in normal subjects. Second, studies of severely amnesic patients, in whom evidence for ERP signs of implicit memory can be sought without the problem of 'contamination' by explicit memory.

5.4.2 Direct tests of recognition memory

The studies reviewed in this section have all compared ERPs evoked by 'old' and 'new' words in tests of recognition memory. Therefore, as with the studies of repetition effects on ERPs discussed above, the basic contrast is between ERPs evoked by items presented for the first versus the second time during the experiment. In most studies, this manipulation was achieved with a study-test procedure, in which items first presented at study are subsequently intermixed in a test series with new items. In some experiments, however, a continuous recognition task was employed. Items in this procedure are presented in a single series, and the requirement is to discriminate between those being shown for the first and the second time.

The investigation of ERPs in tests of recognition memory has the advantage that the ERPs can be related directly to subjects' performance. Against this must be set the disadvantage that since subjects are making differential responses to the items of greatest experimental interest (that is, old and new words), it may prove difficult to isolate a genuine memory effect from the consequences of assigning items to different response categories. This problem can in principle be circumvented by examining ERPs to incorrect responses (misses and false alarms). ERP effects that are associated with old or new responses independently of response accuracy are very likely to reflect processes independent of those responsible for veridical judgements. In practice, two problems arise with this approach. First, it presupposes a sufficient number of error trials to form the appropriate ERP averages; these will not be available when subjects' performance is at a high level. Second, differences between ERPs to correctly and incorrectly classified stimuli are difficult to interpret if they are associated with different levels of performance on such indices as reaction time, reaction time variability, and response confidence (which they often are).

In the light of these problems, Rugg *et al.* (1992) directly addressed the question of whether ERP differences between old and new words are influenced by the assignment of these items to different response categories. In this experiment, the old/new status of words was independent of the response category to which the words had to be assigned. Subjects performed several blocks of continuous recognition, in each of which words were responded to differentially on the basis of whether they were being seen in the block for the first or the second time. From the second block on, some of the items shown within a block for the first time, and therefore requiring a 'new' response, had also been presented in the immediately preceding block. When compared with words that had not previously been encountered in the experiment (and therefore also requiring a 'new' response), ERPs to these items showed the same pattern of differences as those found between ERPs evoked by items shown for the first versus second time *within* a block. Thus it seems unlikely that differences in ERPs evoked by old and new words in tests of recognition memory are strongly influenced by processes associated with the assignment of items to different response categories.

Numerous other studies have described old/new effects in recognition memory tests, including three of those cited in Section 5.3 above (Karis *et al.* 1984; Neville *et al.* 1986; Sanquist *et al.* 1980; see also Friedman 1990*a, b*, 1992; Johnson *et al*, 1985; Paller and Kutas, 1992; Potter *et al.* 1992; Rugg and Doyle, 1992, 1994; Rugg and Nagy, 1989; Rugg *et al.* 1991; Smith, 1993; Smith and Halgren, 1989). The uniform finding is that correctly classified old items evoke more positive-going ERPs than do new items. This finding has often been interpreted in terms of putative functional properties of the P300 component (see Chapter 1), rather than with respect to the light it might shed on recognition memory (e.g. Karis *et al.* 1984). Given this background, the study of Smith and Halgren (1989) is doubly important. First, because it suggested that old/new ERP effects can result from the modulation of multiple ERP components. Second, because the effects were interpreted in the context of a functional model of recognition memory.

Smith and Halgren (1989) recorded ERPs from patients who had undergone left- or right-sided anterior temporal lobectomy, and from normal controls. Following the presentation of a block of words for study, a series of test blocks were presented in rapid succession, each containing the same ten study words and an equal number of new words, which differed from block to block.

As shown in Fig. 5.6, the ERPs of the controls and right-sided patients exhibited old/new effects, whereas those from the left-sided patients did not. On the basis of the differing scalp distributions of the early and late parts of these effects, Smith and Halgren (1989) interpreted them as reflecting the modulation of two components: N400, the amplitude of which was attenuated in ERPs to old items, and a subsequent late positive component (which they identified as the P300), the amplitude of which was enhanced. These two putative components of the old/new effect will be referred to hereafter as the 'early' and 'late' effects respectively.

Smith and Halgren (1989) suggested that both early and late old/new effects

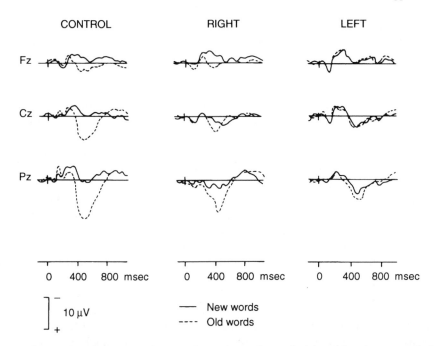

Fig. 5.6 Grand-average ERPs from midline electrodes evoked by old and new words in the recognition memory test of Smith and Halgren (1989). ERPs are depicted separately for unoperated control subjects, and for subjects who had undergone right- or left-sided anterior temporal lobectomy. (Adapted from Smith and Halgren (1989). Copyright © the American Psychological Association 1989.)

reflected processes that played a critical role in the retrieval of episodic (context-specific) memories. By their view (see also Halgren and Smith 1987) the N400 (the ERP component thought to be responsible for the early effect) is generated as the semantic attributes of the evoking item are integrated with the 'cognitive context' pertaining at the time, forming an 'episodic trace' of the item. This process requires the interaction of hippocampal and cortical regions, the neural activity associated with which is reflected in both scalp-recorded and intracerebrally recorded ERPs (Smith *et al.* 1986). Repetition of an item within the same context triggers the retrieval of the episodic trace of its first presentation. This forestalls the generation of N400, and leads instead to an enhanced late positive component. Damage to the left medial temporal lobe prevents these processes from occurring for verbal material, leading to poor episodic memory for such material, and the absence of old/new ERP effects.

Smith and Halgren (1989) noted that although their left-sided patients failed to show old/new ERP effects, they had only a mild deficit in task performance. They accounted for this dissociation by recourse to a dual-process account of recognition memory (see Section 5.1.2). They argued that although their left lobectomy patients were poor at recollecting old words, they were unimpaired at making recognition judgements on the basis of familiarity. Smith and Halgren therefore proposed that the old/new ERP effects in their control and right-operated subjects reflected processes specific to recollection, and that differences in item familiarity are not reflected in ERPs, even when such differences are sufficient to permit accurate recognition judgements.

Smith and Halgren's hypothesis leads to two predictions: both early and late old/new ERP effects should be found whenever recognition judgements are based on recollection of prior encounters with the test item. And when the recollective component of recognition memory is disrupted or weak, and recognition judgements are based predominantly on familiarity, old/new ERP differences should be small or non-existent.

Results from three studies seemingly contradict this hypothesis. Potter *et al.* (1992) investigated the effects of the anticholinergic drug scopolamine in a continuous recognition memory task. Scopolamine impairs performance on direct memory tests, but appears to spare implicit memory, as indexed by performance on indirect tests such as word stem completion (e.g. Kopelman and Corn 1988). In light of the supposed commonality of the processes underlying implicit memory and the familiarity component of recognition memory, Potter *et al.* reasoned that the amnestic effects of scopolamine should result mainly from disruption of recollection. Thus, they argued, both the performance and the ERPs of subjects performing a recognition memory task under scopolamine should resemble those of Smith and Halgren's (1989) left temporal lobectomy patients: recognition performance should be mediated largely by familiarity, and old/new ERP effects should be small.

As expected, scopolamine impaired recognition memory. But early old/new effects were unaffected by the drug, while late effects were enhanced. Potter *et al.* therefore argued that impairment of recollection is not necessarily associated with a reduction in the magnitude of old/new effects on the ERP. They further argued that their findings were consistent with the view that late old/new effects reflected differences in the relative familiarity of old and new items. They argued that since scopolamine selectively impairs recollection, the drug should lead to an increase in the proportion of correct recognition judgements based solely on relative familiarity. Thus old/new differences in ERPs that reflected differences in relative familiarity would also be expected to increase.

The results of Potter *et al.* (1992) clearly demonstrate that both early and late old/new effects are unaffected by the disruption to memory caused by scopolamine. Their conclusion that these effects therefore do not reflect processing related to recollection might, however, be called into question. This conclusion is predicated on the assumption that the deleterious effects of scopolamine on recognition memory are indeed selective for recollection. This assumption is based on circumstantial rather than direct evidence, and Potter *et al.*'s own data do not address the issue. Thus it remains to be determined whether the assumption is correct. If it is not, and scopolamine is shown to disrupt recognition memory non-selectively, Potter *et al.*'s reasoning fails to hold.

A second study relevant to the ideas of Smith and Halgren (1989) involved, like theirs, an investigation of ERPs from left and right temporal lobectomy patients, in this case during a continuous recognition task (Rugg *et al.* 1991). In both patient groups, early old/new effects were abnormally small, despite normal task performance.

Rugg *et al.* considered these findings to contradict Smith and Halgren's (1989) hypothesis relating old/new ERP differences to episodic memory retrieval. As is typically the case (Smith 1989), the left-lobectomy patients showed a significant verbal memory impairment on a standard neuropsychological test, but no impairment was evident in the right-sided patients. Thus, in this latter group, abnormal early old/new ERP differences apparently coexisted with normal verbal memory, calling into question the relationship between early old/new effects and retrieval of episodic memories for words.

Finally, Rugg and Nagy (1989) described findings from healthy subjects that also point to the absence of a strong relationship between early old/new effects and the retrieval of episodic memories. In a continuous recognition task, in which the interval between first and second presentations of each word was about a minute, both early and late effects were apparent in the ERPs, as shown in Fig. 5.7. But when memory was tested over a study-test interval of about 45 min, early effects were no longer apparent, although recognition performance remained well above chance (Fig. 5.7). Rugg and Nagy argued that the early effects were governed more by study-test interval than by the processes responsible for discriminating old from new items. This argument is strengthened by the fact that there is little evidence of early old/new effects in other studies in which the study-test interval is more than a few minutes (see, for example, Neville *et al.* 1986; Paller and Kutas 1992; Rugg and Doyle 1992; Smith 1993).

5.4.2.1 Significance of early old/new effects

In the absence of evidence to the contrary, it seems reasonable to suppose that the processes reflected by the modulation of N400 in the studies reviewed above are the same as those associated with the changes in N400 amplitude that can be found in indirect tests, discussed in Section 5.4.1. The upshot of that discussion was that there was little evidence to link N400 modulation with implicit memory. And the foregoing review indicates that whatever the processes associated with the modulation of the N400 in direct tests of recognition memory, they are not necessary for the explicit discrimination of old and new items. Thus the findings discussed in the preceding section do nothing to modify the conclusion of Section 5.4.1.1: the identity and functional significance of the processes reflected by the modulation of N400 in memory tasks remain unclear.

5.4.2.2 Late old/new effects, familiarity, and recollection

In contrast to early effects, late old/new effects — arising from the modulation of one or more late positive components — remain robust over lengthy study-test intervals, raising the possibility that they reflect processes of functional significance to

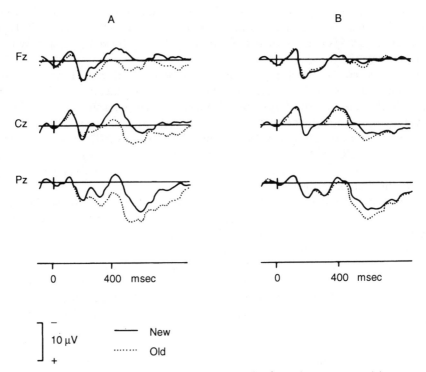

Fig. 5.7 Grand-average ERPs from midline electrodes from the two recognition memory tests employed by Rugg and Nagy (1989). A ERPs evoked by correctly detected new and old words in a continuous recognition memory task, in which 19 items intervened between first and second presentations. B ERPs evoked by correctly detected new and old words after a study–test interval of approximately 45 min.

recognition memory over these intervals. Rugg and Doyle (1992, 1994) addressed the question of whether these effects dissociated the recollective and familiarity components of recognition memory. The motivation for these experiments came from the findings of Rugg (1990), who employed an indirect memory test (non-word detection) in which words of low and high frequencies of occurrence were repeated. Rugg (1990) found that whereas the repetition of low-frequency words enhanced the amplitude of a late positive wave, the same region of the ERP was insensitive to the repetition of high-frequency words (see also Young and Rugg 1992). Rugg accounted for this finding with the same kind of explanation put forward within the dual-process framework to account for the 'word frequency effect' in recognition memory (the fact that low-frequency words give rise to better recognition performance than do those of high frequency). According to this explanation (e.g. Mandler 1980), old low-frequency words engender higher levels of relative familiarity than old high-frequency items, because of a greater disparity between pre- and intra-experimental familiarity. In the light of this account of the word frequency effect on recognition memory, Rugg (1990) suggested

gested that the late positive component was sensitive to the relative familiarity of the item evoking it — the greater the relative familiarity, the more positive-going the component.

In two studies, Rugg and Doyle (1992, 1994) explored the implications of this hypothesis for the understanding of old/new effects in direct tests of recognition memory. In both experiments, the study phase consisted of an incidental lexical decision task, with the test phase following after a delay of about 20 min. In the second experiment only, recognition responses were accompanied by judgements of response confidence. In both experiments, recognition judgements were, as is typical, more accurate for low- than for high-frequency words. The ERPs evoked by correctly classified old words contained larger late positive components than those to the equivalent new items and, critically, these old/new differences were larger for low- than for high-frequency words. The findings remained unchanged when, in the second experiment (Rugg and Doyle 1992), ERPs were formed only from correct trials associated with high response confidence (see Fig. 5.8). Further analysis showed that the differences in the size of the old/new effects evoked by high- and low-frequency words could not be attributed to differences between the two classes of word in the reaction time or reaction time variability of the responses they attracted. Furthermore, ERPs evoked by false alarms and misses resembled those evoked by correctly classified new items. In other words, an enhanced late positive component was observed only for correctly classified old words.

Rugg and Doyle (1992, 1994) concluded that the most parsimonious explanation of their data was that late positive components of ERPs evoked by repeated and unrepeated isolated words do indeed vary as function of the words' relative familiarity. They took this to be strong supporting evidence for dual-process models of recognition memory.

Paller and Kutas (1992) studied old/new effects in the absence of overt old and new responses. Subjects processed words in two study tasks, one requiring orthographic and the other imaginal processing. The test task was indirect, requiring the identification of words presented too briefly to allow error-free performance. Test items consisted of old words from the two study tasks, along with words new to the experiment.

In line with much previous work (see Richardson-Klavehn and Bjork (1988) for review), the type of study task had little effect on identification performance, which was better for words presented in either task than for new items. However, the ERPs evoked at test by correctly identified items differed as a function of study condition. As shown in Fig. 5.9, words from the imagery task evoked the more positive ERPs. This difference resembled previously described late old/new effects, including the tendency for these effects to be larger over the left than the right hemisphere (cf. Neville *et al.*, 1986; Rugg and Doyle 1992, 1994).

Given the well known effects of depth of processing manipulations on retrieval in direct memory tests (Section 5.1.2), Paller and Kutas assumed that words from the imagery task were more likely to have been explicitly recognized as belonging to the study phase than were the words presented in the orthographic task. Thus they argued that the difference between the ERPs evoked at test by items from

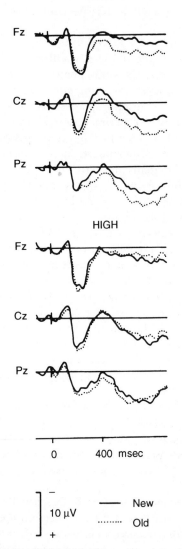

Fig. 5.8 Midline grand-average ERPs evoked by correctly and confidently detected low- and high-frequency old and new words in the recognition memory test of Rugg and Doyle (1992).

the two study tasks could be regarded as an ERP signature for what they termed 'conscious recollection'. According to this view, late old/new ERP effects are largely insensitive to implicit memory, and occur only when there is awareness that an item has recently been experienced.

Paller and Kutas' findings and interpretation are consistent with previous

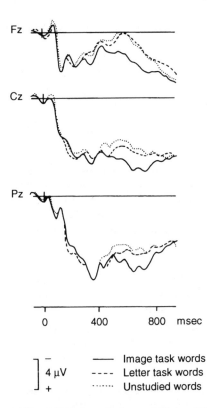

Fz

Cz

Pz

0   400   800   msec

$\left.\begin{array}{l} - \\ 4\ \mu V \\ + \end{array}\right]$

——— Image task words
- - - - Letter task words
········ Unstudied words

Fig. 5.9 Grand-average midline ERPs from Paller and Kutas (1992), evoked by correctly identified test words new to the experiment (unstudied), or which had previously been studied in an imagery or a letter detection task. (Adapted from Paller and Kutas (1992) by permission of The MIT Press, Cambridge, MA, and the authors. Copyright © Massachusetts Institute of Technology 1994.)

observations (e.g. Neville *et al.* 1986; Rugg and Doyle 1992, 1994) that late old/new effects are found only for old words correctly judged as such in tests of recognition memory, items misclassified as new evoking ERPs that closely resemble those evoked by genuinely new items. The findings also provide strong evidence, consistent with the findings of Rugg *et al.*(1992), that old/new ERP effects are a consequence neither of the requirement to assign test items to old and new categories nor of the need to respond differentially to the items. The data do not, however, directly address the question of which of the putative components of recognition memory are most closely associated with late old/new effects. While a necessary condition for these effects may be awareness that the evoking items have recently been experienced, it is unclear from this study whether this need include details of where and when the experience occurred (recollection of the study episode), as opposed to arising from a feeling of familiarity devoid of such contextual detail. This issue is crucial to the question of whether old/new effects are more sensitive to recognition based on recollection or familiarity.

Gardiner and associates (Gardiner 1988; Gardiner and Java 1990, 1991, 1993; Gardiner and Parkin 1990; see also Tulving 1985) have developed a method that attempts to dissociate the contributions of recollection and familiarity to recognition judgements. After each positive judgement on a test item, subjects must indicate whether the item evoked an explicit memory of the context in which it was initially encountered (a 'remember' or 'R' response), or whether instead it was judged old merely on the basis of a feeling of familiarity, with no concomitant recollective experience ('know' or 'K' response). This procedure can be criticized on the grounds that it seems to be based on the questionable assumption that these two forms of recognition judgement are mutually exclusive. None the less, R and K responses are sensitive to a number of variables thought to affect recollection and familiarity-based recognition differentially (e.g. Gardiner and Parkin 1990; Rajaram 1993).

Employing a study-test procedure, Smith (1993) compared ERPs evoked at test by old items attracting R and K judgements. As shown in Fig. 5.10, old/new effects were larger for R responses. Smith (1993) interpreted this finding in favour of the idea that the late old/new ERP effect reflects the operation (or the outcome) of the recollective rather than the familiarity component of recognition memory. However, as is clear from Fig. 5.10, both classes of recognition judgement were associated with old/new effects, the scalp distributions of which were indistinguishable. Smith's (1993) data therefore indicate that while recollection, as operationalized by the R/K procedure, may be associated with the enhancement of late old/new effects, the processes underlying these effects are seemingly not specific to R judgements. These findings could be explained by one of three possible accounts. It could be that Smith's (1993) conclusion is correct, but that the R/K procedure does not neatly dissociate the two bases for recognition memory, and that some proportion of K trials contain items judged old on the basis of recollection. Alternatively, old/new effects might reflect processes associated with both recollective and familiarity-based recognition. Finally, dual-process models of recognition memory might of course be invalid, R and K responses reflecting judgements based not on different bases for recognition but on differing trace strengths in a unitary system.

Irrespective of which of these alternatives is correct, Smith's (1993) findings, taken with the findings of Gardiner and Java (1990), suggest an alternative explanation for the interaction between word frequency and the magnitude of old/new effects to that proposed by Rugg and Doyle (1992, 1994). Rugg and Doyle's explanation depends critically on the assumption that the recognition memory advantage for low-frequency over high-frequency words arises because of the sensitivity of the familiarity component to word frequency, rather than because low-frequency words are easier to recollect.

In contradiction to this assumption, Gardiner and Java (1990) found that the recognition advantage for low-frequency words was carried exclusively by R responses. Thus they argued that, contrary to previous views, low-frequency words

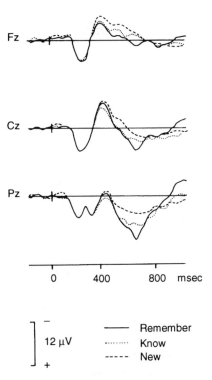

Fig. 5.10 Grand-average midline ERPs from the recognition memory test of Smith (1993), comparing waveforms evoked by correctly judged new items with those evoked by correctly detected old words associated with 'remember' or 'know' judgments. (Adapted from Smith (1993) by permission of The MIT Press, Cambridge, MA, and the author. Copyright © Massachusetts Institute of Technology 1994.)

are better recognized because they are better recollected, and not because they engender higher levels of relative familiarity. Coupled with Smith's (1993) finding that R items evoke larger old/new effects than K items, Gardner and Java's (1990) data suggest an alternative account of the word frequency by old/new interaction described by Rugg and Doyle (1992, 1994). The interaction could have arisen because ERPs evoked by old words are sensitive not to word frequency *per se*, but to the proportion of trials associated with words that would have attracted an R rather than a K response.

Rugg, Wells, and Doyle (unpublished) performed two experiments aimed at assessing the validity of this alternative account of Rugg and Doyle's (1992, 1994) findings. In the first experiment (also described in Rugg 1994), Rugg, Wells, and Doyle employed the Rugg and Doyle (1992) procedure, but substituted an R/K judgement for the confidence judgment of the previous experiment. Replicating Gardiner and Java (1990), they too found that the recognition memory advantage for low-frequency words was restricted to items associated with R judgements. ERPs to these items are shown in Fig. 5.11, where it can be seen

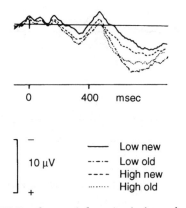

0   400   msec

] ⁻   ——— Low new
    10 µV   ----- Low old
             ---- High new
] ₊   .... High old

Fig. 5.11 Grand-average ERPs, from a left parietal electrode, evoked by correctly detected new and old test items in the R/K experiment of Rugg, Wells, and Doyle's
unpublished study. ERPs are overlaid according to old/new status and word frequency;
only items attracting a 'remember' response were used to form ERPs to old items. Note
the larger late old/new effects for low-frequency words.

that, as in Rugg and Doyle (1992), the old/new effect is larger for low- than for
high-frequency words.

In their second experiment, Rugg, Wells, and Doyle used a procedure permitting a more objective definition of recollection than that given by the R/K
procedure. The rationale for this procedure is that the ability to discriminate
between old items on the basis of study context relies wholly on recollection, while
accurate old/new judgements can be made on the basis of either familiarity or
recollection. Subjects studied lists comprising high- and low-frequency words in
two different incidental study tasks, one requiring them to rate the words for
likeability and the other requiring the generation of a short sentence involving
the word. In the test phase, subjects first judged whether an item was old or new.
When an old judgement was made, they were then required to assign the item
to its correct study task. ERPs were formed from those new items correctly and
confidently judged as such, and from old items for which correct, confident
judgements were made about both their old/new status, and the study task in
which they were originally presented. As shown in Fig. 5.12, these ERPs show
a very similar pattern to that in the preceding R/K study; old/new effects are
considerably larger for low-frequency than for high-frequency words.

These findings suggest that even among recollected items, word frequency
exerts an influence on late old/new ERP effects. Thus Rugg and Doyle's (1992,
1994) original findings are not merely a consequence of the fact that low-frequency
words are more likely to be recognized on the basis of recollection than high-
frequency words are, as was suggested by Smith (1993). The findings do not,
however, directly address the question of whether old/new effects are specific to
one or other of the putative components of recognition memory. This question is
addressed by the findings from two other source memory experiments, conducted
by Wilding, Doyle, and Rugg (submitted).

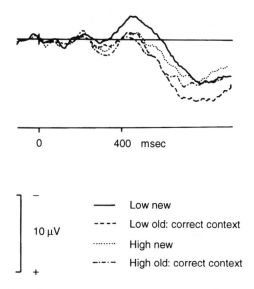

Fig. 5.12 Grand-average ERPs from a left parietal electrode in the context memory experiment of Rugg, Wells, and Doyle's unpublished study. ERPs were formed to new items correctly and confidently judged as such, and to old items both correctly and confidently judged old, and correctly and confidently assigned to study context. Note the larger old/new effects for low- than for high-frequency words.

In the study phase of these experiments, subjects discriminated low-frequency words from non-words, with half the items presented visually and half auditorily. In the test phase, the study words were all presented in only one modality (visual in experiment 1, auditory in experiment 2), along with an equal number of new words. Subjects were required first to make an old/new judgement on each test word and, if the word was judged old, to then judge whether it had initially been presented visually or auditorily. As shown in Fig. 5.13, ERPs evoked by old items differed from those to new words only if both judgements were correct; items judged old, but assigned to the wrong modality, evoked ERPs barely distinguishable from those to new items. Thus these findings strongly suggest that old/new effects do not arise simply when an item is correctly judged old (a judgement that can be based on either familiarity or recollection), but when such a judgement is accompanied by the retrieval of contextual information about the study episode — the hallmark of recollection.

Within the framework of dual-process models of recognition memory, Wilding, Doyle, and Rugg's findings provide direct evidence linking late old/new ERP effects to processes associated with the recollective component of recognition memory. It therefore follows that, contrary to Rugg and Doyle's (1992) hypothesis, the larger old/new effects seen with low-frequency than with high-frequency words do not arise because of the sensitivity of these effects to relative familiarity. Yet the findings of Rugg, Wells, and Doyle (Figs. 5.11 and 5.12) show that these frequency effects are not merely a consequence of the higher probability of

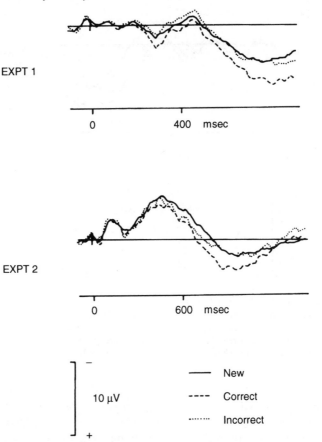

Fig. 5.13 Grand-average left-parietal ERPs from the two experiments of Wilding, Doyle, and Rugg (submitted). The ERPs were elicited by test items correctly judged new, and by correctly detected old items that were either correctly (Correct) or incorrectly (Incorrect) assigned to study modality. Test items were presented visually in experiment 1, and auditorily in experiment 2. Note the different time-bases in the two experiments.

recollection of low-frequency words. This raises the possibility that recollection, or at least those aspects of it reflected in ERP old/new effects, is in some sense graded, with low-frequency words engendering stronger or more intense recollection than high-frequency items. In the light of this possibility, it will be of considerable interest to determine whether there is any correlation between the size of old/new effects and the amount of contextual information retrieved in response to a test item.

It should be noted that although Wilding, Doyle, and Rugg's findings can be interpreted parsimoniously within the framework of dual-processes models, they do not demand an explanation within this framework. An alternative account, based on the assumption that recognition memory is supported by a single mechanism, is also possible. By this account, memories of events can vary in their strength; the stronger a memory, the more information about the event that can be retrieved. On the assumption that less information is required to judge that a word has recently been experienced than to judge when and where it was experienced, it could be argued that to segregate old items on the basis of whether they were correctly assigned to their study context is also to segregate them on the basis of the strength of the memory formed when the items were first presented. Thus the finding of differential old/new effects for these two classes of item may reflect not the operation of qualitatively different memory processes, but the consequences of retrieving strong versus weak memories via a single process.

The validity of this alternative account remains to be determined, and will of course rest to a large degree on the ultimate fate of dual-process models of recognition memory. Taken as a whole, the data from recent studies of late old/new ERP effects in recognition memory tasks do, however, permit some general conclusions to be drawn. First and most important, the evidence points strongly to the conclusion that a necessary, if not a sufficient, condition for the emergence of late ERP old/new effects is awareness that an item has recently been experienced. Thus ERPs might provide a covert method for determining whether old items in indirect (and direct) memory tests are processed with or without awareness that they have recently been experienced. Second, if the framework of dual-process models of recognition memory is accepted, the evidence suggests that old/new effects are specific for only one of the forms that such 'aware memory' can take — recollection — and are insensitive to the processes supporting familiarity-based recognition. Finally, the different sizes of old/new effects observed as a function of word frequency raise the possibility that the effects might provide quantitative as well as qualitative information about memory retrieval.

5.5 CONCLUSIONS

ERP research on memory has progressed in a reasonably cumulative fashion in the last decade or so. The results from studies of encoding give a tantalizing glimpse of the potential of ERPs to provide a new dimension to the question of why items vary in their memorability. And data from recent studies of recognition memory have begun to converge on the idea that differences between ERPs evoked at test are highly sensitive to the nature of the information retrieved in response to a test item. What is lacking in this review is discussion of two critical, interrelated issues: the functional significance and the identity of the neural processes generating the ERP effects under question. This does not reflect a reluctance on the part of the author to address such questions. Rather, it reflects the almost total absence of relevant data. Thus all discussion of the relationship between putative memory processes and ERP modulations has perforce been in the form of correlational statements.

As discussed in Chapter 2, establishing tight correlations between hypothesized cognitive processes and an ERP effect has considerable utility, as well as being an essential step on the way to elucidating the functional significance of the ERP effect. But, again as discussed in that chapter, the absence of information about the neural basis of an ERP effect places strong constraints on the conclusions that could otherwise be drawn. For example, knowledge of the source(s) of the neural activity responsible for the late old/new effect described in Section 5.4.2.2 might allow progress to be made on the critical question of whether the effect reflects neural activity that contributes to, or is consequential upon the conscious recognition of a test item. Such knowledge would also help elucidate the theoretically important question of whether the effect shared any of the generators of other memory-related ERP effects, such as those observed at encoding, and discussed in Section 5.3.

Unfortunately, as already noted, there has as yet been little progress on the question of the neural origins of memory-related ERP effects (see Rugg (in press) for a review of the little that is currently known), and even less progress on the related question of the functional significance of the neural activity they reflect. Since a number of convergent techniques exist with which to address the first question (see Chapters 1 and 2), and since in addition so much is known about the functional neuroanatomy of memory (Zola–Morgan and Squire 1993), there seems no reason why progress on both questions should not be possible. When a significant body of knowledge relevant to these questions has accumulated, ERP studies of human memory will come of age.

ACKNOWLEDGEMENTS

The author's research was supported by the Wellcome Trust. The detailed comments of M. G. H. Coles on earlier versions of the chapter are gratefully acknowledged.

REFERENCES

Baddeley, A. D. (1978). The trouble with levels: a reexamination of Craik and Lockhart's framework for memory research. *Psychological Review*, **85**, 139–52.

Bauer, R. M. and Verfaille, M. (1992). Memory dissociations: a cognitive psychophysiology perspective. In *Neuropsychology of memory* (2nd edn) (ed. L. R. Squire and N. Butters), pp. 58–71. Guilford, New York.

Bentin, S. and Peled B. S. (1990). The contribution of stimulus encoding strategies and decision-related factors to the repetition effect for words: electrophysiological evidence. *Memory and Cognition*, **18**, 359–66.

Bentin, S., McCarthy, G., and Wood, C. C. (1985). Event-related potentials, lexical decision and semantic priming. *Electroencephalography and Clinical Neurophysiology*, **60**, 343–55.

Bentin, S., Moscovitch M., and Heth I. (1992). Memory with and without awareness: performance and electrophysiological evidence of savings. *Journal of Experimental Psychology: Learning, Memory and Cognition*, **18**, 1270–83.

Besson, M. and Kutas, M. (1993). The many facets of repetition: a behavioral and electrophysiological analysis of repeating words in same versus different sentence contexts. *Journal of Experimental Psychology: Learning, Memory and Cognition*, **19**, 1115–33.

Besson, M., Kutas, M., and Van Peten, C. (1992). An event-related potential (ERP) analysis of semantic congruity and repetition effects in sentences. *Journal of Cognitive Neuroscience*, 4, 132–49.

Craik, F. I. M. and Lockhart, R. S. (1972). Levels of processing: a framework for memory research. *Journal of Verbal Learning and Verbal Behavior*, 11, 671–84.

Craik, F. I. M. and Tulving, E. (1975). Depth of processing and the retention of words in episodic memory. *Journal of Experimental Psychology: General*, 104, 268–94.

Donchin, E. (1981). Surprise! . . . Surprise? *Psychophysiology*, 18, 493–53.

Donchin, E. and Fabiani, M. (1991). The use of event-related brain potentials in the study of memory: is P300 a measure of event distinctiveness? In *Handbook of cognitive psychophysiology: central and autonomic system approaches* (ed. J. R. Jennings and M. G. H. Coles), pp. 471–98. Wiley, Chichester.

Dunn, J. C. and Kirsner, K. (1988). Implicit memory: task or process? In *Implicit memory* (ed. S. Lewandowsky, J. C. Dunn, and K. Kirsner, pp. 17–31. Erlbaum, Hillsdale, NJ.

Fabiani, M., Karis D., and Donchin E. (1986). P300 and recall in an incidental memory paradigm. *Psychophysiology*, 23, 298–308.

Fabiani, M., Karis, D., and Donchin, E. (1990a). Effects of mnemonic strategy manipulation in a Von Restorff paradigm. *Electroencephalography and Clinical Neurophysiology*, 75, 22–35.

Fabiani, M., Gratton, G., Chiarenza, G. A., and Donchin, E. (1990b). A psychophysiological investigation of the von Restorff paradigm in children. *Journal of Psychophysiology*, 4, 15–24.

Friedman, D. (1990a). Cognitive event-related potential components during continuous recognition memory for pictures. *Psychophysiology*, 27, 136–48.

Friedman, D. (1990b). ERPs during continuous recognition memory for words. *Biological Psychology*, 30, 61–88.

Friedman, D., Hamberger, M., Stern, Y., and Marder, K. (1992) Event-related potentials (ERPs) during repetition priming in Alzheimer's patients and young and older controls. *Journal of Clinical and Experimental Neuropsychology*, 14, 448–462.

Gardiner, J. M. (1988). Functional aspects of recollective experience. *Memory and Cognition*, 16, 309–13.

Gardiner, J. M. and Java, R. I. (1990). Recollective experience in word and non-word recognition. *Memory and Cognition*, 18, 23–30.

Gardiner, J. M. and Java, R. I. (1991). Forgetting in recognition memory with and without recollective experience. *Memory and Cognition*, 19, 617–23.

Gardiner, J. M. and Java, R. I. (1993). Recognising and remembering. In *Theories of memory* (ed. A. F. Collins, S. E. Gathercole, M. A. Conway, and P. E. Morris), pp. 163–88. Erlbaum, Hove.

Gardiner, J. M. and Parkin, A. J. (1990). Attention and recollective experience in recognition memory. *Memory and Cognition*, 18, 579–83.

Haist, F. O., Shimamura, A. P., and Squire, L. R. (1992). On the relationship between recall and recognition memory. *Journal of Experimental Psychology: Learning, Memory and Cognition*, 18, 691–702.

Halgren, E. and Smith, M. E. (1987). Cognitive evoked-potentials as modulatory processes in human-memory formation and retrieval. *Human Neurobiology*, 6, 129–39.

Hamberger, M. and Friedman, D. (1992). Event-related potential correlates of repetition priming and stimulus classification in young, middle-aged, and older adults. *Journal of Gerontology*, 47, 395–405.

Jacoby, L. L. (1983). Perceptual enhancement: persistent effects of an experience. *Journal of Experimental Psychology: Learning, Memory and Cognition*, 9, 21–38.

Jacoby, L. L. and Dallas, M. (1981). On the relationship between autobiographical memory and perceptual learning. *Journal of Experimental Psychology: General*, 3, 306–40.

Jacoby, L. L. and Kelley, C. (1992). Unconscious influences of memory: dissociations and automaticity. In *The neuropsychology of consciousness* (ed., A. D. Milner and M. D. Rugg, pp. 201–34. Academic, London.

Jernigan, T. L. and Ostergaard, A. L. (1993). Word priming and recognition memory are both affected by mesial temporal lobe damage. *Neuropsychology*, 7, 14–26.

Johnson, R., Pfefferbaum A., and Kopell B. S. (1985). P300 and long-term memory: latency predicts recognition performance. *Psychophysiology*, 22, 497–507.

Karayanidis, F., Andrews, S., Ward, P. B., and McConaghy, N. (1991). Effects of inter-term lag on word repetition: an event-related potential study. *Psychophysiology*, 28, 307–18.

Karis, D., Fabiani, M., and Donchin, E. (1984). P300 and memory: individual differences in the Von Restorff effect. *Cognitive Psychology*, 16, 177–86.

Kopelman, M. D. and Corn, T. H. (1988). Cholinergic 'blockade' as a model for cholinergic depletion. A comparison of the memory deficits with those of Alzheimer-type dementia and the alcoholic Korsakoff syndrome. *Brain*, 111, 1079–110.

Kutas, M. (1988). Review of event-related potential studies of memory. In *Perspectives in memory research*, (ed., M. S. Gazzaniga), pp. 182–217. MIT Press, Cambridge, MA.

Kutas, M. and Hillyard, S. A. (1980). Reading senseless sentences: brain potentials reflect semantic incongruity. *Science*, 207, 202–5.

Mandler, G. (1980). Recognising: the judgment of previous occurence. *Psychological Review*, 87, 252–71.

Mayes, A. R. (1992). Automatic memory processes in amnesia. How are they mediated? In *The neuropsychology of consciousness*, (ed., A. D. Milner and M. D. Rugg), pp. 235–62. Academic, London.

Morris, C. D., Bransford, J. P., and Franks, J. J. (1977). Levels of processing versus transfer appropriate processing. *Journal of Verbal Learning and Verbal Behavior*, 16, 519–33.

Nagy, M. E. and Rugg, M. D. (1989). Modulation of event-related potentials by word repetition: the effects of inter-item lag. *Psychophysiology*, 26, 431–6.

Neville, H. J., Kutas, M., Chesney, G., and Schmidt, A. L. (1986). Event-related brain potentials during initial encoding and recognition memory of congruous and incongruous words. *Journal of Memory and Language*, 25, 75–92.

Noldy, NE., Stelmack, R. M., Campbell, K. B. (1990). Event-related potentials and recognition memory for pictures and words — the effects of intentional and incidental-learning. *Psychophysiology*, 27, 417–28.

Otten, L. J., Rugg, M. D., and Doyle, M. C. (1993). Modulation of event-related potentials by word repetition: the role of selective attention. *Psychophysiology*, 30, 559–71.

Paller, K. A. (1990). Recall and stem-completion have different electrophysiological correlates and are modified differentially by directed forgetting. *Journal of Experimental Psychology: Learning, Memory and Cognition*, 16, 1021–32.

Paller, K. A. and Kutas, M. (1992). Brain potentials during retrieval provide neurophysiological support for the distinction between conscious recollection and priming. *Journal of Cognitive Neuroscience*, 4, 375–91.

Paller, K. A., Kutas, M., and Mayes, A. R. (1987a). Neural correlates of encoding in an incidental learning paradigm. *Electroencephalography and Clinical Neurophysiology*, 67, 360–71.

Paller, K. A., Kutas, M., Shimamura, A. P., and Squire, L. R. (1987*b*). Brain responses to concrete and abstract words reflect processes that correlate with later performance on a test of stem-completion priming. *Electroencephalography and Clinical Neurophysiology*, 40, 360–5.

Paller, K. A., McCarthy, G., and Wood, C. C. (1988). ERPs predictive of subsequent recall and recognition performance. *Biological Psychology*, 26, 269–76.

Potter, D. D., Pickles, C. D., Roberts, R. C., and Rugg, M. D. (1992). The effects of scopolamine on event-related potentials in a continuous recognition memory task. *Psychophysiology*, 29, 29–37.

Rajaram, S. (1993). Remembering and knowing: two means of access to the personal past. *Memory and Cognition*, 21, 89–102.

Richardson–Klavehn, A. and Bjork, R. A. (1988). Measures of memory. *Annual Review of Psychology*, 39, 475–543.

Roediger, H. L., Weldon, M. S., and Challis, B. H. (1989). Explaining dissociations between implicit and explicit measures of retention: a processing account. In *Varieties of memory and consciousness*, (ed., H. L. Roediger and F. I. M. Craik, pp. 3–41. Erlbaum, Hillsdale, NJ.

Rugg, M. D. (1985). The effects of word repetition and semantic priming on event-related potentials. *Psychophysiology*, 22, 642–7.

Rugg, M. D. (1987). Dissociation of semantic priming, word and non-word repetition by event-related potentials. *Quarterly Journal of Experimental Psychology*, 39A, 123–48.

Rugg, M. D. (1990). Event-related brain potentials dissociate repetition effects of high and low frequency words. *Memory Cognition*, 18, 367–79.

Rugg, M. D. Cognitive event-related potentials: intracerebral and lesion studies. In *Handbook of Neuropsychology*, vol. 10, (ed. J. C. Baron and J. Grafman) Elsevier, Amsterdam. (In press.)

Rugg, M. D. and Doyle, M. C., (1992). Event-related potentials and recognition memory for low-frequency and high-frequency words. *Journal of Cognitive Neuroscience*, 4, 69–79.

Rugg, M. D. and Doyle, M. C. (1994). Event related potentials and stimulus repetition in direct and indirect tests of memory. In *Cognitive electrophysiology* (ed. H. J. Heinze., T. Munte, and G. R. Mangun), pp. 124–48. Birkhauser, Boston.

Rugg, M. D. and Nagy, M. E. (1987). Lexical contribution to non-word repetition effects: evidence from event-related potentials. *Memory and Cognition*, 15, 473–81.

Rugg, M. D. and Nagy, M. E. (1989). Event-related potentials and recognition memory for words. *Electroencephalography and Clinical Neurophysiology*, 72, 395–406.

Rugg, M. D., Furda, J., and Lorist, M. (1988). The effects of task on the modulation of event-related potentials by word repetition. *Psychophysiology*, 25, 55–63.

Rugg, M. D., Roberts, R. C., Potter, D. D., Pickles, C. D., and Nagy, M. E. (1991). Event-related potentials related to recognition memory. Effects of unilateral temporal lobectomy and temporal lobe epilepsy. *Brain*, 114, 2313–32.

Rugg, M. D., Brovedani, P., and Doyle, M. C. (1992). Modulation of event-related potentials by word repetition in a task with inconsistent mapping between repetition and response. *Electroencephalography and Clinical Neurophysiology*, 84, 521–31.

Rugg, M. D., Doyle, M. C., and Melan, C. (1993). An ERP study of the effects of intra- versus inter-modal word repetition. *Language and Cognitive Processes*, 8, 337–40.

Rugg, M. D., Doyle, M. C, and Holdstock, J. S. (1994*a*). Modulation of event-related brain potentials by word repetition: effects of local context. *Psychophysiology*, 31, 447–59.

Rugg, M. D., Pearl, S., Walker, P., Roberts, R. C., and Holdstock, J. S. (1994*b*). Word repetition effects on event-related potentials in healthy young and old subjects, and in patients with Alzheimer-type dementia. *Neuropsychologia*, 32, 381–98.)

Sanquist, T. F., Rohrbaugh, J. W., Syndulko K., and Lindsley D. B. (1980). Electrocortical signs of levels of processing: perceptual analysis and recognition memory. *Psychophysiology*, 17, 568–76.

Scarborough, D. L., Cortese, C., and Scarborough, H. J. (1977). Frequency and repetition effects in lexical memory. *Journal of Experimental Psychology: Human Perception and Performance*, 3, 1–17.

Schacter, D. L., Chiu, C.-Y. P., and Ochsner, K. N. (1993). Implicit memory: a selective review. *Annual Review of Neuroscience*, 16, 159–82.

Schmidt, S. R. (1991). Can we have a distinctive theory of memory? *Memory and Cognition*, 19, 523–42.

Shimamura, A. P. (1989). Disorders of memory: the cognitive science perspective. In *Handbook of neuropsychology*, Vol. 3, (ed., L. Squire and G. Gainotti), pp. 35–74. Elsevier, Amsterdam.

Smith, M. E. (1993). Neurophysiological manifestations of recollective experience during recognition memory judgments. *Journal of Cognitive Neuroscience*, 5, 1–13.

Smith M. E. and Halgren, E. (1989). Dissociation of recognition memory components following temporal lobe lesions. *Journal of Experimental Psychology: Learning, Memory and Cognition*, 15, 50–60.

Smith, M. E., Stapleton, J. M., and Halgren, E. (1986). Human medial temporal lobe potentials evoked in memory and language tasks. *Electroencephalography and Clinical Neurophysiology*, 63, 145–59.

Smith, M. L. (1989). Memory disorders associated with temporal-lobe lesions. In *Handbook of neuropsychology*, Vol. 3, (ed. L. Squire and G. Gainotti, pp. 91–106. Elsevier, Amsterdam.

Squire, L. R. (1992). Declarative and nondeclarative memory: multiple brain systems supporting learning and memory. *Journal of Cognitive Neuroscience*, 4, 232–43.

Squire, L. R., Knowlton, B., and Musen, G. (1993). The structure and organization of memory. *Annual Review of Neuroscience*, 44, 453–95.

Sternberg, S. (1966). High-speed scanning in human memory. *Science*, 153, 652–4.

Tulving. E. (1983). *Elements of episodic memory*. Oxford University Press.

Tulving, E. (1985). Memory and consciousness. *Canadian Psychologist*, 26, 1–12.

Van Petten, C., Kutas, M., Kluender, R., Mitchiner, M., and McIsaac, H. (1991). Fractionating the word repetition effect with event-related potentials. *Journal of Cognitive Neuroscience*, 3, 129–50.

Verfaille, M., Bauer, R. M., and Bowers, D. (1991). Autonomic and behavioral evidence of 'implicit' memory in amnesia. *Brain and Cognition*, 15, 10–25.

Verfaille, M. and Treadwell, J. R. (1993). Status of recognition memory in amnesia. *Neuropsychology*, 7, 5–13.

Wilding, E., Doyle, M. C., and Rugg, M. D. Recognition memory with and without retrieval of context: an event-related potential study. Submitted.

Young, M. P. and Rugg, M. D. (1992). Word frequency and multiple repetition as determinants of the modulation of event-related potentials in a semantic classification task. *Psychophysiology*, 6, 664–76.

Zola–Morgan, S. and Squire, L. R. (1993). Neuroanatomy of memory. *Annual Review of Neuroscience*, 16, 547–63.

6 Event-related potentials and language comprehension

Lee Osterhout and Phillip J. Holcomb

6.1 INTRODUCTION

The ability to comprehend language dominates our species-specific activity. Correspondingly, deficits in language function (e.g. the dyslexias and aphasias) are extremely debilitating. Yet, despite its central importance, an adequate understanding of the cognitive and neural processes underlying language comprehension remains elusive. One primary reason for the lack of progress has been a paucity of adequate methodologies. Language comprehension occurs very rapidly (in 'real time') and any sufficient model must describe the process as it unfolds over time (cf. Swinney 1981, 1982). Unfortunately, few methodologies allow for rapid and on-line measurement. Most researchers resort to the use of measurements that are made 'after-the-fact' (e.g. measures of sentence reading times) or that reflect the state of affairs at a discrete moment during comprehension (e.g. cross-modal priming studies; cf. Swinney 1979). Furthermore, these measurements are intrusive; one cannot know for certain the influence the measurement itself has on the phenomenon being investigated.

For these reasons, electrophysiological measurements of event-related brain potentials (ERPs) hold great promise as tools for studying the cognitive processes that underlie language comprehension. ERPs provide a continuous account of the electrical activity in the brain, thereby meeting the need for a continuous on-line measure. Electrophysiological measurement is non-intrusive; and since such measurements provide at least a rough estimate of localization and lateralization of brain activity, ERPs also offer the prospect of tieing behaviour and behavioural models of language comprehension more closely to brain function.

The optimistic view of ERPs as promising tools for investigating language processes stands in contrast to the pessimistic view projected by previous reviewers of the field (Donchin *et al.* 1977; Hillyard and Woods 1979; Picton and Stuss 1984). One reason for this pessimism has been the apparent failure to discover reliable signs of hemispheric specialization, for example the lack of consistent asymmetries in the distribution of language-related effects. Over the past decade, the focus has shifted away from issues of hemispheric specialization and toward an interest in the cognitive processes underlying language comprehension. This shift can be traced in large part to a single study (Kutas and Hillyard 1980c). Kutas and Hillyard reported that semantically inappropriate words (for example 'He spread the warm bread with *socks*') elicited a large-amplitude negative ERP

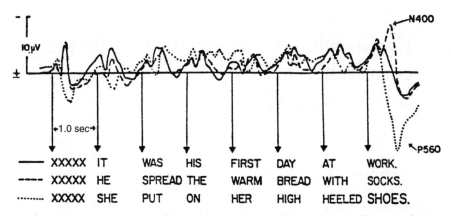

Fig. 6.1 ERPs to sentences ending with a non-anomalous, semantically anomalous, or physically anomalous word. Note in particular the large negative deflection (N400) in the response to the semantically anomalous final words. (From Kutas and Hillyard (1980c). Reprinted by permission of the authors and publishers.)

ERP component with a peak latency of 400 ms (the N400 component), relative to the ERPs elicited by semantically appropriate words (e.g., 'It was his first day at *work*'). In contrast, semantically appropriate but physically abberant words (words printed in larger type) elicited a positive-going potential (P560) in the same temporal window as the N400 (see Fig 6.1). Kutas and Hillyard speculated that the N400 may be an 'electrophysiological sign of the "reprocessing" of semantically anomalous information'. (Kutas and Hillyard 1980c, 203). Although more recent data have suggested alternative interpretations of the N400, Kutas and Hillyard demonstrated that electrophysiological recordings of brain activity covary with meaning-related manipulations to language stimuli. This landmark discovery provided the impetus for an intriguing and rapidly growing literature.

The purpose of the current chapter is to review this literature, pointing out findings of particular import for psycholinguistic models of comprehension. Our review is divided into two primary sections. The first section reviews ERP studies aimed at investigating word-level processes (recognizing isolated words and words in single-word contexts). The second section concerns sentence-level processes (recognizing words in sentence contexts and computing syntactic structure). Throughout the review, we focus on findings that are directly relevant to theoretical issues currently being debated by psycholinguists. The goal is to demonstrate, through example, the utility of ERPs as tools for investigating these issues, particularly in cases where traditional measures have produced conflicting sets of data.

Even though the application of ERPs to the study of language comprehension is in its infancy, we are unable to review all of the relevant literature. Specifically, we will not review studies of phonological processes (e.g. Kramer and Donchin 1987; Polich *et al.* 1983; Rugg 1984 *a,b*, 1985), repetition priming (e.g. Rugg

1985, 1987; Chapter 5, section 5.4.1) and certain single-word tasks (e.g. Neville *et al* 1982; Rugg 1983). The interested reader should consult the original sources or see one of several recent reviews which have covered these topics (Fischler 1990; Fischler and Raney 1991; Kutas and Van Petten 1988).

6.2 METHODOLOGICAL ISSUES

6.2.1 Two strategies for examining comprehension with ERPs

ERP researchers typically adopt one of two approaches in examining the relationship between ERPs and language (see Osterhout (1994); for a somewhat different view see Kutas and Van Petten (1988)). The first approach focuses on the ERP component itself — the researcher tries to identify the cognitive events underlying the component. This can be accomplished, in principle, by investigating the necessary and sufficient conditions for altering the component's waveform characteristics (amplitude and latency). The benefits of this approach are clear. With an electrophysiological marker of a specific cognitive process in hand, changes in the underlying cognitive process can be directly inferred from changes in the ERP component. For example, Van Petten and Kutas (1987) concluded, on the basis of previously collected data, that the amplitude of the N400 component reflects a word's 'activation level' in memory. More specifically, they concluded that highly activated words elicit a small N400, while less-activated words elicit a larger N400. These assumptions allowed them to investigate the effects of context on the processing of polysemous words, by measuring the N400s elicited by target words related to the contextually appropriate and inappropriate meanings of a polysemous word (e.g. 'The gambler pulled an ace from the bottom of the DECK', followed by the target word *cards* or *ship*). The results revealed a larger N400 to contextually inappropriate targets (e.g. *ship*) than to contextually appropriate targets (e.g. *cards*), suggesting that the contextually appropriate meanings of the polysemous words were selectively activated in memory. The strategy of precisely identifying the cognitive events that elicit an ERP component has considerable appeal. However, the mapping between changes in an ERP component and putative cognitive processes is often far from transparent. This point is illustrated by the current controversy over whether changes in N400 amplitude reflect the same set of cognitive processes as do changes in the amplitude of the N2 component, which is elicited by stimuli that do not match preceding stimuli on some attribute (Näätänen and Gaillard 1983). Importantly, experimental designs that assume knowledge of underlying language-related processes carry with them the significant risk associated with a misidentification of these processes. For example, if N400 amplitude reflects processes other than word activation, then the set of interpretations one might entertain in explaining the Van Petten and Kutas data might expand significantly.

A second approach to ERP investigations of language comprehension has been to use a known ERP component to study some aspect of comprehension, *even if the cognitive and neural events underlying the component have not been identified.* This approach becomes feasible once the component is shown to *systematically covary* with manipulations of stimuli, task, or instructions that influence the cognitive process of interest. Having found such a covariation, one can make certain inferences about relevant psychological processes based on between-condition differences in the ERPs. For example, several researchers have observed a slow positive-going wave (labelled the 'P600 effect' by Osterhout and Holcomb (1992)) in the ERP response to syntactically anomalous words (Neville *et al.* 1991; Osterhout 1990; Osterhout and Holcomb 1992; Osterhout *et al.* in press; see below). The specific cognitive events underlying the P600 are not known, and there is no evidence that the P600 is a direct manifestation of sentence comprehension. One possibility is that the P600 is a member of the P300 family of waves often observed following unexpected stimuli (cf. Donchin 1981). The point here is that in order for the P600 to act as a reliable marker of syntactic anomaly (and hence as a useful tool for testing certain theories of comprehension), all that is needed is evidence that it *reliably co-occurs* with syntactic anomaly, regardless of whether or not it directly reflects the processes that parse sentences during comprehension. Using this logic, Osterhout and Holcomb (1992, 1993) (see also Hagoort *et al.* 1993; Osterhout and Swinney 1989; Osterhout *et al.* 1994) have successfully contrasted predictions made by certain parsing models concerning when and where syntactic anomaly will be encountered, employing the P600 as an electrophysiological marker of syntactic anomaly.

6.2.2 ERPs and the timing of linguistic processes

ERPs promise to reveal a great deal about the timing and ordering of language-related processes. In temporal evaluations of ERPs, the critical issue often concerns the moment in time at which the ERPs from two conditions begin to diverge significantly, rather than the peak latency of a particular ERP component (see Chapter 2, section 2.3). For example, the peak of the N400 component reliably occurs at about 400 ms after presentation of the word. However, divergences in the waveforms elicited by contextually appropriate and contextually inappropriate words can begin to emerge as early as 50 ms (Holcomb and Neville 1991) and typically emerge around 200–250 ms following word onset (Kutas and Hillyard 1980c). The importance of this distinction becomes clear when considering whether the N400 is sensitive to the process of lexical access. The available evidence indicates that lexical access occurs in the range of about 200 ms (Sabol and DeRosa 1976). If the peak latency of the N400 is taken as the temporal marker of its occurrence, then many would argue that the component occurs too late to reflect lexical access. However, if the onset of divergences in waveforms is taken as the temporal marker, then the N400 is much closer to the time window suggested for lexical access (see Fischler (1990) for more discussion of this issue).

A related issue concerns the sorts of inferences about the timing of cognitive processes that are licensed by ERP data. Unless one knows with certainty the cognitive events underlying a given ERP effect, such inferences can be risky. This is particularly true of ERP effects with relatively late occurring onsets. For example, the P600 effect elicited by syntactically anomalous words (Osterhout and Holcomb 1992) typically has an onset around 500 ms. This finding does not necessarily license the inference that the assignment of syntactic roles to words occurs around 500 ms after word onset. The P600 might only indirectly reflect the assignment of syntactic structure; the cognitive events that do in fact underlie the P600 might be temporally removed from the syntactic processes themselves.

Conversely, very early onsets of ERP effects can sometimes license strong inferences about the timing of language processes. For example, the ERPs to contextually inappropriate words in spoken sentences begin to diverge from those to contextually appropriate controls long before the entirety of the word has been encountered by the listener (Holcomb and Neville 1991). These data clearly indicate that an interaction between word recognition and context occurs long before the word can be recognized solely on the basis of the acoustic stimulus.

6.3 ERPS AND WORD RECOGNITION

Some of the most heavily researched questions in cognitive psychology concern the mental operations and processes underlying word recognition. What are the information processing steps that lead to recognition? Are these steps arranged in a discrete series, with a strictly bottom-up progression? Or are they highly parallel and interactive? What is the nature and organization of the stored mental representations with which incoming sensory information is compared? What aspects of stored information become available to subsequent linguistic processes? What is the time course of word recognition?

A number of researchers have examined word recognition by recording ERPs to words presented in lists (that is, without a sentence context). In almost all cases this has involved presenting subjects with between 20 and 60 visually displayed items in each of several conditions. Typically, subjects have been asked to perform a task concurrent with reading the words. The most frequently used task has been the lexical decision task (LDT), in which the subject must rapidly decide if a letter string is a legal English word or a non-word (e.g. FLARK). Unfortunately, the other task frequently used to study word recognition, the naming task, is not suitable for use while collecting ERPs. Muscle 'artefact' is produced when the mouth and tongue are moved during speaking; this artefact interferes with reliable recording of ERPs.

6.3.1 Semantic priming

Several ERP researchers have investigated *semantic priming* (cf. Meyer and Schvaneveldt 1971). In a typical semantic priming experiment, pairs of letter strings are presented. The first letter string (the prime word) is followed by a semantic associate of the prime word (the related target), a word unrelated to the prime (the unrelated target), or a non-word. Numerous behavioural studies have shown that a subject's processing of related targets (e.g. DOCTOR–*NURSE*) is enhanced or facilitated, in comparison with the processing of the unrelated targets (e.g. WINDOW–*NURSE*). This facilitation has typically taken the form of faster reaction times (RTs) to related targets than to unrelated targets during a lexical decision task. Several mechanisms have been proposed to account for such semantic priming. One of the earliest and most enduring accounts, automatic spreading activation (Collins and Loftus 1975), proposes that representations of words in the mental lexicon are organized semantically and that related words are either located closer together in the lexicon or have stronger links relative to unrelated words. When a prime word's representation is accessed due to 'bottom-up' processing of the sensory information, activity passively spreads to semantically related items, boosting their activation beyond normal resting levels. When a target word is presented a short time later, it will be processed more quickly or efficiently if its representation is one of those passively activated by the prime. In contrast, processing of the target will not benefit if the target is unrelated to the prime. We should note that the locus of this type of automatic priming has generally been assumed to occur prior to the actual recognition of the target word — hence the term *pre*- or *interlexical priming*.

As the literature on semantic priming has grown, the pattern of observed effects has become more difficult to account for via a purely passive spreading activation process. For example, in experiments in which the proportion of related items was high and/or the interval between target and prime was relatively long (more than 500 ms), RTs were reported to be longer than expected when the target and prime were unrelated (e.g. den Heyer *et al.* 1983; Neely 1976, 1977; Tweedy *et al.* 1977). This suggested that in addition to the facilitatory spreading activation process, an inhibitory mechanism was operating under certain circumstances. Because automatic spreading activation was supposed to function without costs or inhibition, Neely (1977), among others, proposed a second, limited-capacity priming mechanism to account for inhibition effects. According to this view, so-called attentional or strategic priming occurs when the subject actively anticipates the occurrence of the target item based upon the meaning of the prime word (cf. Becker 1980). This further facilitates RT beyond automatic levels when the prime and target are related, but slows RT when they are unrelated, because attention, which is relatively slow, must be shifted from the anticipated related representation to the appropriate unrelated one (Posner and Snyder 1975).

The locus of such attentional priming effects is not clear. For example, Neely (1991) has suggested that they are pre-lexical, implying that attentional processes can direct the lexical access process. Others (e.g. Seidenberg *et al.* 1984) have argued that attentional priming is post-lexical because larger effects are found in the LDT than in the naming task (as used here, post-lexical implies that the process operates after an item's representation has been activated in the lexicon). Seidenberg *et al.* assume that naming is primarily sensitive to pre- or inter lexical influences (but see Balota and Chumbley 1985).

For a number of years much of the literature on semantic priming seemed consistent with one or both of the above processes. However, recent data from both the naming task and the LDT have cast doubt on the ability of these two mechanisms to fully explain semantic priming. Neely and Keefe (1989) have suggested that a third process may be important under certain circumstances when the lexical decision task is involved. Their argument is based on the assumption that LDT reaction times are influenced by post-lexical 'decision' factors as well as by pre-lexical factors. (Note that according to Neely this is not the same as the attentional mechanism, which he argues is a pre-lexical effect). In other words, the decision process occurs after an item has activated its representation in the lexicon. But how do subjects actually decide to respond 'non-word?' An exhaustive search of the lexicon would appear to be inefficient and too time-consuming. This issue has never been convincingly resolved, but it increasingly looks as though non-word responses might be made in different ways under different conditions (e.g. Balota and Chumbley 1984). Neely and Keefe (1989) have suggested that in semantic priming experiments subjects can sometimes use a relatedness strategy to help make the lexical decision. In effect, subjects might ask themselves, 'Are the prime and target related?' If yes, respond 'word', if not then consider responding 'non-word'. Note that this strategy works best if the ratio of non-word to unrelated word trials is relatively high, and if non-word targets are not paired with semantically related primes (e.g. DOCTOR–NARSE).

In an extensive review of the priming literature, Neely (1991) concluded that a combination of three of the above reviewed factors contributes to the pattern of priming in the LDT: automatic spreading activation, attentional expectancy, and the non-word ratio. However, it should be pointed out that this conclusion is partly based on the assumption that automatic spreading activation and attentional priming are separate pre-lexical mechanisms and that the non-word ratio mechanism is post-lexical. An alternative possibility is a modified two-process account that assumes that attentional expectancy and cognizance of the non-word ratio are two of a host of possible post-lexical strategies that subjects might use in making a lexical decision. In other words, in addition to automatic spreading activation it might be most parsimonious to assume a single flexible process (we will call it 'strategic attention') that can deal with information from a variety of sources depending on the demands of the task in hand. In procedures such as the LDT, the ways in which subjects strategically employ and combine these various pieces of information might account for the somewhat different patterns of priming effects seen across studies.

A potential promise of ERPs is that some aspect (component) of these measures might prove uniquely sensitive to one or more of the processes involved in word recognition (e.g. automatic spreading activation), whereas others might reflect post-lexical processes (e.g. strategic attentional factors). The advantages of such a find are clear. Since RT results are frequently ambiguous with respect to the locus of the information process(es) responsible for an effect, the existence of a measure that is sensitive to a specifiable, restricted set of these processes would provide valuable data for modellers of word recognition.

Bentin *et al.* (1985) were one of the first groups to record ERPs to visually presented word pairs in a semantic priming/lexical decision experiment. They found that all three of their target types (related to the prime, unrelated to the prime, and non-word) elicited a large ERP positivity (550 to 650 ms). However, two types of targets (targets unrelated to the prime and non-word targets) produced a large negative-going wave which peaked at approximately 400 ms. Bentin *et al.* suggested that the negative-going activity might be related to the N400 component previously observed following contextually inappropriate words (Kutas and Hillyard 1980*c*; see above). Similar findings have been reported by Rugg (1985) and Holcomb (1986, 1988). In another study (Bentin 1987), subjects made either antonym judgements or lexical decisions about targets preceded by a prime word or non-word. Targets that were antonyms of the prime produced almost no negativity in the N400 region. In contrast, targets that were unrelated to the prime produced a clear N400. Pronounceable non-words generated the largest N400 response.

Subsequent work has been aimed at determining whether these modulations to N400 amplitude reflect a pre- or post-lexical process. For example, Holcomb (1988) manipulated both the instructions given to subjects and the proportion of related prime–target pairs (17 per cent versus 67 per cent) within the list. In one block, the instructions and the relatively small proportion of related prime–target pairs were ideally suited for producing only automatic priming. In a second block, the instructions and the larger proportion of related prime–target pairs encouraged subjects to attend to the semantic relationship between prime and target words; that is, the second condition presumably induced subjects to employ strategic processes in responding to the targets. In both blocks, target words that followed an unrelated word or a neutral prime (a row of x's) elicited larger N400s than targets that were related to the prime (see Fig. 6.2). However, this N400 effect was larger in the 'attentional' block than in the 'automatic' block. If the N400 is sensitive to the 'inhibition' or 'interference' associated with processing a target word that is unrelated to the prime, one might predict that targets following an unrelated prime should elicit larger N400s than targets following a neutral prime. No such difference in N400 amplitude was observed. One interpretation of this finding is that N400 amplitude is sensitive to processes that facilitate target processing (e.g. spreading activation) but not to processes that inhibit or interefere with target processing (e.g. conscious expectations generated only by attending to the prime–target relationships). Interestingly, a later 'slow wave' differentiated the neutral and unrelated targets, but only in the attentional condition. Holcomb concluded that these results are in agreement with the substantial literature that supports the dual-process account of semantic priming. Specifically, the N400 may be sensitive to priming due to automatic spreading activation and to the additional priming that results from the allocation of attentional resources, but not to the inhibitory or interference effects of unrelated targets. Conversely, differences in the late slow wave might reflect the interference effects engendered by target words that were unrelated to the preceding prime word.

Other studies have attempted to determine whether N400 amplitude reflects one specific pre-lexical process, namely, automatic spreading activation. Evidence that N400 amplitude is sensitive to automatic spreading activation would be

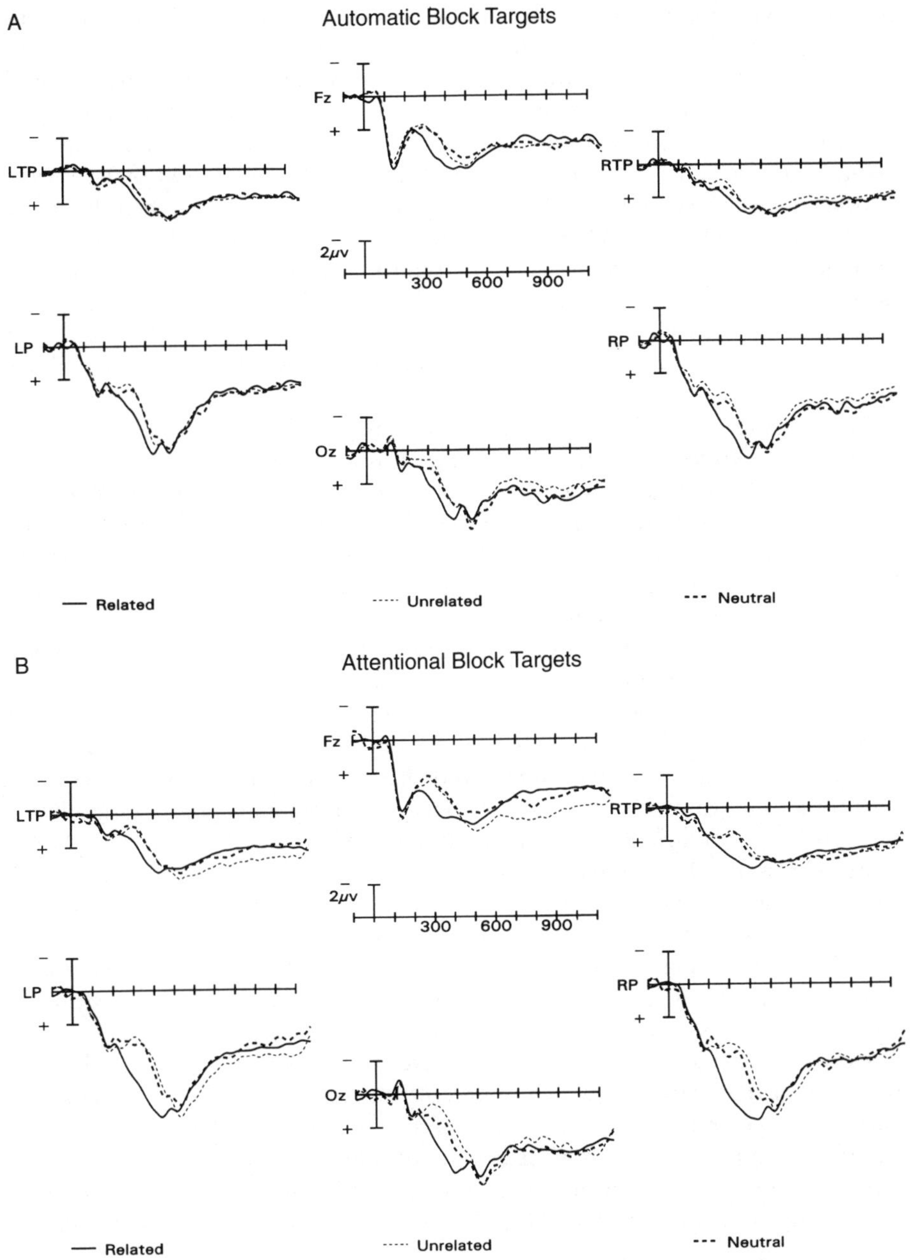

Fig. 6.2 ERPs to related, unrelated, and neutral target words in a semantic priming lexical decision task. The ERPs in panel A are from the 'automatic' block of trials and those in panel B are from the 'attentional' block. Stimulus onset in this and all subsequent figures is the vertical calibration bar. Each tick mark is 100 ms. LP and RP are left and right parietal sites, LTP and RTP are left and right temporal-parietal sites, Fz is frontal midline, and Oz is occipital midline. (Adapted from Holcomb 1988.)

consistent with the claim that this component is sensitive to activation of word representations (lexical access or some other word-level recognition process). One possibility is that N400 amplitude is sensitive to the number of resources utilized in pushing a word's detector past its recognition threshold (as in Morton's (1969) logogen model). According to this account, N400 is small to primed target words because the lexical detector for the target benefits from the 'spread of activation' associated with the processing of the prior prime word. However, when the target word is preceded by an unrelated prime there is no such benefit and more resources are required to drive the target word's detector past its recognition threshold. The utilization of these extra resources might be what is reflected by the larger N400 to these words.[1] This view of the N400 (or one very close to it) is favoured by a number of ERP researchers (e.g. Fischler and Raney 1991, Van Petten and Kutas 1991).

The possibility that the N400 is sensitive to an automatic lexical process is bolstered by two recent studies. Kutas and Hillyard (1989) instructed subjects to determine if a target letter was present in either the first or second member of a word pair (delayed letter search task). The ERPs to second words produced the following pattern: N400 was largest when the preceding prime word was semantic-ally unrelated, intermediate when the semantic relationship was relatively weak, and smallest when pairs were highly related (see Fig. 6.3). Because this task does not appear to require the subject to process either word for meaning, it is possible to argue that the obtained priming effects were due to automatic spreading activation.

More recently, Besson *et al.* (1992) demonstrated that the N400 is larger to unrelated than to related targets when the subject's task involved a graphemic judgement (do the prime and target words have similar or dissimilar initial and final consonant–vowel characteristics), even at relatively short prime–target inter-vals (300 ms stimulus onset asynchrony (SOA)). Neely (1977) has argued that at short SOAs only the automatic spreading activation process, which is relatively fast, has time to become active. So, the finding of N400 priming effects at short intervals suggests that this component is sensitive to automatic spreading activa-tion. This conclusion is bolstered by a study by Boddy (1986) who also found similarly large N400 effects for long (1000 ms) and shorter (200 ms) stimulus onset asynchronies in a lexical decision task (LDT).

However, the fact that in all of the above studies both the prime and target were part of the active task structure prevents us from concluding that the N400 effects were not mediated by a strategic post-lexical process. Even in the case of the 300 ms SOA of Besson *et al.* it is still possible that subjects might have used attentional resources to aid in the processing of the prime–target relationship — particularly since the target N400 peaks at such a relatively late point (700 ms

---

[1] Note that we have carefully avoided talking about differences in the duration of the lexical process as is customary in models dealing with RT priming differences. The reason for this is that latency differences in the N400 have not been reported in priming studies (but see Kutas 1987). From the available data it seems most likely that the process reflected by the N400 is one with a relatively fixed duration and time-course and that modifications in this process are in terms of the amount of activity it expends. However, this assumption has never been carefully tested by, for example, looking at differences in the time-course of the N400 to different items.

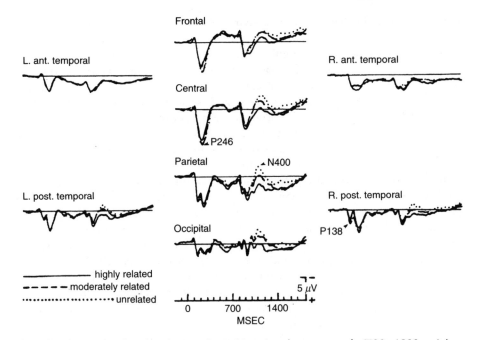

Fig. 6.3 ERPs to prime words (the first 700 ms) and target words (700–1800 ms) in a delayed letter search task. Note particularly the large N400 to the unrelated targets and the somewhat smaller N400 to moderately related targets. (From Kutas and Hillyard (1989). Reprinted with permission of the authors and the publishers.)

post-prime onset in the Besson *et al.* study). To more conclusively determine if the N400 is sensitive to strictly automatic processes would require a procedure which prevents attentive processing of the prime. Masking of the prime at the level of identification, which presumably prevents the subject from attending to the meaning of the prime word, has been shown to produce purely automatic behavioural priming in lexical decision (e.g. Fowler *et al.* 1981; Marcel 1983). Two such studies have been conducted with ERPs. Brown and Hagoort (1993) failed to obtain an N400 effect between related and unrelated words in a masked prime LDT even though they did find evidence of RT priming (they found typical N400 effects when the prime was not masked). In a second study Neville *et al.* (1989) found robust N400 semantic priming effects in the LDT at both long (533 ms) and relatively short (100 ms) prime–target intervals when the prime and target were identifiable. However, they failed to find an N400 semantic priming effect when the prime was obscured by a prior pattern mask, although there was an earlier left-hemisphere negativity (200 to 300 ms) that distinguished unrelated from related targets.[2] The results of these two masking studies cast doubt on the

[2] Neville *et al.* did find an N400-like effect for targets that were repeats of the prime, even when the prime was masked. This suggests that the mechanisms involved in repetition and semantic N400 priming may not be exactly the same.

hypothesis that the N400 reflects activity in an automatic spreading activation, pre-lexical process.

Another candidate for the cognitive process underlying the N400 is some type of post-recognition process. At least two possibilities exist. First, N400 may reflect activity in a post-lexical conceptual memory system. In some comprehension models conceptual/semantic knowledge is separated from lexical knowledge, primarily for reasons of cognitive economy. For example, Ellis and Young (1988) have proposed that each modality (spoken words, written words, and possibly pictures) has its own input lexicon that feeds into an amodal semantic system. In this type of model semantic priming might occur at the lexical level (e.g. due to lexical items being organized semantically) and/or at the conceptual/semantic level (e.g. due to related concepts sharing features). N400 could be sensitive to processes at either or both of these levels (although the masked priming studies suggest that lexical priming is unlikely; see above). The rapid onset of N400 semantic priming effects between spoken and written words (Holcomb and Anderson 1993), and between words and pictures (e.g. Nigam *et al.* 1992; see below), can be construed as evidence favouring the claim that modulations in N400 amplitude reflect an amodal conceptual/semantic level process. According to this account, such cross-modal effects result because both input modalities tap a common set of conceptual knowledge representations.[3]

A second possibility is that N400 reflects an even higher-level 'integrative' process (Holcomb 1993; Rugg 1990; Rugg *et al.* 1988) In some psycholinguistic models, integrative processes are used by the language comprehension system to help coalesce information provided by a variety of 'lower' processes (e.g. lexical/semantic, syntactic, pragmatic, etc.) into an ongoing discourse representation (e.g. Kintsch 1988; Marslen-Wilson 1987). There are at least two possibilities as to how N400 could reflect priming-like operations at this level. First, integration may be directly affected by up-stream word recognition operations, such as the number of resources required to activate a lexical or conceptual representation. For example, the processes that integrate the language input may receive semantic and syntactic output from the lexicon, as well as information on how easily this information could be activated. Integration (and N400) might then be sensitive to this latter information. However, at a functional level, this characterization does not differ significantly from the above proposal for a word-level locus of N400 priming. A more reasonable possibility, *vis-à-vis* the integration hypothesis, is that N400 amplitude reflects the ease with which various knowledge sources (e.g. lexical, syntactic and semantic) are used to form an integrated discourse representation; the more difficult it is to integrate a given piece of information into the ongoing representation, the larger the N400 effect elicited by that information.

A host of behavioural studies have shown that degraded linguistic stimuli slow down the speed of word processing. Meyer *et al.* (1975) were the first to show

---

[3] One possibility is that the modalities (spoken words, written words, and pictures) maintain separate input lexicons that feed into a common conceptual memory system where a single amodal semantic representation is maintained.

that stimulus degradation interacts with semantic priming. In their experiment the difference in RT between target words preceded by semantically related primes and targets preceded by unrelated primes was greater when the targets were degraded by an overlaid matrix of dots. This pattern of results was true for both lexical decision and naming latency. Based on additive factors logic, Meyer *et al.* concluded that priming and degradation affect a common process, which they argued was an initial encoding stage (that is, lexical access). If this conclusion is correct, and if N400 is closely tied to this level, then N400 amplitude, like RT, should produce a larger difference between primed and unprimed words when the words are degraded than when they are intact. On the other hand, if N400 is more closely associated with a mechanism that is not directly affected by degradation, such as a later post-lexical process, then the difference between primed and unprimed words should not necessarily increase in amplitude when these items are degraded.

Recently, Holcomb (1993) conducted such an ERP study using intact and degraded targets in a semantic priming LDT. The behavioural results replicated the basic degradation/priming interaction seen in the Meyer *et al.* study (that is, priming was greater under degraded conditions). Analyses of the ERP data indicated that degrading the target had a small but non-significant effect on the overall time-course of the N400. However, and more importantly, there was no difference in the size of the ERP priming effects (amplitude or latency) for intact and degraded targets. In other words, the larger priming effect seen in RT for degraded targets was not present in the N400. Moreover, this lack of a priming-by-degradation interaction was accompanied by a large main effect of priming on N400 (amplitude and latency — see Fig. 6.4). Holcomb argued that these data are most consistent with the view that the mechanism underlying the N400 is a relatively late (post-lexical) process. However, the data from this study cannot distinguish between the two above-mentioned post-lexical accounts (conceptual versus integration) of the N400.

6.3.2 Recognizing spoken words

Most researchers investigating word recognition have presented visual stimuli. This preference for visual presentation of language stimuli is understandable, given the relative difficulty of presenting language auditorily in a controlled experimental situation. However, several recent experiments have recorded ERPs to auditorily presented words. For example, Holcomb and Neville (1990) directly compared and contrasted semantic priming in the visual and auditory modalities. Subjects participated in two versions (one visual, one auditory) of a lexical decision task, in which stimuli were word pairs consisting of a prime word followed by a semantically related word, an unrelated word, or one of two kinds of non-words: pseudowords, and 'backwords', words either spelled (visual) or played (auditory) backward. N400s were larger to unrelated words than to related words in both modalities (see Fig. 6.5). However, this ERP 'priming effect' began earlier and lasted longer in the auditory modality than in the visual modality. Holcomb and

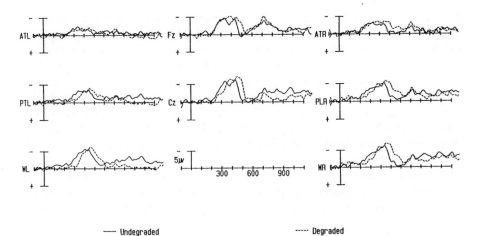

— Undegraded   ----- Degraded

Fig. 6.4 Difference waves, computed by subtracting ERPs to targets preceded by a related prime from those preceded by an unrelated prime, showing N400 amplitude in a task in which subjects performed a lexical decision task. Targets were either 'undegraded' or 'degraded'. ATL and ATR are left and right anterior temporal sites, PTL and PTR are left and right posterior temporal sites, and Fz and Cz are frontal and central midline sites. Note that the N400 effect is not larger in the degraded condition, but that N400 onset is shifted later in time. (Adapted from Holcomb (1993).)

Neville concluded that there may be overlap in the set of processes that underlie priming in each modality but that these processes are not identical. In particular they noted that the earlier onset of the N400 in the auditory modality was consistent with the model of speech comprehension proposed by Marslen-Wilson (Marslen-Wilson and Welsh 1978; Marslen-Wilson 1987) — that auditory word processing can begin prior to the arrival of all of the acoustic information in a spoken word and that the time-course of this processing can be influenced by semantic properties of a prior word.

6.3.3 Is the N400 specific to linguistic stimuli?

In the experiment discussed above, Holcomb and Neville (1990) reported that in both modalities pseudowords produced large N400s, but that 'backwards' words (words spelled or played backward) showed no evidence of an N400 response in either modality; the related words actually had a larger N400 response than the backward words. They argued that these data were consistent with the hypothesis that the N400 is elicited only by linguistic stimuli; that is, they claimed that the component is *language specific*. The reasoning behind this argument is that if the N400 is a generic mismatch response (i.e. an N2) that responds to any kind of discrepancy between prime and target stimuli (e.g. Polich 1985), then both kinds of non-words should have produced equivalent negativities. Since un-word-like non-words (backward words) failed to show any hint of N400 activity,

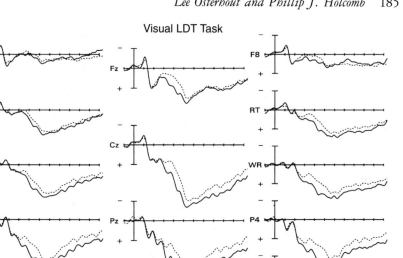

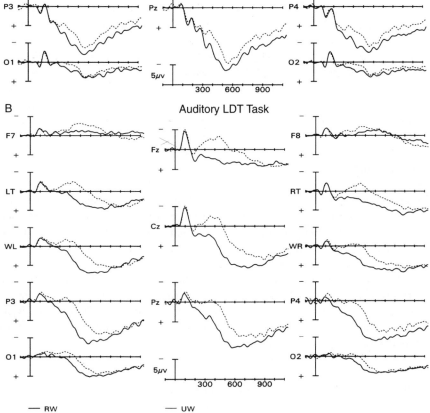

Fig. 6.5 ERPs elicited in a lexical decision task under conditions of semantic priming. Panel A plots ERPs recorded to visually presented target words. Panel B plots ERPs elicited under identical conditions with auditory stimuli. RW and UW refer to related and unrelated targets respectively. F7 and F8 are left and right frontal sites, LT and RT are left and right temporal sites, WL and WR are left and right temporal parietal sites (approximately over Wernicke's area and its right-hemisphere analogue), P3 and P4 are left and right parietal sites, and O1 and O2 are left and right occipital sites. (Adapted from Holcomb and Neville (1990).)

they concluded that the N400 is selectively sensitive to language-like stimuli (see Fig. 6.6).

The language-specificity hypothesis is supported by the results of other studies as well. Besson and Macar (1987) had subjects listen to well-known melodies that ended either with the expected note or with an unexpected note (that is, the musical version of a priming task), and to sentences that ended in the expected final word or an incongruous word (the Kutas and Hillyard paradigm). In comparison to the expected final note, the unexpected notes did not produce an N400-like response, but rather produced an enhanced positivity (P3). A similar pattern was obtained with geometric shapes and musical scales. Comparison of the expected and incongruous sentence final words revealed a large N400 response for the incongruous words, replicating the original Kutas and Hillyard (1980c) result.

Recently, several priming studies have shown N400-like effects to pairs of related and unrelated pictures (Barrett and Rugg 1990; Holcomb and McPherson 1994) or a combination of words and semantically appropriate and inappropriate pictures (Nigam *et al.* 1992). These findings would appear to cast some doubt on the language specificity of the N400. However, if pictures and words are represented in a common representational system (e.g. in conceptual memory), or if picture and word representations are separate but highly interconnected, then priming between input domains might be viewed as contradictory only to a strong specificity hypothesis.

6.3.4 Summary

Although specific ERP components (e.g. the N400) are clearly sensitive to important aspects of word recognition, the precise cognitive processes underlying such ERP effects remain undetermined. In particular, the evidence available to date does not allow one to divide these effects into 'pre-lexical' and 'post-lexical' categories. One might tentatively conclude from the data reviewed here that the N400 component is not solely a direct reflection of the cognitive processes underlying lexical access. Rather, N400 amplitude appears to be quite sensitive to relatively late-occurring processes. (For a dissenting view see Fischler and Raney (1991).) Identification of the specific nature of the processes underlying the N400 component will require additional research.

6.4 ERPS AND SENTENCE COMPREHENSION

Words only occasionally appear in isolation. Usually, words are embedded within sentences, and the meaning of a sentence is determined in part by the specific combination of words within the sentence. A number of questions immediately arise when one attempts to describe how readers and listeners successfully comprehend a sentence. Some of these questions concern the relationship between word processing and sentence context. For example, does sentence context influence the earliest stages of word recognition, or are these processes isolated from

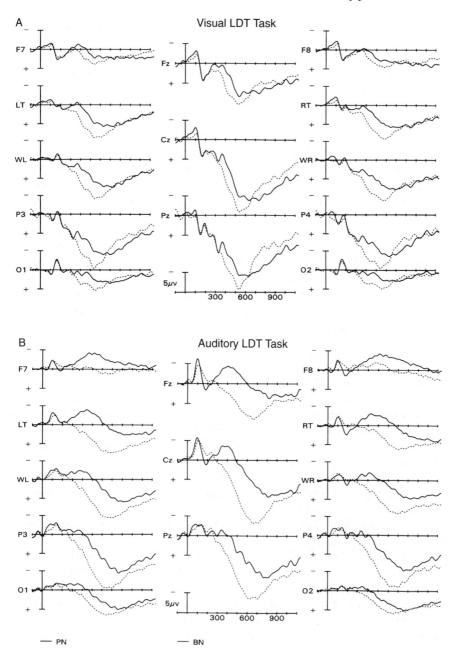

Fig. 6.6 ERPs to pseudowords (PNs) and 'backward' non-words (BNs) for the visual (panel A) and auditory (panel B) modalities. (Adapted from Holcomb and Neville (1990).)

the effects of context? Other questions concern the determination of relations between words in the sentence, that is, the computation of syntactic structure. (The processes underlying syntactic analysis are often referred to as *parsing*.) Do readers and listeners compute syntactic representations that are distinct from semantic representations? Assuming that syntactic representations are indeed computed, then precisely *how* are such representations arrived at? In particular, how does the sentence parser deal with the ubiquitous syntactic indeterminism present in natural languages?

An important methodological concern in any study of sentence processing is the mode of stimulus presentation. Since measurement of ERPs does not require an intrusive 'secondary' task (e.g. pressing a button after each word or sentence), this method allows researchers to more closely approximate a normal comprehension environment. A number of recent studies have presented connected natural speech (Holcomb and Neville 1990, 1991; McCallum *et al.* 1984; Osterhout and Holcomb 1993). Others have linked ERP measurements with eye saccades during 'normal' reading (Marton and Szirtes 1988). However, the standard method in most of the work to date (and of most of the work reviewed below) has involved the visual presentation of sentences in a sequential, word-by-word manner. Intervals between the onset of words have ranged from about 100 ms to over 1 s, with typical word onset asynchronies of 300 to 1000 ms.

6.4.1 ERPs in sentences

Before reviewing the ERP literature relevant to psycholinguistic models of sentence comprehension, we will briefly consider the typical ERP response to sentences. Sentences elicit a sustained and increasing negativity; this negativity has been associated with the contingent negative variation (CNV) (Rohrbaugh and Gaillard 1983; see Chapter 1, section 1.3.2). ERPs to individual words within the sentence are superimposed on the negative-going activity (Fischler *et al.* 1983; Kutas and Hillyard 1980*c*; Kutas *et al.* 1988; Neville *et al.* 1982). When the temporal separation between words is sufficiently large, the early 'exogenous' components (e.g. the P1–N1–P2 complex) are clearly observable in grand averages. Later-occurring 'endogenous' components are also visible; for example, most words within the sentence elicit the N400 component (Kutas *et al.* 1988; Van Petten and Kutas 1990, 1991). Hemispheric asymmetries have been observed, both for exogenous and for endogenous components elicited by words. Specifically, the P1, P2, and N400 components all appear to be slightly larger over the right hemisphere (Kutas *et al.* 1988). Finally, sentence-ending words in grammatical, coherent sentences are often followed by a slow positive wave (Friedman *et al.* 1975). This wave is greatly reduced when the sentence is ungrammatical or incoherent (Herning *et al.* 1987; Osterhout and Holcomb 1992; Van Petten and Kutas 1991).

6.4.2 Word recognition in sentence contexts

When subjects are asked to name or make lexical decisions about words in sentences, they respond more quickly to words preceded by related context than to words preceded by unrelated context (Fischler and Bloom 1979; Schuberth and et al. 1981; Stanovitch and West 1983). This and other evidence indicates that word processing is influenced by the sentence context in which it occurs. Various mechanisms have been proposed to account for such influences. One hypothesis is that these effects reflect the automatic spread of activation from 'active' concepts to related concepts within the lexicon or conceptual knowledge store (see Section 6.3). A second hypothesis is that context engenders expectations concerning the identity of subsequent words (cf. Becker 1980). More recently, this issue has been couched in terms of a dichotomy between *interactive* models, in which context influences early (pre-lexical) stages of word processing (cf. Marslen-Wilson 1987), and *modular* models, in which the early-occurring word recognition processes are isolated from the influences of context (Swinney 1979). According to the modular model, sentence context has its effects on late-occurring, post-lexical processes. Efforts to uncover the locus of sentence context effects with behavioural measures have produced a substantial literature but no consensus. The continuous, on-line nature of ERPs would appear to make them ideal tools for investigating the time-course of sentence context effects on word recognition.

6.4.2.1 *Priming within sentences*

The pioneering work of Kutas and her associates (Kutas and Hillyard 1980*a,b,c*) clearly demonstrated that the N400 component of the ERP is sensitive to the semantic relationship between a word and preceding sentence context. In their study described above, Kutas and Hillyard (1980*a,b,c*) observed that contextually inappropriate words elicit a larger N400 component than do contextually appro-priate words (see Fig. 6.1). Subsequent studies have indicated that N400 amplitude is responsive to word expectancy. For example, Kutas and Hillyard (1984) man-ipulated the expectedness of sentence-final words by varying 'the cloze probability' of these words. (Cloze probability is determined by requiring a large group of subjects to fill in the missing final word in a set of sentences.) Although all of the sentence-final words were semantically acceptable, less-expected final words (e.g. 'The bill was due at the end of the *hour*') elicited a larger N400 than more likely or predictable completions (e.g. 'The bill was due at the end of the *month*'). In addition to demonstrating that N400 amplitude can be influenced by word expectancy, these results indicate that semantic anomaly, although perhaps a sufficient condition, is not a necessary condition for eliciting the N400 effect.

Other data appear to indicate that both word expectancy *and* automatic activa-tion within the lexicon play a role in determining N400 amplitude. Kutas *et al.* (1984) compared the N400 elicited by three types of sentence-ending words (e.g. 'The pizza was too hot to *eat/drink/cry*'). The first type (*eat*) was the high-cloze (that is, most expected) completion to the sentence. The second type (*drink*) was related to the high-cloze completion, but was itself an anomalous ending. The third type (*cry*) was both unrelated to the high-cloze completion and semantically anomalous with respect to context. Unrelated anomalous endings elicited a large N400 and expected words elicited a small N400. Of more interest was the response to the anomalous endings which were related to the most likely completions. The N400 to these words was larger than the N400 to the most likely completions, but smaller than the N400 to anomalous words unrelated to the high-cloze word. These results were taken to indicate that N400 amplitude is responsive to both (i) word expectancies engendered by context, and (ii) associations between individual words (e.g. the association between *eat* and *drink*), not all of which need to be physically present in the sentence (cf. Kutas and Van Petten 1988).

Another question receiving quite a bit of attention in the psycholinguistic literature is whether the effects of single-word contexts on word processing are distinct from the effects of sentence or discourse context. Put differently, the question is whether 'lexical' and 'sentential' priming result from a single mechanism or from distinct mechanisms. The prevailing view has been that lexical and sentential priming reflect qualitatively distinct processes. For example, one common claim is that lexical priming results from the spread of activation among related items in the lexicon, whereas sentential priming reflects processes that integrate individual words into a conceptual representation of the discourse (for a review see Van Petten (1993)). This standard view was examined by Kutas (1993), who reasoned that if lexical and sentential priming do indeed occur via qualitatively distinct mechanisms, then the effects of such priming might take the form of qualitatively distinct changes in the ERP waveform. However, Kutas (1993) found no such evidence when she directly compared the ERP manifestation of lexical and sentential priming. Both types of priming had remarkably similar effects. Specifically, both types of context reduced the amplitude of the N400 component, and neither the latency nor the scalp distribution of these effects differed as a function of context. Kutas interpreted these findings as indicating that there is a qualitative similarity between the processes underlying lexical and sentential priming.

This conclusion, however, is at least partially at odds with the results of another recent study. Van Petten (1993) also directly compared lexical and semantic priming, but did so by recording ERPs to associated and unassociated word pairs that were embedded in semantically anomalous or coherent sentences. Van Petten found what could be construed as evidence that qualitatively distinct processes underlie in the two effects. For example, the sentential context effect had a longer duration but smaller amplitude than the lexical context effect. Furthermore, these effects appeared to be additive, perhaps indicating some degree of independence. Finally, the sentential context effect was predictive of subsequent recognition accuracy, whereas the lexical effect was not.

6.4.2.2 Interaction between sentence context and word frequency

As noted above, subjects respond more quickly to words preceded by related context than to words preceded by unrelated context. Similarly, subjects respond more quickly to frequent words than to less frequent words. The interaction between context and word frequency has implications for models of lexical access. Given the simplifying assumptions of additive-factors logic, interactive models predict an interaction between the effects of word frequency and context on responses to targets, because both factors are presumed to influence a common processing stage (e.g. the processes associated with lexical access). In contrast, modular models predict that these effects should be additive, since word frequency is presumed to influence lexical access, whereas context is presumed to influence post-access processes.

Behavioural tests of these predictions have produced conflicting results, with some studies reporting additive effects (Schuberth and Eimas 1977; Schuberth *et al.* 1981; Stanovitch and West 1983) and others reporting interactive effects (Becker 1979; Cairns and Foss 1971; Forster 1981). Van Petten and Kutas (1990) examined this issue with ERPs by measuring N400 amplitude to words in grammatical, semantically coherent sentences. The ERP responses to open-class words (e.g. nouns and verbs) were sorted and averaged according to word frequency and ordinal position within the sentence. Words occurring in early positions within their sentences were associated with larger N400s than words occurring later in the sentences. The authors interpreted this as indicating that as contextual constraints became stronger (simply by the addition of more sentence material), N400s to words in the sentence decreased in amplitude. Furthermore, less frequent words elicited larger N400s (relative to more frequent words) when they occurred in early positions in their respective sentences, but this frequency effect disappeared for words occurring in later positions. Van Petten and Kutas argue that this interaction between sentence position and word frequency is most compatible with an interactive model of lexical access in which the effects of contextual constraints can supersede the effects of word frequency during early stages of word recognition.

A subsequent study (Van Petten and Kutas 1991) isolated the effects of semantic and syntactic constraints on the N400 effect. The word position and frequency effects observed by Van Petten and Kutas (1990) were replicated in semantically coherent, grammatical sentences. But in sentences that were grammatical but semantically incoherent, (e.g. 'They married their uranium in store and cigarettes'), word position had no effect on N400 amplitude. One reasonable interpretation of this finding is that although semantic constraints interact with lexical access, the constraints imposed by sentence structure do not.

6.4.2.3 *Sentence context and lexical ambiguity*

Another means for contrasting interactive and modular models of lexical access focuses on lexical ambiguities, that is, words associated with two or more meanings. According to interactive models (Marslen-Wilson and Tyler 1980), contextual information can be used to selectively retrieve information from the lexicon. Given adequately biasing context, interactive models predict that only the contextually relevant meaning of a lexical ambiguity will be retrieved. In contrast, modular models (Swinney 1979) propose that lexical access operates independently of context; hence, such models predict that multiple meanings of a lexical ambiguity will be retrieved, regardless of the semantic content of context.

Attempts to resolve this issue with behavioural measures have provided compelling evidence that multiple meanings of lexical ambiguities are accessed, even in the presence of strongly biasing context (Onifer and Swinney, 1981; Seidenberg *et al.* 1982; Swinney 1979). Swinney and his associates employed a cross-modal priming technique, in which sentences containing biasing context and a subsequent ambiguous word were presented auditorily, while a visual target word (related to one meaning of the ambiguous word) was presented concurrently with the offset of the ambiguous word. Lexical decisions were facilitated to targets related to *either* the contextually relevant or the contextually inappropriate meaning of the ambiguous word, suggesting that context did not prevent both meanings from being accessed.

Such interpretations have been criticized for failing to take into account the possibility of *backward priming* — the effects of the target word on the processing of the preceding ambiguous word (Kiger and Glass 1983). Specifically, the close temporal proximity of the target to the ambiguous word might allow the target to act as a context for the ambiguous word, encouraging the activation of the meaning related to the target word (see Glucksberg *et al.* 1986). Conceivably, this backward priming process could occur rapidly enough to affect subjects' responses to the targets.

Given the continuous, millisecond-by-millisecond nature of ERP recordings, ERPs might provide a better test of the backward priming hypothesis than discrete measures such as reaction time. For example, one might predict that the response facilitation due to backward priming would have a later onset than that due to the effects of context preceding the ambiguous word. Van Petten and Kutas (1987; see above) adopted an all-visual variation of Swinney's method. The ambiguous word appeared as the final word in the sentence, and was followed (after a 200 ms delay) by the target word. Van Petten and Kutas made the crucial assumption that N400 amplitude is a metric of the activation level of a word's meaning. The contextually inappropriate targets elicited a larger-amplitude N400 than did the contextually appropriate words, and (within the window normally associated with the N400) ERPs to inappropriate targets did not differ from those to unrelated control words. However, later in the epoch the ERPs to the inappropriate words did become more negative-going than ERPs to controls. These results were taken to indicate that only the contextually relevant meaning was active prior to presentation of the target words (accounting for the absence of a difference in N400 amplitude to inappropriate targets and controls early in the epoch). Furthermore, the relatively late occurring differences in the ERPs to inappropriate and control targets could be accounted for by a backward priming mechanism.

6.4.3 Syntax and sentence comprehension

Sentence comprehension involves more than simply retrieving word meanings. It is generally (although not universally) agreed that sentence comprehension also requires an analysis of constituent structure, that is, an analysis of the relative ordering of words in the sentence and of the grammatical roles played by these words. Over the past decade, one of the primary goals of psycholinguistic research has been to specify the psychological processes underlying syntactic analysis. Do readers and listeners compute separable syntactic and semantic representations of a sentence during comprehension, or can the meaning of a sentence be derived directly, without an intervening syntactic representation? Assuming that syntactic representations do play a role, then exactly how are such representations constructed by the reader or listener? And how do the syntactic and semantic representations of a sentence interact during comprehension?

6.4.3.1 *The syntax/semantics distinction*

From a linguist's point of view, sentences that violate syntactic constraints (e.g. 'John hoped the man to leave') are quite distinct from sentences that violate semantic or pragmatic constraints (e.g. 'John buttered his bread with socks'). Whether or not these anomaly types are distinct with respect to the *psychological* and *neurological processes* engaged during comprehension remains a point of dispute. A common assumption in much recent psycholinguistic work is that separable cognitive processes derive syntactic and semantic interpretations of a sentence (cf. Berwick and Weinberg 1983; Fodor *et al.* 1974). However, other theorists claim that purely syntactic processes play no role in comprehension (cf. Ades and Steedman 1982; Riesbeck and Schank 1978). This fundamental question has been difficult to address with standard measures, largely because these measures tend to respond similarly to anomalies at different levels. The multidimensional nature of ERPs might make them a more efficacious tool for addressing this question, given two reasonable assumptions. One assumption is that the processes associated with a given level of analysis are distinct from those associated with other levels. The second assumption is that cognitively distinct processes are mediated by neurally distinct systems. Given these assumptions, evidence that syntactic and semantic anomalies elicit dissimilar patterns of brain response could be construed as evidence that separable syntacic and semantic processes exist (cf. Hagoort *et al.* 1993; Neville *et al.* 1991; Osterhout 1994; Osterhout and Holcomb 1992).

Previous work, discussed above, has been taken to indicate that one type of semantic anomaly (contextually inappropriate words) elicits a large N400 component. Several recent studies have examined the ERP response to syntactic anomalies. Kutas and Hillyard (1983) presented sentences containing errors in bound morphemes that designated word number or verb tense (e.g. 'As a turtle grows its shell grow too'). Few reliable differences were found between the ERPs to agreement-violating and control words, although the errors were associated with an increased negativity between 200 and 500 ms post-stimulus at some sites.

However, errors of number and tense agreement are quite distinct from anomalies associated with the determination of sentence structure. Osterhout and Holcomb

(1992) examined the ERP response to violations of constraints on permissible verb arguments, as in sentence (2):

(1)   The broker hoped <u>to</u> sell the stock.
      (intransitive-verb sentence)
(2)* The broker persuaded <u>to</u> sell the stock.[4]
      (transitive-verb sentence)

The clausal complement *to sell the stock* can be easily attached to the sentence fragment *The broker hoped* in (1). However, when used in its active form the transitive verb *persuade* does not allow an argument beginning with the word *to* (that is, a prepositional phrase or an infinitival clause) to occur immediately adjacent to the verb. Such restrictions on verb arguments are known as *subcategorization restrictions*. Hence, the word *to* in (2) is likely to be perceived as syntactically anomalous, that is, a violation of verb subcategorization. Figure 6.7 plots the ERPs elicited by the critical word *to* in each sentence type. This word in sentences like (2) elicited a widely distributed positive-going wave with an onset around 500 ms. Since the midpoint of the positivity was near 600 ms, Osterhout and Holcomb labelled this effect 'P600'. Importantly, the P600 is quite distinct from the N400 elicited by semantically anomalous words.

In a second experiment, Osterhout and Holcomb presented lengthened versions of sentences like (1) and (2). An extra phrase (*was sent to jail*) was added onto the end of each sentence, as indicated below:

(3)* The broker hoped to sell the stock <u>was</u> sent to jail.
      (intransitive-verb sentence)

(4)   The broker persuaded to sell the stock <u>was</u> sent to jail.
      (transitive-verb sentence)

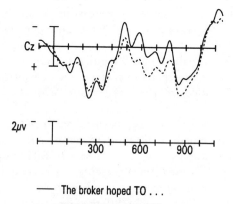

— The broker hoped TO . . .
····· The broker persuaded TO . . .

Fig. 6.7 ERPs from the Cz (midline central) electrode site to apparent violations of verb subcategorization (broken curve) and grammatical control words (full curve). (Adapted from Osterhout and Holcomb (1992).)

---

[4] Sentences with an asterisk indicate the sentence is typically judged to be ungrammatical.

In (3) the added phrase cannot be attached to the initial part of the sentence. (The phrase cannot be attached to the preceding sentence fragment without violating English phrase structure rules.) Thus, sentence (3) is ungrammatical, and it becomes ungrammatical at the auxiliary verb *was*. Conversely, the added phrase can be attached to the initial part of sentence (4); the verb *persuade* can be passivized, and this allows a reduced relative clause interpretation of the sentence ('The broker (who was) persuaded to sell the stock was sent to jail'). Under such an analysis, the auxiliary verb *was* can be attached as part of the main clause ('The broker was sent to jail'). Therefore, if the P600 is associated with syntactic anomaly, then the word *was* in (3) should elicit a P600 relative to ERPs to the same word in (4). The ERP response to auxiliary verbs in the two sentence types is shown in Fig. 6.8. As predicted, the auxiliary verbs in sentences like (3) elicited a large positive-going wave with an onset around 500 ms (the P600) relative to the response to the same words in sentences like (4). These words also elicited a left-hemisphere negativity between 200 and 500 ms, largest over frontal and temporal regions.

Although these findings appear to indicate that syntactically anomalous words elicit a brain response that is quite distinct from the response to semantically inapprorpriate words, it is unclear whether or not the P600 is in any sense 'language-specific'. One possibility is that the P600 is a member of the family of late positive components (P300 and related components) often observed following unexpected, task-relevant events (Donchin 1981; see Chapter 1, section 1.3.). One might assume that readers anticipate grammaticality, and that syntactically anomalous words are an 'unexpected event'. Furthermore, subjects in the Osterhout and Holcomb study were asked to make 'acceptability' judgements after each sentence; hence, the syntactically anomalous words were clearly task-relevant. However, the possibility that the P600 is 'just another' P300 is made less likely given the recent findings of Hagoort *et al.* (1993). Hagoort *et al.* visually presented

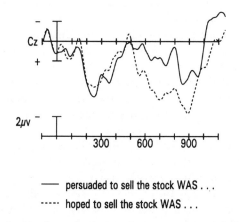

—— persuaded to sell the stock WAS . . .

····· hoped to sell the stock WAS . . .

Fig. 6.8 ERPs from the Cz electrode site to phrase structure violations (broken line) and grammatical controls (full curve). (Adapted from Osterhout and Holcomb (1992).)

Dutch sentences containing several types of syntactic anomalies. Subjects were asked to silently read each sentence and were not required to make explicit grammaticality or acceptability judgments. Under these conditions, the syntactically anomalous words were no longer as clearly task-relevant. Even so, two types of anomaly (phrase structure and agreement violations) elicited a positive-going wave very similar to the P600 observed by Osterhout and Holcomb.

Based on these and similar findings, several researchers have speculated that the N400 and P600 are general responses to semantic and syntactic anomalies, respectively (Hagoort *et al.* 1993; Osterhout 1994; Osterhout and Holcomb 1992). However, this generalization is seemingly inconsistent with some recently reported findings in which syntactic anomalies have been associated with a negative-going wave, rather than the P600. For example, Munte *et al.* (1993) recorded ERPs to word pairs. In the semantic condition, these pairs were either semantically related (*gangster — robber*) or unrelated (*parliament — cube*). In the syntactic condition, the pairs were either 'grammatical' (*you — spend*) or 'ungrammatical' (*your — write*). Target words (the second word in each pair) in the semantically unrelated condition elicited a negative-going wave with a centro-parietal distribution (an enhanced N400), whereas targets in the ungrammatical condition elicited a negative-going wave that was largest over frontal and left-hemisphere sites, relative to controls. In a separate study, Rosler *et al.* (1993) presented sentences that ended either in a semantically or a syntactically anomalous word. Subjects made lexical decisions to the final words. Both anomalies elicited a negative-going wave. As in the Munte *et al.* paper, the response to semantic anomalies was posteriorly distributed whereas the response to ungrammaticality was frontal and largest over the left hemisphere.

Given the distinct scalp distributions of the responses to syntactic and semantic anomalies, the authors concluded that separable processes underlie each type of processing. However, these data are seemingly at odds with the claim that the P600 is a *general* marker of syntactic processing difficulty. We believe that the proper interpretations of these findings, and the caveats they might necessitate with respect to the claim that syntactic anomalies elicit the P600, are not yet clear. For example, word pairs might not fully engage the syntactic processing system. Nor do we know how the lexical decision task might interact with the detection of and response to the syntactic anomaly. But perhaps most importantly, the critical word in both studies was the *last stimulus presented* prior to the subject's response, and in the Rosler *et al.* study the critical word appeared in sentence-final position. There are a number of reasons for suspecting that such a placement introduces the possibility of confounding the response to the anomaly with sentence wrap-up, decision, and response factors. For example, recent work (Hagoort *et al.* 1993; Osterhout and Holcomb, 1992, 1993) has indicated that the final words in sentences that are typically judged to be unacceptable, regardless of the cause of the unacceptability, elicit an enhanced N400-like component. Thus, a sentence containing a syntactic anomaly embedded within the sentence typically elicits two responses, relative to well-formed controls: a P600-like response to the anomalous word, and an N400-like response to the sentence-final word. One speculation is that these two effects co-occur in the same epoch when the anomalous word is in sentence-final position. Given the effects of temporally overlapping components, the resulting waveform might look like neither the P600 nor N400 when these effects occur in isolation.

Taken together, then, recent ERP data appear to indicate that the brain response to certain types of syntactic anomaly is quite distinct from the brain response to semantically inappropriate words. This, in turn, supports the claim that separable cognitive/neural processes are involved in syntactic and semantic processing during comprehension. Neville and her associates have reached a similar conclusion based on quite different evidence. Neville *et al.* (1992) contrasted the ERP response to 'open class' words (e.g. nouns, verbs, and adjectives) and 'closed class' words (e.g. prepositions, articles, and conjunctives). Open class words carry semantic information by referring to specific objects and events, while closed class words serve primarily as indicators of sentence structure. Several lines of evidence suggest that these two word classes are treated differently during comprehension. One frequent claim has been that open and closed class words are associated with different modes of lexical access (Bradley *et al.* 1980). Clinical evidence has been interpreted to suggest that different neural systems are associated with the comprehension of open and closed class words. Specifically, lesions to anterior regions in the left hemisphere appear to disrupt the use and comprehension of closed class vocabulary, while lesions of posterior regions in the left hemisphere disrupt the use and comprehension of open class vocabulary (Friederici 1985; Swinney *et al.* 1980).

By examining the ERP response to visually presented words in sentences, Neville *et al.* (1992) have shown that open and closed class words are associated with dissimilar ERP responses. Open class words elicited a bilateral, posterior negativity in the 400 ms range (the 'classic' N400 component). In contrast, closed class words elicited a negative peak around 280 ms (N280) that was most evident over anterior regions in the left hemisphere. One might speculate that the N280 component reflects the special grammatical function of closed class words (and perhaps the activation of neural systems associated with the construction of syntactic representations). If so, then one reasonable prediction is that the N280 should be reduced or absent in comprehenders who do not have full grammatical competence. Neville *et al.* (1992) tested this prediction by presenting sentences to deaf subjects who had not fully acquired the grammar of English. Although the open class items elicited a posterior, bilateral N400 component, ERPs to closed class words did not display the N280 component. In contrast, ERPs from deaf readers who had acquired a full competence in English grammar showed both the N280 over left anterior regions to closed class words and the N400 over posterior regions to open class words. These results are consistent with the claim that non-identical semantic and syntactic processes operate during sentence comprehension.

The basic distinction between syntax and semantics is not the only relevant distinction made by current theories of grammar. For example, government and binding (GB) theory (Chomsky 1981, 1986) posits the existence of multiple modules of grammatical knowledge. GB includes one module specifying constraints on the phrase structure of sentences, and other modules constraining the 'movement' of sentence elements for question and relative clause formation. It is conceivable that a direct mapping exists between the grammar and the comprehension system, such that there is one 'processing module' for each module in the grammar. This possibility was examined by Neville *et al.* (1991), who contrasted the ERP response to several types of syntactic anomaly, as exemplified by sentences (5)–(7):

(5)* The man admired Don's <u>of</u> sketch the landscape.
   (phrase structure violation)
(6)* What$_i$ was a sketch of ___$_i$ <u>admired</u> by the man?
   (subjacency violation)
(7)* What$_i$ did the man admire Don's sketch <u>of</u> ___$_i$?
   (specificity violation)

The underlined word in each sentence represents the point at which a specific grammatical constraint is violated. The blank spaces in sentences (6) and (7) represent 'gaps' formed by the movement of a sentence constituent from its canonical position to another position within the sentence during question formation. The subscripts index the gap to the moved constituent. In both (6) and (7) the gap is co-indexed with the moved constituent *what*. The violations in the above sentences are as follows. In (5), the string *The man admired Don's of* cannot be assigned a well-formed phrase structure. The question in (6) has been formed by movement out of the subject noun phrase, which is not allowed in English. In GB, the ungrammaticality of such movement has been subsumed under the *subjacency condition*, which is the central constraint on constituent movement. The ill-formedness of (7) reflects the fact that questions cannot be formed by moving a specified or definite noun phrase from its canonical position, a principle known as the *specificity constraint*. Within the GB framework, phrase structure rules, the subjacency condition, and the specificity constraint reflect the operation of three distinct modules of grammatical knowledge.

Neville *et al.*'s data revealed differences in the brain response to each type of anomaly. ERPs elicited by the underlined words in sentences similar to (5)–(7) were compared with ERPs elicited by non-violating control words. Phrase structure violations elicited both an enhanced negativity between 300 and 500 ms over regions of the left hemisphere, and a subsequent positive-going wave (largest over posterior sites) beginning at about 500 ms. This pattern of brain activity was strikingly similar to that observed by Osterhout and Holcomb (1992) (discussed above) following phrase structure anomalies. Violations of the subjacency constraint elicited a broad-based positivity with an onset at about 200 ms that lasted for the duration of the epoch. Violations of the specificity constraint produced a slow negative potential, largest at anterior sites in the left hemisphere, with an onset as early as 125 ms. Hence, each violation type was associated with a distinct brain response.

6.4.3.2 *Sentence parsing*

Given evidence that ERPs are sensitive to syntactic aspects of sentence comprehension, it becomes feasible to use ERPs as on-line tools for investigating the processes engaged in deriving syntactic representations during comprehension. One topic attracting considerable experimental interest in recent years is the processing response to syntactic ambiguity, that is, situations in which more than one well-formed syntactic analysis is available for one string of words. How does the processing system deal with the indeterminism introduced by such ambiguity? Competing theories of sentence parsing provide different answers to this question. Proponents of serial parsing models (e.g. Frazier and Rayner 1982) claim that a single 'preferred' structure is initially constructed, with subsequent reanalysis when the preferred structure turns out to be the incorrect one. Others have claimed that no grammatical roles are assigned until the correct ones are known with certainty (Marcus 1980), or that all possible structures are built in parallel (Gorrell 1989).

Data from the few ERP studies that have examined this issue are, by and large, consistent with the serial parsing model. Osterhout *et al.* (1994) presented sentences containing a syntactically ambiguous noun phrase, as in (8):

(8) The lawyer charged the defendant <u>was</u> lying.

(9) The lawyer charged that the defendant <u>was</u> lying.

In sentence (8) the proper grammatical role of the noun phrase *the defendant* is temporarily uncertain; it can serve either as object of the verb, or as the subject of an upcoming clause. The fact that the noun phrase is playing the subject role in (8) becomes clear only after the syntactically disambiguating auxiliary verb *was* is encountered. In contrast, the overt complementizer in sentence (9) unambiguously indicates that the noun phrase is the subject of a forthcoming clause. Considerable psycholinguistic evidence (cf. Frazier 1987*b*; see below) has indicated that readers experience processing difficulty upon encountering the auxiliary verb in sentences like (8), relative to sentences like (9). For example, Frazier and Rayner (1982) observed longer eye fixations and more eye regressions in the disambiguating region of sentences like (8) than in the corresponding region of sentences like (9) (the so-called *garden-path effect*). These results have been interpreted as indicating that readers initially assign the object role to the ambiguous noun phrase in sentences like (8).

If readers erroneously assign the object role to the noun phrase *the defendant* in (8), then the disambiguating auxiliary verb will be perceived to be syntactically anomalous; under a direct object analysis the auxiliary verb cannot be attached to the preceding material. Osterhout *et al.* observed the ERP response to the auxiliary verb in sentences like (8) and (9). The auxiliary verbs in sentences like (8) elicited the P600 effect, relative to ERPs to the same words in unambiguous sentences like (9). Assuming that the P600 is a metric of syntactic anomaly, this finding is fully consistent with the serial parsing model proposed by Frazier and her associates. At the same time, these data suggest that the P600 can be elicited by syntactic anomaly resulting from strategies employed by the comprehender, as well as by anomaly resulting from outright violations of grammatical constraints.[5]

If readers initially pursue a single analysis for syntactically ambiguous sentences, as claimed by the serial parsing model, then what factors determine which path is attempted first? Frazier and her colleagues (Frazier 1987*b*; Frazier and Rayner 1982) have persuasively argued for a 'minimal attachment' model in which the simplest analysis (as defined by the number of nodes in the phrase structure) is always attempted first, with backtracking and reanalysis when the simplest structure turns out to be inappropriate. Others have argued for a 'lexical preference' model in which information about the main verb in the sentence dictates the initial parse (Holmes *et al.* 1989). Implications of these two approaches are illustrated by sentences (10)–(13):

(10)   The doctor hoped the patient <u>was</u> lying.
          (pure intransitive verb)
(11)* The doctor forced the patient <u>was</u> lying.
          (pure transitive verb)
(12)   The doctor believed the patient <u>was</u> lying.
          (intransitively biased verb)
(13)   The doctor charged the patient <u>was</u> lying.
          (transitively biased verb)

These sentences can be distinguished in terms of the subcategorization information associated with the main verb in each sentence. The subcategorization properties of the verbs in (10) and (11) unambiguously indicate the proper role of the noun phrase *the patient*. Specifically, the intransitive verb *hope* in (10) does not allow a direct object noun phrase, unambiguously indicating that the noun phrase is the subject of an upcoming clause. The transitive verb *force* in (11) *requires* a direct object, so the noun phrase must be assigned the direct object role. Sentence (11) becomes ungrammatical at the auxiliary verb, since the sentence-final phrase *was lying* cannot be attached to the sentence unless the noun phrase is assigned the subject role.

The verbs in (12) and (13) can be used with or without a direct object. This introduces temporary syntactic ambiguity when the noun phrase *the patient* is encountered; the noun phrase might be acting as the direct object of the verb, or as the subject of a forthcoming clause. Because the direct object analysis is syntactically simpler than the subject-of-a-clause analysis, a minimal attachment parser would initially assign the object role to the noun phrase in both sentence

---

[5] The data reported by Osterhout and Holcomb (1992) are also consistent with a serial parser, since the infinitival markers in their materials would have been perceived to be syntactically anomalous only under a simple active analysis. Another (grammatical) analysis was possible at the point of the infinitival marker, that is, the infinitival marker could have be attached as part of a reduced relative clause (e.g. 'The broker (who was) persuaded to sell the stock . . .'). Assuming that the P600 reflects syntactic anomaly, the observation that the infinitival markers in such sentences elicited the P600 effect suggests that readers did not attempt the reduced relative clause analysis during their first parse of these sentences. This interpretation is consistent with the minimal attachment model proposed by Frazier and her colleagues (e.g. Frazier and Rayner 1982), since the simple active analysis is less complex than the reduced relative clause analysis.

types. This will lead to parsing difficulty and reanalysis when the parser encounters the auxiliary verb in both sentence types. In contrast, the lexical preference model predicts that the initial analysis attempted by the parser will be determined by the subcategorization 'preferences' of the main verb. The verb in (12) is biased toward intransitive use (use without an object noun phrase) while the verb in (13) is biased toward transitive use (use with a direct object noun phrase) (Connine *et al.* 1984). Hence, according to the lexical preference model the subject role will be correctly assigned to the noun phrase in (12), since the verb *believe* 'prefers' to be used without a direct object. But the direct object role will be erroneously assigned in (13), since the verb *charge* 'prefers' to be used *with* a direct object. This will lead to parsing diffculty at the auxiliary verb in sentences like (13). To summarize: the minimal attachment model predicts that the parser will encounter syntactic anomaly at the auxiliary verb in sentences like (11), (12), and (13), while the lexical preference model predicts anomaly only in sentences like (11) and (13).

Osterhout *et al.* (1994) presented sentences similar to (10)–(13). Sentences were presented visually in a word-by-word manner, with word onset asynchronies of 650 ms. ERPs to the auxiliary verb (e.g. *was*) in each sentence type are shown in Fig. 6.9. As expected, when these words followed 'pure' transitive verbs, such as in sentence (11), they elicited a large positive-going wave that was largest over parietal sites (the P600). More importantly, auxiliary verbs that followed transitively biased verbs, as in sentence (13), also elicited a P600, although the amplitude of this effect was much smaller than that elicited in sentences with pure transitive verbs. Auxiliary verbs that followed either an intransitive verb (sentence (10) or an intransitively biased verb (sentence (12)) did not differ from

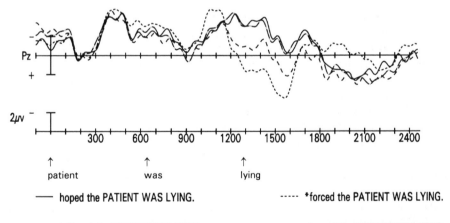

Fig. 6.9 ERPs from Pz (parietal midline) to the final three words in each of four sentence types: intransitive (full curve), transitive (small-dash curve), intransitively biased (dot-dash curve) and transitively biased (medium-dash curve). Onset of the critical word, the auxiliary verb, is indicated by the second arrow under the horizontal axis. (Adapted from Osterhout *et al.* 1994.)

each other and did not elicit this positive-going activity. Again assuming that the P600 is a metric of parsing difficulty, then these findings are consistent with the claim that the structural analysis readers initially pursue is determined by lexical preferences, rather than by syntactic complexity.[6]

Another type of syntactic ambiguity involves the processing of 'filler-gap' relationships within sentences. As noted above, certain structures contain constituents which have been 'moved' from one location to another within the sentence. The moved constituent is called the 'filler', and its original location is called the 'gap' (Fodor 1978). Presumably, the comprehension system must match up each filler with the appropriate gap before the sentence can be fully understood. However, this process is far from trivial, largely due to uncertainty over the proper location of the gap. For example, the fragment 'The mother found out which book the child read . . .' can be continued in several ways, each with a different gap location (e.g. 'The mother found out which book$_i$ the child read $\_\__i$ in school'; 'The mother found out which book$_i$ the child read about $\_\__i$ in school'). How does the processing system deal with such uncertainty? Two models have been contrasted in the recent literature. A *first-resort parser* assigns a filler to the first possible gap, while a *last-resort parser* waits until there is unambiguous information about the location of the true gap location.

Garnsey *et al.* (1989) conducted a clever experiment to contrast these parsing models. They presented sentences similar to (13) and (14):

(13) The businessman knew which customer the secretary <u>called</u> $\_\__i$ at home.
  (plausible filler)
(14) The businessman knew which article$_i$ the secretary <u>called</u> $\_\__i$ at home.
  (implausible filler)

The first possible gap location in these sentences is after the verb, in direct object position. However, the sentences could have continued in such a way that a later gap location existed ('The businessman knew which article the secretary called about $\_\_\_\_$'). A first-resort parser would attempt to assign the filler to the direct object position in (13) and (14) as soon as the verb *called* is encountered, while a last-resort parser would wait until the location of the gap could be assigned with certainty (that is, no filler-gap assignments would be made until words subsequent to the embedded verb had been encountered). The noun *customer* is a plausible filler for a gap in direct object position, while the noun *article* is not. The logic of the experiment was as follows: if the parser associates the filler with a gap in direct object position immediately after seeing the verb, and if the filler

---

[6] The auxiliary verbs in the 'transitive' condition also elicited an enhanced N400 component. This observation is a challenge to the claim that the P600 and N400 effects reflect syntactic and semantic anomaly, respectively. One reasonable explanation that allows us to maintain this claim hinges on the observation that the auxiliary verbs in these sentences rendered the sentence unequivocally ungrammatical, hence uninterpretable. Thus, ERPs to these words might contain two effects: a larger P600 due to the syntactic anomaly, and a larger N400 due to the semantic anomaly. However, given such an interpretation the onset of these effects seems somewhat paradoxical, with the response to the semantic anomaly preceding that to the syntactic anomaly. See Osterhout *et al.* 1994) or Osterhout (1994) for a discussion of this apparent paradox.

is implausible for that gap, then there should be an N400 in the response to the verb. If the parser waits until later in the sentence to make a filler-gap assignment, then the N400 should not occur in response to the verb but may appear later in the sentence. The results indicated that the verb in sentences like (14) (*called*) elicited a larger N400 than the same verbs in sentences like (13), providing support for the first-resort parsing model.

In a more recent ERP study involving sentences containing 'filler-gap' relationships, Kluender and Kutas (1993) recorded ERPs to words intervening between the filler and the gap, and compared these with ERPs elicited by the same words in sentences without a filler-gap relationship. For example, they examined the ERPs to the pronoun *he* in sentences like (15) and (16):

(15) Can't you remember that <u>he</u> advised them against it on previous occasions? (sentence without filler-gap relationship)
(16) Can't you remember who_i <u>he</u> advised _____i against it on previous occasions? (sentence containing filler-gap relationship)

ERPs to *he* in sentences like (16) (that is sentences containing a filler-gap relationship) were more negative-going over left anterior regions, compared with ERPs elicited by *he* in sentences like (15) (sentences without a filler-gap relationship). Although the correct interpretation of this effect is uncertain, one possibility is that it reflects the added processing load associated with holding a filler in memory (cf. Wanner and Maratsos 1978).

6.4.4 Comprehending spoken sentences

A sceptical observer might readily object to the mode of stimulus presentation used in the studies described above. Visual word-by-word presentation of sentences, at rates ranging up to 1 s per word, is far from a 'normal' comprehension environment. One way to address this objection is to present sentences in the form of natural, continuous speech. Such experiments not only provide a replication of the visual studies; they also allow investigations of processes that are by their nature restricted to auditory input (e.g. speech segmentation). They also provide an opportunity for directly contrasting visual and auditory sentence comprehension. Although auditory studies are at present few in number, the preliminary data are largely consistent with their visual analogues.

6.4.4.1 Speech segmentation

A considerable amount of theorizing has been directed at the problem of speech segmentation (e.g. Cole and Jakimik 1980; Cutler 1987; Frazier 1987*a*; Pisoni and Luce 1987). It has been known for many years that the speech signal is not composed of a series of discrete words, but rather is a continuous flow of sound with few breaks or pauses (e.g. Pisoni and Luce 1987). Two important questions that arise from this observation are: how do listeners segment the complex spoken signal into individual units and what are the basic units of speech perception?

The ERP technique permits the recording of brain-wave activity time-locked to the onset of each word in a sentence. Numerous studies have shown a consistent pattern of early 'sensory' components in ERPs recorded to isolated non-linguistic (e.g. Picton *et al.* 1974) and linguistic (e.g. Holcomb and Neville 1990) sounds. A reasonable preliminary question then is: do words in connected speech generate a consistent pattern of sensory ERP components? Evidence from Holcomb and Neville (1991) suggests that they do. In their study all open class words in the middle of naturally spoken sentences were averaged together to form a single ERP. The resulting waveforms, although small in overall amplitude, revealed a clear set of early ERP components. That these waves represent the P1, N1, and P2 components frequently seen to other auditory stimuli was supported by their scalp distributions, latencies, and relative positions in the ERPs. The existence of a relatively normal set of early ERP components time-locked to the onset of words in natural continuous speech is consistent with the hypothesis that speech segmentation occurs on-line and at a relatively early point in the processing of speech stimuli. However, whether these ERP findings directly reflect the segmentation process at work or whether they indicate that segmentation is complete prior to the occurrence of these early waves is unclear.

6.4.4.2 Comprehending words in spoken sentences

McCallum *et al.* (1984) performed an auditory replication of the original Kutas and Hillyard (1980c) visual sentence study. They included sentences spoken by a male with best completion endings (e.g. 'The pen was full of blue ink'), semantically anomalous endings (e.g. 'At school he was taught to snow'), and best completion endings that had a physical deviation (the final word spoken by a female). As in previous visual studies, ERPs to the anomalous endings produced a negative component (peak latency 456 ms), while ERPs to appropriate endings produced a relatively flat response between 200 and 600 ms and ERPs to physically deviant endings produced a large positivity in this latency band. McCallum *et al.* noted that while their auditory N400s had a similar scalp distribution to those recorded by Kutas and Hillyard (1980c) in the visual modality, they were also somewhat less peaked.

Holcomb and Neville (1991) also replicated an earlier Kutas *et al.* (1984) study with auditory stimuli. However, unlike McCallum *et al.* their sentences were spoken as natural 'connected' speech. McCallum used natural speech for all but their final words, which were spliced in from other sentences. This removes the effects of between-word speech cues such as co-articulation and prosody that can be used by the listener to help decode the speaker's message. Even though the average duration of final words was 561 ms in the Holcomb and Neville study, the ERPs at posterior electrode sites reliably registered a difference between sentence-final words that were contextually appropriate and those that were contextually anomalous as early as 50 ms post-word-onset (see Fig. 6.10). As with their earlier word-pair study (Holcomb and Neville 1990) this result is consistent with Marslen-Wilson's (1987) claim that contextual factors can have an effect on

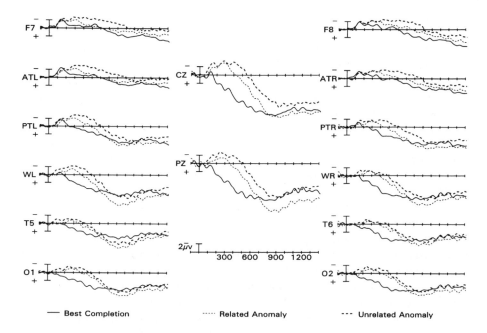

— Best Completion   ····· Related Anomaly   --- Unrelated Anomaly

Fig. 6.10 ERPs from six pairs of lateral electrodes and two midline sites. Best completions were final words that fit with the context of the sentence (e.g. He spread the warm bread with *butter*), unrelated anomalies were final words that did not fit with the sentence context and were semantically unrelated to the best completion (e.g. He spread the warm bread with *socks*), and related anomalies were final words that although anomalous were semantically related to the best completeion (e.g. He spread the warm bread with *milk*). (Adapted from Holcomb and Neville (1991).)

auditory word processing prior to the point at which all the acoustic information about a given word is available. This finding is particularly striking when compared with similar data from procedurally equivalent visual studies (see above), where all of the information about a given final word is available at stimulus onset. In these studies the difference between best completion and anomalous final words typically does not start prior to 200 ms. It is also noteworthy that the latency of Holcomb and Neville's (1991) effects were 100 to 150 ms earlier than the onset of the first effects visible in the McCallum *et al.* (1984) study. A likely possibility for this finding is the presence of non-semantic contextual cues (that is, prosody and across-word co-articulation) in the natural speech stimuli from the Holcomb and Neville study. To check this possibility Holcomb and Neville ran a second experiment in which the impact of prosodic and co-articulatory factors was minimized (an artificial 750 ms interval (ISI) was introduced between the words of the spoken sentences). Although there were still N400-like effects in this experiment, the onset of these effects was 100 to 150 ms later.

6.4.4.3 Syntax and spoken sentence comprehension

Only one study has explicitly examined syntactic analysis during the comprehension of connected, natural speech. Osterhout and Holcomb (1993) replicated their earlier visual study (Osterhout and Holcomb 1992), in which sentences like (1)–(4) above were presented. Apparent violations of subcategorization and phrase structure constraints elicited a positive-going wave (P600) similar to that observed during visual presentation (Fig. 6.11). However, this effect tended to have an earlier onset (between 50 and 300 ms post-stimulus) during spoken language comprehension, relative to the effects observed during reading (around 500 ms). Furthermore, the P600 appeared to have a more posterior distribution in the auditory experiment than in the visual experiment. Since the effects observed during the reading experiment were closely replicated in its auditory analogue, it is tempting to conclude that (at least under certain conditions) the parsing strategies employed during spoken language comprehension closely mirror those employed during reading. In both modalities, comprehenders show signs of using a serial parser with a proclivity for building simple structures. The sensitivity of ERPs to aspects of syntactic analysis during auditory comprehension also opens the door to investigation of phenomena difficult to study with more traditional measures. For example, it should be possible to carefully examine the influence of prosodic and other phonological information on the on-line syntactic analysis of sentences.

6.4.5 Summary

ERP studies of word processing in sentence contexts were initially motivated by the seminal findings of Kutas and Hillyard (1980*a*, *b*, *c*), who found that con-

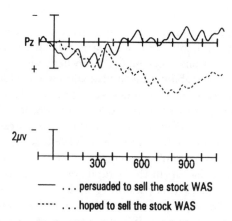

Fig. 6.11 ERPs from site Pz to phrase structure violations and grammatical controls. Stimuli were presented as continuous natural speech. (Adapted from Osterhout and Holcomb (1993).)

textually inappropriate words elicit the N400 effect. Subsequent studies have examined the sentence-level factors that influence the size of the N400 effect. It is now generally agreed that (i) most words within a sentence elicit an N400 component (cf. Kutas *et al.* 1988; Van Petten and Kutas 1991); (ii) the amplitude of the N400 is sensitive to semantic aspects of sentence context (although exactly *which* aspects remains a point of contention; see Fischler (1990) and Kutas and Van Petten (1988)); and (iii) N400 amplitude appears to be influenced by a complex interaction between lexical and contextual factors (Van Petten and Kutas 1991).

Changes in N400 amplitude resulting from principled manipulations to linguistic stimuli have been used to arbitrate between modular and interactive models of word recognition. For example, an apparent interaction between word frequency and sentence context on N400 amplitude has been taken to indicate support for interactive models of word recognition (Van Petten and Kutas 1990).

ERPs have also been used to examine syntactic processes. Perhaps the most intriguing outcome of these studies is the dramatic difference in the ERP response to deviations from semantic and syntactic well-formedness. Deviations from semantic well-formedness (e.g. contextually inappropriate words) generally elicit a large N400 component. Several types of syntactic deviations are associated with an ERP response, but none of these elicits a 'classical' N400-like effect. Furthermore, although the syntactic anomalies examined to date have elicited a variety of ERP responses, three types of anomaly (phrase structure violations, apparent subcategorization violations, and violations of subjacency) have been associated with a long-lasting, widely distributed positive-going wave. Although the precise cognitive processes reflected in these components are unknown, these observations allow one to speculate that, at least under certain experimental conditions, the N400 and the slow positive-going wave (the 'P600') are elicited as a function of the representational level of the anomaly (semantic and syntactic respectively). In general, the ERP studies reviewed above provide rather striking evidence of a correspondence between the neural and cognitive processes involved in comprehension, and distinctions made within formal theories of language.

These studies also demonstrate that ERP measures are sensitive to at least an interesting subset of the neural and cognitive processes engaged during sentence comprehension. The available ERP evidence is largely consistent with a parsing model in which a single structural analysis is pursued initially, even when the parser is confronted with uncertainty about the correct analysis. Preliminary data suggest that the parser's early decisions can be influenced by word-specific information (e.g. verb subcategorization knowledge), rather than solely by biases in the application of phrase structure knowledge. This parsing model appears to hold regardless of the modality of input (visual or auditory).

6.5 CONCLUSIONS

We began our review by noting that previous reviewers have projected a noticeably pessimistic view concerning the use of ERPs as tools for comprehending language comprehension. This view has been shared by many psycholinguists, who have (seemingly) looked upon ERPs as something akin to an intriguing but largely unfulfilled promissory note. We believe that the literature reviewed here justifies a decidedly more optimistic view. It is now clear that ERPs are sensitive to relevant aspects of the processes underlying comprehension, and that this sensitivity can be exploited to reveal a great deal about these processes. Indeed, given their unique combination of properties (on-line, non-intrusive, multidimensional measurement), ERPs are ideally suited to address certain questions that would be difficult or impossible to address with more conventional measures. For example, given their multidimensional nature, ERPs have a better chance (in principle and, it appears, in practice) of distinguishing between distinct cognitive states. This allows the researcher to determine (to a first approximation) not only *when* an anomaly has been detected, but also *what kind* of anomaly has been perceived. Similarly, it appears that meaningful language-sensitive changes in the ERP can be obtained under extremely natural comprehension conditions; for example, under conditions in which subjects are asked to simply process the language without a secondary task (Hagoort *et al.* 1993), or when the stimulus is presented as continuous natural speech (Osterhout and Holcomb 1993). To all appearances, the forseeable future will offer a productive marriage between the tools of cognitive psychophysiology and the theoretical richness of modern psycholinguistics.

Of course, ERPs are not a panacea for the difficulties afflicting psycholinguistic research, and in all likelihood certain questions will remain largely unilluminated by ERP measurement. The observant reader might have noted that much of the work reviewed here has examined aspects of comprehension that occur early in the information processing flow (e.g. word recognition, integrating a word into context, and syntactic analysis). These 'early occurring' processes can be contrasted with 'later-occurring' processes (for example making inferences, integrating propositional content into the discourse representation, and interpretating non-literal speech acts). As noted by Fischler (1990) and others, this is an appropriate and perhaps inevitable focus for ERP studies of language comprehension. Event-related potentials represent brain activity averaged over both items and subjects, typically time-locked to the presentation of a stimulus. The most observable and reliable ERP effects are those that have an invariant temporal relation to the onset of the stimulus. A priori, it seems likely that early occurring processes, such as those involved in word recognition, maintain a more consistent temporal relation to stimulus onset (across both items and subjects) than do later-occurring processes. The interesting question of how far down the 'path of comprehension' ERPs will take us remains to be answered.

In sum, ERPs have been shown to be sensitive measures of a number of language-related processes. The literature reviewed here allows us to hope that the success or failure of the ongoing effort to comprehend comprehension by recording event-related potentials will be determined largely by the imagination and skill of the researchers, rather than by limitations inherent in the measures themselves.

REFERENCES

Ades, A. and Steedman, S. (1982). On the order of words. *Linguistics and Philosophy*, 6, 517–58.

Balota, D. A. and Chumbley, J. I. (1984). Are lexical decisions a good measure of lexical access: the role of word frequency in the neglected decision stage? *Journal of Experimental Psychology: Human Perception and Performance*, 10, 340–57.

Balota, D. A. and Chumbley, J. I. (1985). The locus of word frequency effects in the pronunciation task: lexical access and/or production? *Journal of Memory and Language*, 24, 89–106.

Barrett, S. E. and Rugg, M. D. (1990). Event-related potentials and the semantic matching of pictures. *Brain and Cognition*, 14, 201–12.

Becker, C. (1979). Semantic context and word frequency effects in visual word recognition. *Journal of Experimental Psychology: Human Perception and Performance*, 5, 252–9.

Becker, C. (1980). Semantic context effects in visual word recognition: an analysis of semantic strategies. *Memory and Cognition*, 8, 493–512.

Bentin, S. (1987). Event-related potentials, semantic processes, and expectancy factors in word recognition. *Brain and Language*, 31, 308–27.

Bentin, S., McCarthy, G., and Wood, C. C. (1985). Event-related potentials associated with semantic priming. *Electroencephalography and Clinical Neurophysiology*, 60, 343–55.

Berwick, R. and Weinberg, R. (1983). The role of grammars as components of models of language use. *Cognition*, 13, 1–61.

Besson, M. and McCar, F. (1987). An event-related potential analysis of incongruity in music and other non-linguistic contexts. *Psychophysiology*, 24, 14–25.

Besson, M., Fischler, I., Boaz, T., and Raney, G. (1992). Effects of automatic associative activation on explicit and implicit memory tests. *Journal of Experimental Psychology: Learning, Memory and Cognition*, 18, 89–105.

Boddy, J. (1986). Event-related potentials in chronometric analysis of primed word recognition with different stimulus onset asynchronies. *Psychophysiology*, 23, 232–45.

Bradley, P. C., Garrett, M. F. and Zurif, E. B. (1980). Syntactic deficits in Broca aphasia. In Biological studies of mental processes (ed. D Caplan). MIT Press Cambridge, MA.

Brown, C. M. and Hagoort, P. (1993). The processing nature of the N400: evidence from masked priming. *Journal of Cognitive Neuroscience*, 5, 34–44.

Cairns, H. S. and Foss, D. J. (1971). Falsification of the hypothesis that word frequency is a unified variable in sentence processing. *Journal of Verbal Learning and Verbal Behaviour*, 10, 41–3.

Chomsky, N. (1981). *Lectures on government and binding*. Foris, Dordrecht.

Chomsky, N. (1986). *Knowledge of language*. Praeger, New York.

Cole, R. A. and Jakimik, J. (1980). A model of speech perception. In *Perception and production of fluent speech* (ed. R. A. Cole), pp. 133–64. Erlbaum, Hillsdale, NJ.

Collins, A. M. and Loftus, E. F. (1975). A spreading-activation theory of semantic processing. *Psychological Review*, 82, 407–28.

Connine, C., Ferreira, F., Jones, C., Clifton, C., and Frazier, L. (1984). Verb frame preferences: descriptive norms. *Journal of Psycholinguistic Research*, 13, 307–19.

Cutler, A. (1987). Speaking for listening. In (Eds.) *Language perception and production: relationships between listening, speaking, reading and writing* (ed. A. Allport, D. MacKay, W. Prinz and E. Scheerer) pp. 23–40. Academic, New York.

den Heyer, K., Briand, K., and Dannenbring, G. (1983). Strategic factors in a lexical decision task: evidence for automatic and attention-driven processes. *Memory and Cognition* 25, 19–42.

Donchin, E. (1981). Surprise? . . . Surprise! *Psychophysiology*, 18, 493–513.

Donchin, E., Kutas, M., and McCarthy, G. (1977). Electrocortical indices of hemispheric utilization. In *Lateralization of the nervous system* (ed. S. Harnad *et al.*), pp. 339–84 Academic, New York.

Ellis, A. W. and Young, A. W. (1988). *Human cognitive neuropsychology*. Erlbaum, Hillsdale, NJ.

Fischler, I. S. (1990). Comprehending language with event-related potentials. In *Event-related brain potentials* (ed. J. W. Rohrbaugh, R. Parasuraman, and R. Johnson, jun.) pp. 165–170 Oxford University Press, New York.

Fischler, I. and Bloom, P. (1979). Automatic and attentional processes in the effects of sentence contexts on word recognition. *Journal of Verbal Learning and Verbal Behavior*, 18, 1–20.

Fischler, I., Bloom, P. A., Childers, D. G., Roucos, S. E., and Perry, N. W. (1983). Brain potentials related to stages of sentence verification. *Psychophysiology*, 20, 400–9.

Fischler, I., and Raney, G. E. (1991). Language by eye: behavioral, autonomic and cortical approaches to reading. In *Handbook of cognitive psychology: central and autonomic nervous system* (ed. J. R. Jennings and H. G. H. Coles). Wiley, New York.

Fodor, J. A., Bever, T. G., and Garrett, M. F. (1974). *The psychology of language*. McGraw-Hill, New York.

Fodor, J. D. (1978). Parsing strategies and constraints on transformations. *Linguistic Inquiry*, 9, 427–73.

Forster, K. I. (1981). Priming and the effects of sentence and lexical contexts on naming time: evidence for autonomous lexical processing. *Quarterly Journal of Experimental Psychology*, 33A, 465–495.

Fowler, C. A., Wolford, G., Slade, R. and Tassinary, L. (1981). Lexical access with and without awareness. *Journal of Experimental Psychology: General*, 110, 341–62.

Frazier, L. (1987a). Structure in auditory word recognition. *Cognition*, 25, 157–89.

Frazier, L. (1987b). Sentence processing: a tutorial review. In *Attention and performance XII* (ed. M. Coltheart), pp. 559–85. Erlbaum, Hillsdale, NJ.

Frazier, L. and Rayner, K. (1982). Making and correcting errors during sentence comprehension: eye movements in the analysis of structurally ambiguous sentences. *Cognitive Psychology*, 14, 178–210.

Friederici, A. D. (1985). Levels of processing and vocabulary types: evidence from on-line comprehension in normals and agrammatics. *Cognition*, 19, 133–66.

Friedman, D., Simson, R., Ritter, W., and Rapin, I. (1975). The late positive component (P300) and information processing in sentences. *Electroencephalography and Clinical Neurophysiology*, 38, 255–62.

Garnsey, S. M., Tanenhaus, M. K., and Chapman, R. M. (1989). Evoked potentials and the study of sentence comprehension. *Journal of Psycholinguistic Research*, 18, 51–60.

Glucksberg, S., Kreuz, R. J., and Rho, S. H. (1986). Context can constrain lexical access: implications for models of language comprehension. *Journal of Experimental Psychology: Learning, Memory, and Cognition*, 12, 323–35.

Gorrell, P. (1989). Establishing the loci of serial and parallel effects in syntactic processing. *Journal of Psycholinguistic Research*, 18, 61–71.

Hagoort, P., Brown, C., and Groothusen, J. (1993). The syntactic positive shift as an ERP measure of syntactic processing. *Language and Cognitive Processes*, 8, 439–84.

Herning, R. I., Jones, R. T. and Hunt, J. S. (1987). Speech event-related potentials reflect linguistic contex and processing level. *Brain and Language*, 30, 116–29.

Hillyard, S. A. and Woods, D. L. (1979). Electrophysiological analysis of human brainl function. In *Handbook of behavioral neurobiology*. Vol. 2, (ed. M. S. Gazziniga), pp. 345–78 Plenum, New York.

Holcomb, P. J. (1986). Electrophysiological correlates of semantic facilitation. *Electroencephalography and Clinical Neurophysiology*, 38, 320–22.

Holcomb, P. J. (1988). Automatic and attentional processing: an event-related brain potential analysis of semantic priming. *Brain and Language*, 35, 66–85.

Holcomb, P. J. (1993). Semantic priming and stimulus degradation: implications for the role of the N400 in language processing. *Psychophysiology*, 30, 47–61.

Holcomb, P. J. and Anderson, J. (1993). Cross-modal semantic priming: a time-course analysis using event-related brain potentials. *Language and Cognitive Processes*, 8, 379–412.

Holcomb, P. J. and McPherson, W. B. (1994). Event-related brain potentials reflect semantic priming in an object decision task. *Brain and Cognition*, 24, 259–76.

Holcomb, P. J. and Neville, H. J. (1990). Semantic priming in visual and auditory lexical decision: a between modality comparison. *Language and Cognitive Processes*, 5, 281–312.

Holcomb, P. J. and Neville, H. J. (1991). The electrophysiology of spoken sentence processing. *Psychobiology*, 19, 286–300.

Holmes, M., Stowe, L., and Cupples, L. (1989). Lexical expectations in parsing complement-verb sentences. *Journal of Memory and Language*, 28, 668–89.

Kiger, J. I. and Glass, A. L. (1983). The facilitation of lexical decisions by a prime occuring after the target. *Memory and Cognition*, 11, 356–365.

Kintsch, W. (1988). The use of knowledge in discourse processing: a construction-integration model. *Psychological Review*, 95, 163–82.

Kluender, R. and Kutas, M. (1993). Bridging the gap: evidence from ERPs on the processing of unbounded dependencies. *Journal of Cognitive Neuroscience*, 5, 196–214.

Kounios, J. and Holcomb, P. (1992). Structure and process in semantic memory: evidence from event-related brain potentials and reaction times. *Journal of Experimental Psychology: General*, 121, 459–79.

Kramer, A. and Donchin, E. (1987). Brain potentials as indices of orthographic and phonological interaction during word matching. *Journal of Experimental Psychology: Learning, Memory, and Cognition*, 13, 76–86.

Kutas, M. (1987). Event-related brain potentials (ERPs) elicited during rapid serial visual presentation of congruous and incongruous sentences. In *Current trends in event-related potential research* (ed. R. Johnson, J. W. Rohrbaugh, and R. Parasuraman), pp. 406–11.

Kutas, M. (1993). In the company of other words: electrophysiological evidence for single-word and sentence context effects. *Language and Cognitive Processes*, 8, 533–72.

Kutas, M. and Hillyard, S. A. (1980a). Event-related brain potentials to semantically inappropriate and surprisingly large words. *Biological Psychology*, 11, 99–116.

Kutas, M. and Hillyard, S. A. (1980b). Reading between the lines: event-related brain potentials during natural sentences processing. *Brain and Language*, 11, 354–73.

Kutas, M. and Hillyard, S. A. (1980c). Reading senseless sentences: brain potentials reflect semantic incongruity. *Science*, 207, 203–5.

Kutas, M. and Hillyard, S. A. (1983). Event-related brain potentials to grammatical errors and semantic anomalies. *Memory and Cognition*, 11, 539–50.

Kutas, M. and Hillyard, S. A. (1984). Brain potentials during reading reflect word expectancy and semantic association. *Nature*, 307, 161–3.

Kutas, M. and Hillyard, S. A. (1989). An electrophysiological probe of incidental semantic association. *Journal of Cognitive Neuroscience*, 1, 38–49.

Kutas, M. and Van Petten C. (1988). Event-related brain potential studies of language. In *Advances in psychophysiology* (ed. P. K. Ackles, J. R. Jennings, and M. G. H. Coles), pp. 138–87, JAI Press, Greenwich, CT.

Kutas, M., Lindamood, T., and Hillyard, S. A. (1984). Word expectancy and event-related brain potentials during sentence processing. In *Preparatory states and processes*, (ed. S. Kornblum and J. Roquin), pp. 217–38. Erlbaum, Hillsdale, NJ.

Kutas, M., Van Petten, C., and Besson, M. (1988). Event-related potential assymetries during the reading of sentences. *Electroencephalography and Clinical Neurophysiology*, 69, 218–33.

McCallum, W. C., Farmer, S. F., and Pocock, P. K. (1984). The effects of physical and semantic incongruities on auditory event-related potentials. *Electroencephalography and Clinical Neurophysiology*, 59, 447–88.

McClelland, J. L. (1979). On the time relations of mental processes: an examination of systems of processes in cascade. *Psychological Review*, 86, 287–330.

Marcel, A. J. (1983). Conscious and unconscious perception: experiments on visual masking and word recognition. *Cognitive Psychology*, 15, 197–237.

Marcus, M. P. (1980). *A theory of syntactic recognition for natural language*. MIT Press, Cambridge, MA.

Marslen-Wilson, W. (1987). Functional parallelism in spoken word-recognition. *Cognition*, 25, 71–102.

Marslen-Wilson, W. and Tyler, L. K. (1980). The temporal structure of spoken language comprehension. *Cognition*, 8, 1–71.

Marslen-Wilson, W. D. and Welsh, A. (1978). Processing interactions and lexical access during word recognition in continuous speech. *Cognitive Psychology*, 10, 29–63.

Marton, M. and Szirtes, J. (1988). Context effects on saccade-related brain potentials to words during reading. *Neuropsychologia*, 3, 453–63.

Meyer, D. and Schvaneveldt, R. (1971). Facilitation in recognizing pairs of words: evidence of a dependence between retrieval operations. *Journal of Experimental Psychology*, 90, 227–34.

Meyer, D., Schvaneveldt, R., and Ruddy, M. (1975). Loci of contextual effects on word recognition. In *Attention and performance*, Vol. 5 (ed. P. M. A. Rabbit & S. Dornic), pp. 98–118. Academic, New York.

Morton, J. (1969). Interaction of information in word recognition. *Psychological Review*, 76, 165–78.

Munte, T. F., Heinze, H. and Mangun, G. (1993). Dissociation of brain activity related to syntactic and semantic aspects of language. *Journal of Cognitive Neuroscience*, 5, 335–44.

Näätänen, R. and Gaillard, A. W. K. (1983). The orienting reflex and the N2 deflection of the event-related (ERP). In *Tutorials in ERP research: endogenous components* (ed. A. W. K. Gaillard and W. Ritter). pp. 119–42. Elsevier, Amsterdam.

Neely, J. H. (1976). Semantic priming and retrieval from lexical memory: evidence for facilitory and inhibitory processes. *Memory and Cognition*, 4, 648–654.

Neely, J. H. (1977). Semantic priming and retrieval from lexical memory: roles of inhibitionless spreading activation and limited capacity attention. *Journal of Experimental Psychology*, 106, 226–54.

Neely, J. H. (1991). Semantic priming effects in visual word recognition: a selective review of current findings and theories. In *Basic processes in reading: visual word recognition* (ed. D. Besner and G. Humphreys), pp. 264–336 Erlbaum, Hillsdale, NJ.

Neely, J. H. and Keefe, D. E. (1989). Semantic context effects on visual word processing: a hybrid prospective/retrospective processing theory. In G. H. Bower (Ed.), *The psychology of learning and motivation: advances in research and theory*, Vol. 24 (ed. G. H. Bower), pp. 207–48. Academic, New York.

Neville, H. J., Kutas, M., and Schmidt, A. (1982). Event-related potentials studies of cerebral specialization during reading: II studies of congenitally deaf adults. *Brain and Language*, 16, 316–37.

Neville, H. J., Pratarelli, M. E., and Forster, K. I. (1989). Distinct neural systems for lexical and episodic representations of words. *Society for Neuroscience Abstracts*, 15, abstract No. 101.11.

Neville, H. J., Nicol, J., Barss, A., Forster, K. I., and Garrett, M. F. (1991). Syntactically based processing classes: evidence from event-related brain potentials. *Journal of Cognitive Neuroscience*, 3, 151–65.

Neville, H. J., Mills, D. L., and Lawson, D. L. (1992). Fractionating language: different neural subsystems with different sensitive periods. *Cortex*, 2, 244–58.

Nigam, A., Hoffman, J. E., and Simons, R. F. (1992). N400 to semantically anomalous pictures and words. *Journal of Cognitive Neuroscience*, 4, 15–22.

Onifer, W. and Swinney, D. A. (1981). Accessing lexical ambiguity during sentence comprehension: effects of frequency on meaning and contextual bias. *Memory and Cognition*, 9, 225–36.

Osterhout, L. (1990). Event-related potentials elicited during sentence comprehension. Unpublished doctoral dissertation. Tufts University.

Osterhout, L. (1994). Event-related brain potentials as tools for comprehending language comprehension. In *Perspectives on sentence processing* (ed. C. Clifton, jun., L. Frazier, and K. Rayner), pp. 15–44. Erlbaum, Hillsdale, NJ.

Osterhout, L. and Holcomb, P. J. (1992). Event-related brain potentials elicited by syntactic anomaly. *Journal of Memory and Language*, 31, 785–806.

Osterhout, L. and Holcomb, P. (1993). Event-related potentials and syntactic anomaly: evidence of anomaly detection during the perception of continuous speech. *Language and Cognitive Processes*, 8, 413–38.

Osterhout, L. and Swinney, D. A. (1989). On the role of the simplicity heuristic during language processing: evidence from structural and inferential processing. *Journal of Psycholinguistic Research*, 18, 553–62.

Osterhout, L., Holcomb, P. J., and Swinney, D. A. (1994) Brain potentials elicited by garden-path sentences: Evidence of the application of verb information during parsing. *Journal of Experimental Psychology: Learning, Memory, and Cognition* 20, 786–803.

Picton, T. W. and Stuss, D. T. (1984). Event-related potentials in the study of speech and language: a critical review. In *Biological perspectives on language* (ed. D. Caplan, A. Roch Lecours, and A. Smith), pp. 303–60. MIT Press, Cambridge, MA.

Picton, T. W., Hillyard, S. A., Krausz, H. I., and Galambos, R. (1974). Human auditory evoked potentials. I: evaluation of components. *Electroencephalography and Clinical Neurophysiology*, 36, 179–90.

Pisoni, D. B. and Luce, P. A. (1987). Acoustic-phonetic representation in word recognition. In *Spoken word recognition* (ed. U. H. Frauenfelder and L. K. Tyler), pp. 21–52. MIT Press, Cambridge, MA.

Polich, J. (1985). Semantic categorization and event-related potentials. *Brain and Language*, 26, 304–21.

Polich, J., McCarthy, G., Wang, W. S., and Donchin, E. (1983). When words collide: orthographic and phonological interference during word processing. *Biological Psychology*, 16, 155–80.

Posner, M. and Snyder, C. (1975). Attention and cognitive control. In *Information processing and cognition* (ed. R. Solso), pp. 55–85. Erlbaum, Hillsdale, NJ.

Riesbeck, C. K. and Schank, R. C. (1978). Comprehension by computer: expectation-based analysis of sentences in context. In *Studies in the perception of language* (ed. W. J. M. Levelt and G. B. Flores d'Arcais). pp. 247–293. Wiley, New York.

Rohrbaugh, J. and Gaillard, A. W. K. (1983). Sensory and motor aspects of the contingent negative variation. In *Tutorials in ERP research: endogenous components* (ed. A. W. K. Gaillard and W. Ritter), pp. 269–310. Elsevier, Amsterdam.

Rosler, F., Friederici, A., Putz, P., and Hahne, A. (1993). Event-related brain potentials while encountering semantic and syntactic constraint violations. *Journal of Cognitive Neuroscience*, 5, 345–62.

Rugg, M. D. (1983). The relationship between evoked potentials and lateral asymmetries of processing. In *Tutorials in event-related potential research: endogenous components* (ed. A. W. K. Gaillard and W. Ritter), pp. 369–384. Elsevier, Amsterdam.

Rugg, M. D. (1984a). Event-related potentials in phonological matching tasks. *Brain and Language*, 23, 225–40.

Rugg, M. D. (1984b). Event-related potentials and the phonological processing of words and nonwords. *Neuropsychologia*, 22, 435–43.

Rugg, M. D. (1985). The effects of semantic priming and word repetition on event-related potentials. *Psychophysiology*, 22, 642–47.

Rugg, M. D. (1987). Dissociation of semantic priming, word and non-word repetition effects by event-related potentials. *Quarterly Journal of Experimental Psychology*, 39A, 123–48.

Rugg, M. D. (1990). Event-related brain potentials dissociate repetition effects of high- and low-frequency words. *Memory and Cognition*, 18, 367–79.

Rugg, M. D., Furda, J., and Lorist, M. (1988). The effects of task on the modulation of event-related potentials by word repetition. *Psychophysiology*, 25, 55–63.

Sabol, M. A. and De Rosa, D. V. (1976). Semantic encoding of isolated words. *Journal of Experimental Psychology: Human Learning and Memory*, 2, 58–68.

Schuberth, R. E. and Eimas, P. D. (1977). Effects of context on the classification of words and nonwords. *Journal of Experimental Psychology: Human Perception and Performance*, 3, 27–36.

Schuberth, R. E., Spoehr, K. T., and Lane, D. M. (1981). Effects of stimulus and contextual information on the lexical decision process. *Memory and Cognition*, 9, 68–77.

Seidenberg, M. S., Tanenhaus, M. K., Leiman, J. L., and Bienkowski, M. (1982). Automatic access of the meanings of ambiguous words in context: some limitations of knowledge-based processing. *Cognitive Psychology*, 14, 489–537.

Seidenberg, M. S., Waters, G. S., Sanders, M., and Langer, P. (1984). Pre-and post-lexical loci of contextual effects on word recognition. *Memory and Cognition*, 12, 315–28.

Stanovitch, K. E. and West, R. F. (1983). On priming by a sentence context. *Journal of Experimental Psychology: General*, 112, 1–136.

Swinney, D. A. (1979). Lexical access during sentence comprehension: (re)consideration of context effects. *Journal of Verbal Learning and Verbal Behavior*, 18, 645–59.

Swinney, D. A. (1981). The process of language comprehension: an approach to studying issues in cognition and language. *Cognition*, 10, 307–12.

Swinney, D. A. (1982). The structure and time-course of information interaction during speech comprehension: lexical segmentation, access, and interpretation. In *Perspectives on mental representation*. (ed. J. Mehler, E. C. T. Walker, and M. Garrett), pp. 151–68. Erlbaum, Hillsdale, NJ.

Swinney, D. A., Onifer, W., Prather, P., and Hirshkowitz, M. (1979). Semantic facilitation across sensory modalities in the processing of individual words and sentences. *Memory and Cognition*, 7, 159–65.

Swinney, D. A., Zurif, E. B., and Cutler, A. (1980). Interactive effects of stress and form class in the comprehension of Broca's aphasics. *Brain and Language*, 10, 132–44.

Tweedy, J. R., Lapinski, R. H., and Schvaneveldt, R. (1977). Semantic-context effects on word recognition: influence of varying the properties of items presented in an appropriate context. *Memory and Cognition*, 5, 84–9.

Van Petten, C. (1993). A comparison of lexical and sentence-level context effects in event-related potentials. *Language and Cognitive Processes*, 8, 485–32.

Van Petten, C. and Kutas, M. (1987). Ambiguous words in context: an event-related potential analysis of the time course of meaning activation. *Journal of Memory and Language*, 26, 188–208.

Van Petten, C. and Kutas, M. (1990). Interactions between sentence context and word frequency in event-related brain potentials. *Memory and Cognition*, 18, 380–93.

Van Petten, C. and Kutas, M. (1991). Influences of semantic and syntactic context on open-and closed-class words. *Memory and Cognition*, 19, 95–112.

Van Petten, C. and Kutas, M. (1991). Electrophysiological evidence for the flexibility of lexical processing. In *Word and sentence* (ed. G. Simpson), pp. 129–74. North Holland, Amsterdam.

Wanner, E. and Maratsos, M. (1978). An ATN approach to comprehension. In *Linguistic theory and psychological reality* (ed. M. Halle, J. Bresnan, and G. A. Miller), pp. 119–161. MIT Press, Cambridge, MA.

Index